D1701192

THE MASTERPIECES OF EUSTACE COCKRELL
VOLUME II

Copyright © 2021 by Eustace Cockrell
All world rights reserved.

No part of this book may be reproduced, stored in a retrieval system, or transmitted in any form or by any means electronic, mechanical, photocopying, recording or otherwise, without the prior consent of the publisher.

Readers are encouraged to go to www.MissionPointPress.com to contact the author or to find information on how to buy this book in bulk at a discounted rate.

Published by Mission Point Press
2554 Chandler Rd.
Traverse City, MI 49696
(231) 421-9513
www.MissionPointPress.com

ISBN: 978-1-954786-01-1 (softcover)
ISBN: 978-1-958363-11-9 (hardcover)
Library of Congress Control Number: 2021902035

Printed in the United States of America

The Masterpieces of Eustace Cockrell

Collected Works, Volume II

Mission Point Press

For Leacy, Geoffrey, Frederick and Elizabeth —
In honor of their dad — "famed writer" Eustace Cockrell.

Collier's

MAY 8, 1948   TEN CENTS

Beginning
SHADOW OF FU MANCHU
By SAX ROHMER

Hate—With Russian Dressing
PAGE 20

Contents

xi
INTRODUCTION

SHORT STORIES

2
THE SHAME OF THE CECILIA
The Star Weekly, July 27, 1946
(Co-authored with Daniel Gordon)

7
TOO HOT TO HANDLE
Argosy, September 1946

15
"THAT WYNNE GIRL"
This Week, December 15, 1946

18
NIGHTMARE
The American Magazine, March 1947

23
NO REST FOR THE MEDIUM
Esquire, April 1948

29
CODE OF THE WEST
Colliers, May 8, 1948

35
FOR DIVERS REASON
Colliers, July 31, 1948
(Co-authored with Daniel Gordon)

38
THE KEYHOLE ARTIST
This Week, August 8, 1948

41
HOT PILOT
Detective Tales, September 1948
(Co-authored with Daniel Gordon
using pseudonym, Nick Spain)

47
BEAUTY AND THE DROP KICK
Colliers, October 30, 1948

53
NO ONE BUT YOU
The American Magazine, April 1949

57
HIS BROTHER'S KEEPER
Blue Book, June 1949
(Co-authored with Daniel Gordon)

63
ROCKY'S ROSE
The American Magazine, October 1949

71
IT'S ALWAYS THE WAY
Blue Book, October 1949

75
TAFFY'S TWO LOVES
Cosmopolitan, November 1951

79
THE CAT AND THE CONSTITUTION
Antioch Review, Autumn 1956

85
THE EAGLEBIRD
Argosy, January 1957

91
THE LONG WAY HOME
Collier's, January 4, 1957

NOVELETTES

101
THE TIMID ANGEL
Esquire, March 1949
(Co-authored with Herbert Dalmas
using pseudonym, Jeff Conover)

119
THE POWER DEVIL
The American Magazine, December 1949
(Co-authored with Herbert Dalmas)

APRIL, 1948

Esquire
THE MAGAZINE FOR MEN

PRICE 50¢
CANADA 55¢

ARTICLES
PAUL GALLICO
HARRY N. SPERBER
SIDNEY CARROLL
JOE LAURIE, JR.
O. E. SCHOEFFLER
HERB GRAFFIS
ALEXANDER E. FOX
HERBERT KUBLY
J. B. RICE
ROBERT ULRICH GODSOE
DON WHITEHEAD

BOOK
JOHN EVANS

FICTION
WILLIAM FRANCIS
ROBERT SWITZER
PATRICK NICHOLSON, III
BARNEY R. MILLER
MICHAEL MacDOUGALL
HAMILTON BENZ
EUSTACE COCKRELL
JOSEPH E. KELLEAM
WILLIAM VALRICK

SPORTS
JIMMY CANNON
BARNABY CONRAD
ROBERT W. MINTON

POETRY
CARL SANDBURG
JAMES MENZIES BLACK, Jr.

ART
BEN-HUR BAZ
GLENN GROHE
CHESLEY BONESTELL
GUSTAV REHBERGER
VICTOR KALIN
BERNARD SIMPSON
MARTIN BURNISTON

PHOTOGRAPHY
DON CHRISTIE
BOB SMALLMAN
ADRIAN J. SALVAS
LOWNDS
WILLIAM STONE
ARNOLD GLANTZ

CARTOONS
B. SHERMUND
D. McKAY
E. SIMMS CAMPBELL
PAUL WEBB
HOWARD BAER
ELDON DEDINI
GARRETT PRICE
SAM COBEAN

INDEX ON PAGE 5
ADV. INDEX ON PAGE 190

SPECIAL BOOK-LENGTH FEATURE
If You Have Tears
a murder mystery by JOHN EVANS

EUSTACE COCKRELL

(1909 – 1972)

*They all told me that writing is nice work if you can get it,
and I always was gullible. Well I still think it's nice work
— if and when you can get it.*

INTRODUCTION

One Christmas, we received an unexpected gift from my wife's cousin, Nancy Cockrell. Opening it, Elizabeth and I found several yellowed and very fragile copies of *Blue Book* magazine from the 1930s and '40s. Included, too, was a note that began, "I thought you might be interested...." To our surprise, each issue featured a short story by Elizabeth's father, Eustace Cockrell.

This gift has led to an extensive 20-year search to track down and collect all of Cockrell's stories. These were written between 1932 and 1957 prior to his more recognized careers as a screen writer for Warner Brothers, a magazine editor and a script writer for many early television shows. The latter included westerns like "Have Gun, Will Travel," "Maverick" and "Gunsmoke." He also wrote for "Alfred Hitchcock Presents" (two episodes in the highly acclaimed first year written with his older brother, Francis Cockrell), "The Loretta Young Show," "Philco Television Playhouse," "This Man Dawson," "I Spy" and "Naked City." In 1953, while managing editor of *Fortnight Magazine* in Los Angeles, Cockrell was part of a team nominated for an Academy Award in the documentary category.

As with any search, the excitement is often in the seeking rather than in any grand plan for what to do with the treasure once discovered. Cockrell wrote over 100 short stories and novelettes. Many were published in pulp fiction magazines including *Blue Book, Argosy, Detective Tales, All-American Fiction* and *Adventure Magazine*. Others appeared in "slicks" like *Colliers, Saturday Evening Post, The American Magazine, Coronet, Cosmopolitan* and *Esquire*. Several of his stories became screenplays.

These included *Fast Company* (1953) starring Howard Keel and Polly Bergen and *Tennessee Champ* (1954) with Charles Bronson and Shelly Winters. He was the ghostwriter of *The Stardust Road*, an autobiography of songwriter Hoagy Carmichael.

Every generation discovers its own form of entertainment. Today it might be streamed movies or video games. For an earlier generation, it may have been television sit-coms. I grew up with comic books and Saturday morning western movies. Prior to these, however, it was the inexpensive pulp fiction magazines with their exciting and well-illustrated tales offering escape from the Great Depression sandwiched between two world wars. In addition to Eustace Cockrell, other regular pulp fiction contributors included familiar names like Edgar Rice Burroughs, Ray Bradbury, Max Brand, Dashiell Hammett, Sax Rohmer, Raymond Chandler and H. Rider Haggard.

Pulp magazines are often associated with detective stories, science fiction and adventures in foreign lands (or planets), featuring covers with scantily clothed women needing to be rescued from some devilish fiend. While Cockrell's writings covered a variety of genres, his primary medium was sports-based stories – football, baseball, horse racing, tennis, golf, wrestling and especially boxing. Often there is a heroine (or an orphaned child) to remind the hero that relationships, not wealth or fame, are the values to be treasured. The women in Cockrell's stories did not need to be rescued, however. Far from it. For the most part, they are out-spoken and independent-minded. This focus allowed him to become more than a writer of pulp fiction: it also allowed him to make the transition to other mainline publications. Here again, Cockrell was surrounded by the most esteemed writers of his day including Willa Catha, J.D. Salinger, F. Scott Fitzgerald, Ernest Hemingway, Jack London, Zane Grey, Andre Gide and Sinclair Lewis.

Eustace Williams Cockrell was born in 1909 in the small mid-Missouri town of Warrensburg. His was from a distinguished family. His grandfather, Francis Marion Cockrell, was a general in the Army of the Confederacy and served as U.S. Senator from Missouri for five terms from 1875 to 1905. Prior to this, Cockrell was a practicing attorney in Warrensburg. His law partner, Thomas T. Crittenden, went on to become governor of Missouri and was most famous for rounding up Jessie James and his gang of bank robbers that had given Missouri a national reputation for lawlessness.

In 1906, following his retirement from the Senate, Cockrell was nominated for President at the Democratic National Convention in Kansas City, Missouri but lost to the eventual nominee, Alton P. Parker. Senator Cockrell's third wife and Eustace Cockrell's grandmother was Anna Ewing, daughter of Judge Ephram Brevard Ewing from Missouri. Many considered her the more socially prominent member of the family.

Eustace Cockrell's parents were Ewing and Leacy Williams Cockrell. Like his father, Ewing was an attorney and later became a circuit court judge before moving to Washington, D.C. Judge Cockrell was nominated for the Nobel Peace Prize on three occasions for his work in developing the Federation of Justice, an organization formed by Judge Cockrell in 1928 to promote successful court practices throughout the United States. Judge Cockrell was nominated for the Nobel Peace Prize on several occasions for his work in developing the Federation of Justice, an organization he formed in 1928 to promote world peace. In 1938, Cockrell also published a book, Successful Justice, that became a major resource for law school curriculums in the U.S. In 1938, Cockrell published a book, *Successful Justice*, that became a major resource for law school curriculums.

Eustace Cockrell was literally surrounded by a family of writers. As he wrote in the introduction to one of his stories, "It was inevitable... that he end up as a writer: his sister married a writer; his brother was a writer, married a writer; another sister was also a writer." In 1939, Eustace himself married a writer, Betty Barnett. Together they had four children —Leacy, Geoffrey, Frederick. and Elizabeth.

As a young writer, Eustace Cockrell followed in his older brother's footsteps. His first major published work was a boxing story co-authored with Francis Cockrell. It appeared in *Blue Book* magazine in 1932. Eustace Cockrell was 22 years old when the story was published.

Cockrell developed a style that set him apart from other writers of his time. In addition to highlighting strong, independent women, Cockrell was one of the first writers to introduce a black hero in the person of boxer Refugee Smith. (He also featured the first women to play on a men's college football team in "Beauty and the Drop Kick," a story included in Volume I.) Refugee Smith appeared in 13 of Cockrell's stories, most published in Colliers. It was the purchase of the movie rights to the Refugee Smith series by MGM in 1942 that brought Cockrell to Hollywood and his initial work with the film industry.

Many of Cockrell's later stories were co-authored with friends including Herb Dalmas and Daniel Gordon. As was the custom, they sometimes wrote under pseudonyms including Jeff Conover (Cockrell and Dalmas) and Nick Spain (Cockrell and Gordon) to broaden their publishing opportunities.

While in Hollywood, Cockrell did not always get credit for his work, especially when under contract with Warner Brothers. Writers often worked in teams with little individual acknowledgement. He did get credit from one person, however. The detective writer, Sue Grafton, most famous for her "alphabet series" of murder mysteries (*A is For Alibi*, etc.), sent a copy of her first book, *Keziah Dane* (1967) to Cockrell with the inscription: "To Eustace without whom...."

In 1950, Cockrell was invited to write for Armed Forces Radio. This coincided with a period in U.S. history when Senator Joseph McCarthy was leading efforts to identify and persecute suspected Communist sympathizers. As a result, many Hollywood writers, producers and other artists were blackballed and unable to work. As Cockrell testified in one of his biographical statements, "I have never belonged to any political or semi-political organization except the Democratic Party but lived in New York during the 1930s and was an interested observer of many "front" groups and knew many Communists intimately."

Still, Cockrell passed the tight military security clearance and went on to write a series of half hour dramas for the Armed Forces Radio. A photo recently added to the National Archives Catalog shows Capt. John Quinn on board the *US Norton Sound* with "famed writer" Eustace Cockrell. While on board, Cockrell wrote about Project Reach, the highly secretive testing of the Viking rocket and the only test performed aboard an actual vessel.

By the mid-1950s, television began to replace magazines as a source of entertainment, leading Cockrell to spend more time with the latter and to establish himself as a major presence in Hollywood. His career was brief, however. Cockrell died in 1972 at the age of 62.

Eustace Cockrell was a gifted writer for whom everyone, even the most hard-hearted and downtrodden, received a second chance. Hope came not from the power of wealth or prestige but from the innocence of children (or childlikeness in the case of Refugee Smith); the integrity of women; and the insights of those often on the fringes of society. Though he spent most of his life in New York and Los Angeles, Cockrell maintained his small-town values and lived with the same sense of honesty, humility, and fair play that infused his writing.

As mentioned, no plan had been envisioned for what to do with Cockrell's stories except for a vague idea that a collection might someday be published. As this became a more serious possibility, it was soon apparent that more than one volume would be needed to cover the diversity of Cockrell's subject matter and the broadness of publications in which his stories appeared. There, too, can be found a division within Cockrell's writings. His early stories (1932-1945) reflect the darkness of the Great Depression and the coming of World War II. Here, orphans, ex-cons and soldiers often serve as sources of inspiration. His later stories (1946-1957) express greater awareness of social issues and a rebellion against restrictive attitudes, especially those limiting the roles of women and minorities. The distinction between short story and television script begins to fade in his later writings, however, and one can sense that television is replacing magazines as Cockrell's writing focus.

In these two volumes, Cockrell's works are presented with little editing and reflect the style of the times in which they were written. Because some of the stories include "Negroes," "Jews" and other minorities, wording has been changed on several occasions to avoid offensive stereotypes. In addition, while over half of Cockrell's published works are sports-related, the number included in this collection has been reduced to allow for greater diversity of plots, settings and publications.

During the years spent collecting these stories, my computer has crashed and been replaced so often that many of the names of those assisting me have been lost. The cooperation, however, from librarians and magazine collectors from the '30s, '40s and '50s has been extensive. In addition to Nancy Cockrell's original gift, Fred Cockrell was kind enough to loan me his father's personal correspondence. Having access to telegrams and letters from his long-time New York agent, Paul Reynolds, and his Hollywood agent, H. N. Swanson, was a major asset in locating Cockrell's early works. Elizabeth Cockrell Coleman and her love and respect for her father was the inspiration that kept me in touch with the person and not just the stories he told.

We all go through life looking for treasures — hidden mysteries about the meaning of life. Then, if we are lucky, we wake up one morning and find that the treasures were never hidden. It is we who have been lost. The treasure is always in the relationship. That's the gift "famed writer" Eustace Cockrell continues to bring to his readers.

Roger Coleman

Edenton, North Carolina

Eustace Cockrell (third from right) on board the USS Norton Sound with Capt. John Quinn (center.)

Short Stories

Douglas Kent, pointing out to sea, said drily, "It seems we have visitors."

THE SHAME OF THE CECILIA

A SONG came to Douglas Kent in the swift tide-race of Placentia Gut, came in the voice of water tugging with his dory, in the answering surge of his muscles as he threw his weight on the oars. It was singing of the men of Newfoundland. Of fishing and fighting and courage; of joy and battle with the timeless enemies, the water and the wind.

Placentia Gut is a narrow cleft between two hills cut by centuries of surging tide, and through the cleft pour cold Atlantic waters.

Douglas Kent, feathering those oars, chuckled; a pleasure-sound deep in his throat, echoing the song he heard. He made to the sloping beach and his father helped pull the dory well beyond the reach of tide. "She's strong today," his father said.

"Aye, but it was fun."

"Fun." He heard the strident voice and looked up and saw the looming figure of John Drake. He heard Drake's laughter.

His father glanced at his son then with vague distaste at the approaching figure. "An economical pleasure," he said drily.

John Drake came abreast of them, laughed again, echoing the word: "Fun!"

Douglas Kent felt the back of his neck burning in helpless rage as he followed his father up the cliff.

At supper, his father reading his thoughts said finally: "Don't act like a child, my son, because a man laughs at you. John Drake is a …"

"John Drake is no good," Douglas said.

"He's new here," his father said amiably. "Don't judge him too quickly."

Douglas didn't answer and his father smiled again. "Kate Arnold doesn't judge him with such haste."

Douglas felt the color come up in his face again and his father turned the subject. "We're going out to the grounds next week." For Douglas Kent there was happiness in this news.

NERVOUSNESS BEFORE A GIRL

Hadn't the old one promised that the money from the next catch would be his? A little luck would make a haul worth $500, and $500 was the goal he'd set himself before asking Kate Arnold to marry. Thinking of Kate he thought of John Drake and found some comfort in the thought that John Drake's Cecilia was still in; he wouldn't be at St. John's soon. Kate still lived at St. John's. But still the thought of John Drake blackened his mood.

The old man said, "Fine schooner that lad Drake has got."

Douglas Kent grunted.

"Hear he has a fine lass, too, in St. John's."

"He probably stole the schooner," growled Douglas. "The lass he has not got yet."

It was with the old soaring delight in his heart that he stood at the helm of the Mary K., nudging the rudder ever so carefully that the tiny ship might swoop through the narrow entrance on the lift of the outgoing tide to the sea and the fishing grounds. His cap rode carelessly on the back of his head and a black shock of hair leaped in the breeze that sent whitecaps scampering over the waste of gray water.

In the week that followed he thought with alternate chagrin and amusement the day he had spoken of rowing as fun. The old man kept him in the dory until he felt the oars were but extensions of his arms. But the shimmering fish filled the hold and grew high on the deck. At last, as Douglas swept the dory aside with a final load. The old one nodded contentedly and said, "If you're caught up on your fun, my boy, we'll take 'em in."

And so Douglas sailed the Mary K. into St John's and Kate Arnold answered his knock on her door.

"I'm back," Douglas said, and blushed at his foolishness. He'd seen her scarce two weeks ago.

"Are you now?" Kate queried solemnly. "You should have given fair warning that we might have a proper welcome. Perhaps a band …"

"Don't tease me now," Douglas said pleading, then waited for the girl to sit down but she remained standing.

"Kate!"

"Yes?"

He took a deep breath. "I'm thinking of taking a wife."

"Where are you thinking of taking her?" Kate asked politely, laughter behind her voice.

"Back to Placentia — where else? We have a fine house there."

"I don't envy the girl, but then every woman to her taste."

This was not the way of it! If he could tell of the song — tell her of the leap of heart when he thought of her. How she made the oars light in his hands. How work was fun working for her. Yes, fun! Instead he said doggedly, "You'll come to love it."

His father came then. He nodded to Kate, and spoke to his son. His voice was flat with bitterness. "The fish," he said, "are gone."

"You mean someone stole them?" Douglas asked incredulously.

"Worse. They are covered with oil. The fuel line's still there leading from the dock to the hold. We've not only lost the fish but we've a mighty mess to clean."

"Did you see anyone?"

"No one."

Douglas' eyes blazed black with fury. Together, father and son walked out of the house.

Then his father said: "I didn't want to say it there, son, but John Drake's boat lies in the harbor. I wouldn't be doing nothing hasty now."

Douglas Kent gave brief inspection to the Mary K. and then said curtly, "Let's clean her up."

"But son, it will be dark 'ere we finish."

"Then we'll rig a light. We've got to get out and take another catch while the luck and fish are running. I'll take care of John Drake later — for he's the one."

Standing in the hold Douglas Kent forked the fish to his father on the deck above, but there was no song in his heart.

When the fish were all out they flushed the hold with salt water, then pumped the water out. Still the compartment smelled of cod, hatefully of oil.

"Never mind," the old man said wearily, "we'll scrub it out well tomorrow."

"It'll have fish in it tomorrow," his son said. "Cast off and head her out. I'll rig a lantern and scrub as we go."

The old one sighed wistfully. Yesterday his lad — today a man. A sad realization, but a proud one too. He slacked the sheet and set a course for the harbor entrance.

The old one's silent compliance might have puzzled Douglas Kent had he had time to think of it. But his mind was on other things. He found pail and soap and rigged a lantern in the freezing hold.

This, the second cruise, was a weary business. Gone was the buoyancy that marked the first. Silently they baited up and silently they worked the lines. But the fish were there and they caught them. And, as before, the little ship grew heavy beneath the weight of the catch.

Douglas dropped into the dory and extended his arms for the baskets that held the baited lines. As he lifted up his arms he suddenly felt that something was desperately amiss. He looked at the Mary K.

"The schooner," he yelled. "She's too far down."

MORE BITTER TROUBLE

He plunged into the hold and crawled inside the top layer of fish. As he exposed the first seam, the schooner rolled to starboard — and a thin sheet of water spurted into a narrow open space between the planks.

"Caulking's washed out!" He shouted to his father.

"Look at the next strake!"

Douglas burrowed deeper into the slippery cargo. "The same," he called. "Best start the pump, she's feeling logy."

He scrambled topside, almost fell as he stepped on a round yellow object, and he picked it up and put it in his pocket as he heard his father say flatly: "My caulking don't wash out."

Douglas Kent, on the pump, called to his father: "She's coming up to blow — how much longer?"

"It's bad," the voice came faintly from below.

Then there was a long silence broken only by the monotonous thunk thunk of the pump. Finally the gray head appeared above the coaming of the hatch. "Can't be done," said the old one. "Have to heave the fish over."

Douglas Kent stopped pumping and began to undress. His father looked at him — too incredulous for query.

"Going over the side," Douglas said, and he tried to keep his voice level. "Maybe I can caulk her from outboard!"

The wind painted his torso purple as he drew off his shirt and then he had draped a bight of line over the side, and straddled the line and the sea put out her arms to him and her arms were icy cold.

Loosely suspended in the water he was flung against the side. The water washed over his head, then fell away to give the wind a chance at him.

Hold the line, line up the soft yarn and tap her in with chisel and hammer. But you can't see. Let her sink.

The decision was a relief and he tried to pass the tools to his father. He dropped them and smiled at his concern over the tools now he had decided to let her sink.

He tried to lie on the deck after his father helped him aboard, but the old man made him dress and wanted him to fork fish. Douglas Kent reeled on the tilting deck and forked the fish over the side as his father shot them up from the hold.

And while he forked there rode up out of the grayness John Drake standing life-size on the deck of the Cecilia, the hateful boat that had a motor, that used oil… and then John Drake called to him, suggesting salvage. John Drake said aloud above the wind that he would help him. He laughed at John Drake. A wild laugh. And he screamed his refusal in exaggerated phrases, exquisitely polite, and the old man called to him, worried. Douglas reassured him — he was talking to himself. And then the Cecilia was gone. And he forked the fish that came up from the hold over the side, back from where they had been too painfully twice taken.

And at last the tiny craft rode so high in the water that no open seams went under when she rolled, and together they manned the pumps and at last the hold was dry. Dry and empty.

"Slack away, we're going in."

Douglas went first to Kate Arnold's. There was no laughter in her eyes when she greeted him this time, for the struggle of the second cruise had had its way with him and he didn't inspire laughter.

"Kate," he said, "come with me." And she came.

They reached the dock and there was the Cecilia. He motioned Kate into the dory, climbed in after her and pulled toward the craft. Aboard, he went below and Kate followed, too curious now for protest.

John Drake's boat was empty. John Drake was gone. The galley stove was long cold. John Drake's mate was gone. Douglas Kent came above, frustration in him more than he could contain.

Kate looked at him. "I'll thank you to take me home," she said. It was the wrong thing for her to say.

Douglas looked at her. His helpless rage boiled up in him. He walked over, axe in hand, and cut the anchor line with one vicious swing.

Freed of her mooring, the Cecilia drifted quickly down wind. Douglas let her gather speed, then brought her about sharply. He spun the wheel and headed for the open sea.

"I'll take you home, blast you," he said.

The storm had abated and the moon shone and lighted the frightened figure of Kate Arnold as she huddled against the cabin top, her face white, upturned to the sky.

"You'll be warmer below."

Kate Arnold didn't move, nor did she make reply.

All that night they sailed. Douglas Kent felt grudging admiration for the quality of his enemy's boat. She was a taut craft, and no mistaking. No matter if she had a hateful engine in her hull.

Dawn showed the sails hanging slackly in a rare calm.

"The breeze is dead," Douglas said.

"Your powers of observation," Kate Arnold said, moving from the foredeck where the cut anchor line lay limply, "are equaled only by your technique as a lover."

Douglas blushed guiltily. "We'll have to stay here until she blows up again …"

"Go down and start the engine."

"I know naught of engines …"

"How do you cook in this fine mansion in Placentia you own?" Kate Arnold asked in bitter sarcasm. "With forked twigs over the fireplace?"

"We own a fine stove," Douglas said, then bit his lips. "We have as fine a house as your own, except the clutter of needless gear about."

Kate didn't answer him but turned down the companionway. In a moment he heard the beat of the little motor and the boat started into motion.

Kate appeared and walked back to him and took the wheel. "Go below," she said, mimicking his tone of the night before. "You'll be warmer."

Douglas Kent, pointing out to sea, said drily, "It seems we have visitors."

A launch was drawing near and on its deck a constable and John Drake were visible. Douglas Kent's father joined them from the cabin.

The launch came close to the Cecilia and John Drake, followed by the elder Kent and the constable, leaped aboard.

The constable said uncomfortably: "You're charged with the stealing of this craft, Douglas Kent."

Douglas Smiled. "Twas just a bit of a good turn I was doing for John Drake. The chock chafed through the anchor line and Kate and myself see her drifting helpless, so we row like mad to board her and take to the open sea for safety."

"Bah …" but the constable stopped John Drake.

"And 'tis convenient that Drake is here. I have a couple of matters to take up with him and the law. He sprayed our load of fish with oil, came aboard out craft and leaning over the port gunwale, he loosened the caulking down as far as he could reach. Thus, when we put out the second time and took on a full catch below she started leaking badly.

"And so," Douglas went on, "when we were in dire trouble, he comes alongside and asks if he could help. The salvage would have brought him more even than the load of fish we had aboard. But I was out of my head and thought the Cecilia a haunt, having been overside trying to caulk from outboard."

He heard Kate Arnold take her breath in horror but he went on. "So the old one and I, we brought her in empty, having thrown the catch overside — and lucky we were, too."

John Drake laughed. "Lies," he said, "all lies. True, I gave him offer of help and he laughed at me, but he stole this boat. I'll lay the anchor line's cut clean, yonder on the foredeck."

Douglas Kent felt his heart stop for so it was,

but he said calmly: "He didn't want me to marry Kate. He wanted her for himself, and he thought — most wrongly — that I would have a chance with her if I had the money from a catch."

"Most wrongly?" Kate Arnold said.

"Let's look at the anchor line," John Drake said. "'Tis all a cock and bull story from first to last."

They walked then to the foredeck and Douglas Kent walked most slowly of them all. There lay the rope. Its end was frazzled as convincingly as if it had been chafed through in months of service.

The song came to his heart then with a burst that drowned out all else and he looked at Kate Arnold and her eyes were shining. One of them slowly closed.

"And look at the coat on Drake," Douglas said, "the shining buttons there. And note the frazzled thread that held the missing one till he leaned over my father's ship and loosened the caulking and snapped the button off. For it fell just inside the coaming of the Mary K."

He reached inside his pocket and held the button he took there from against the coat of John Drake. It was a perfect match.

John Drake's stammer and his face told of his guilt. "We'll take him to St. John's," the constable said grimly, "and you can prefer charges against him."

"No," Douglas Kent said airily, "not if he'll give me the deed to the Cecilia. I have a big salvage claim against her, and the fish he spoiled for my father and me — 'twill be a fair deal."

John Drake nodded dumb assent and Douglas' father spoke: "Ye can trade her to me, for the Mary K., lying at St. John's. I have no objection to the aid of a motor now and again."

"No," Douglas said, "a motor is very nice — especially when you have a wife who can start it." He moved toward Kate Arnold and said over his shoulder, "And that will be tomorrow."

McLoughlin's Sassoon Democrat was all his dreams come true.
It would either print all the news—or, by God and Uncle Henry!
—it would print none.

TOO HOT TO HANDLE

THE MAN in the little coupé drove slowly through the streets of Sassoon, refraining from hurry much as a small boy will prolong an all-day sucker. Here was the square. Around a corner and halfway down the block was his goal: a dingy brick building with a plate-glass front. Slowly the man in the coupe' approached it. He stopped his car across the street.

He sat and watched a sign painter working on the glass front. The man had removed one line, repainted the one above it. He stepped back to survey his work. The first line became visible to the man watching. It was large, bold. *The Democrat*, it said.

The next line began to take form. After a time the painter stepped back again and surveyed the finished job.

The man across the street could see it all now. A grin of pure boyish delight appeared on his face. The complete sign read:

The silent silver-hooded figures strung a large washtub full of tar across the fire.

The Democrat

Lindsay McLoughlin, Prop.

Lindsay McLoughlin climbed down from the coupé. He walked across the street, took a key from his pocket, opened the door and entered the home of the *Democrat,* Coldwater County's only newspaper. He went behind the counter and sat down at the littered desk with the telephone on it. He waited.

Miss Fosbinder was the first to arrive. She was neat in her linen suit, and her prematurely gray hair gave her a regal look. Her quick smile made her surprisingly pretty. "Good morning," she said. "We didn't expect you so early."

Archie Bottom, the Linotype operator, appeared then. Archie Bottom looked as if he had been run through a wringer at some time in his life and had never been ironed out. He tucked his cud of tobacco in the back of his cheek and grunted something that might have been "Hello."

The front door banged and Bingo Gannett appeared, young and red-haired. In another era he could have been accurately called a "printer's devil."

Lindsay McLoughlin said, smiling, "I want to tell you all that you don't have to worry about your jobs. I even hope to give you all a raise soon. We are going to make this an even finer weekly paper, print all the news, have lots of names in our copy, get lots of advertising and have lots of fun."

"Gee," Bingo Gannett said. "Thanks."

Archie Bottom nodded and shuffled back to the press room. Bingo followed him reluctantly.

Lindsay McLoughlin said briskly, "Please give me the names and telephone numbers of our county correspondents. I want to make next Thursday's paper a banner one. I want to call them all up and give them a pep talk. I won't be able to see them all."

Miss Fosbinder walked over to her desk and returned with a slip of paper. "First is Sally Blaine, out in Columbus township. Sally hasn't been getting many items lately but she's about to have a baby and it wouldn't pay to change."

"Have her list all the stuff she gets at her showers and who gave it to her," Lindsay said.

Miss Fosbinder smiled. She continued methodically down her list.

Later, with Miss Fosbinder accompanying him, Lindsay walked around the square. The people were fine. It was great to be a newspaper owner in a fine little town like Sassoon, where people were so friendly. It was, in fact, even better than he had expected and he told Miss Fosbinder as much when they were back at the office.

"I'M AFRAID Sassoon will seem awfully dull to you," she said.

"That," Lindsay said, "will be just fine." He stopped, lit a cigarette.

"When I was seventeen," he said, "I lived in a little town like this one. There was another boy in the town the same age I was. We wanted to go to the city and work on a newspaper. We went and we both got jobs on the River City *Free Press*. I wanted to be a great reporter and then write a great novel — or anything, just so long it was great. As a dream it was practically standard." Lindsay paused.

"And so?" Miss Fosbinder asked, smiling.

"My friend," Lindsay said, "started out selling want ads. I started out scanning hotel registers. By the time I was a full-fledged reporter, I had discovered I couldn't write. But I could report, and so I have journeyed hither and yon and worked where I wanted, but my friend stayed on. When I left he was the assistant circulation manager."

Miss Fosbinder kept attentively silent.

"I hope I'm not boring you," Lindsay said. "I just feel expansive."

"No, indeed," she said hastily.

"So finally," Lindsay said, "I wound up back on the *Free Press*. And by then I had another dream, also standard. I wanted to own a small-town paper. I had practically become a museum piece, being slightly over a half century. My friend had never been with any paper but the *Free Press*, and when I got back to it he owned it. He helped me make a down payment on this paper and when I quit to come here he gave me a watch."

Lindsay took a small hunting case out of his pocket. "It says in the front — I can't read it without my glasses — 'To the best reporter I ever knew, from his last and most grateful employer — Walter Garand.'"

"Oh," Miss Fosbinder said, "the famous Mr. Garand."

Lindsay grinned. "In thirty-five years," he said, "I wind up with a watch. Walt winds up with a big paper. I am attacking the matter this time from the publisher's angle in the hope that the next thirty-five years will be more fruitful."

"But people in small towns," Miss Fosbinder said, "are pretty much like people in big towns, and some of them are resentful to outsiders."

"But I don't want to be an outsider," Lindsay said.

"People so often," Miss Fosbinder said, "see faults in little towns and want to jump right in and crusade for what they consider to be improvements. It sometimes leads to trouble."

"I quite agree with you," Lindsay said. "I'm not a crusader or a reformer or anything. I'm just a reporter. I crave to collect the news and print it. That's all."

Miss Fosbinder looked relieved. She smiled and said, "I mean that there is more to running a county newspaper than having three days to write that John Doe won a blue ribbon at the fair with a Belted Poland China shout. I don't want you to get all worked up about something and then realize it would hurt somebody and maybe make some advertiser mad. I don't want you to get caught because you'll be both the advertising and the editorial departments."

LINDSAY INTERRUPTED her. "What's your name?" he asked.

"Miss Fos — Oh you mean my first name? It's Vivian."

"Well, Vivian, my name is Lindsay. We might as well watch my last illusion perish on a somewhat less formal basis."

"Yes, Mr. — yes, Lindsay."

"And as for the advertising and the editorial getting at cross purposes, don't worry about that. 'The Truth shall make us free.' If it makes us free of advertisers, I'll teach you cribbage. And," Lindsay concluded, "I promise not to crusade a single crusade."

Miss Fosbinder smiled and walked over to her desk.

Lindsay picked up last week's copy of the paper, envisioned his name on the masthead above the editorial column, then ground a piece of copy into his machine and happily started rewriting "Post Oak Notes (By Our Correspondent)." The Post Oak correspondent loved too dearly the words that ended in "ly." Lindsay hoped she wouldn't object to his modest efforts toward brevity.

The first edition of the Sassoon *Democrat*, Lindsay McLoughlin, Prop., was a banner one. The correspondents, goaded gently by phone, had done themselves proud. Ike Ledyard's coal yard had been badly damaged by fire, though fully covered by insurance, and Old Man Clark, a member of Lee's army of Northern Virginia, had died in his sleep and had reaped an obituary which included a detailed account of his conduct at Spotsylvania Courthouse that would have made him proud.

Having been assured by Miss Fosbinder that everybody wanted the street around the Courthouse Square resurfaced, Lindsay gently editorialized on this theme. Miss Fosbinder acquired a new national advertiser on a good contract. She got four new subscribers, and the Marcuses paid their bill for their wedding announcements and ordered a hundred birth announcements. Bingo ran off a thousand dodgers for an auction sale. Max Handley, out Post Oak way, left a half bushel of prime Jonathon apples.

Lindsay looked for a house.

Gradually he got to know the people, gradually he got to admire Miss Fosbinder a little more. Bingo plainly worshiped him, and only Archie Bottom remained reserved. Lindsay wrote to Walter Garand:

DEAR WALT:

A short screed on 'Contentment Come To The Typewriter Tramp.' I have gone to press and the situation is well in hand.

It was a swell issue without a harmful word about anyone therein. When I think of you up there fighting civic corruption, breaking extras on the war, murder, rape and sudden death, etc. etc., I pity you.

I have a new national advertiser, four new subscribers, and an advertising and circulation department that is strictly the mahokus. Its name is Vivian Fosbinder. Do you suppose at my age…?

I'm sending you a copy of last Thursday's paper. Don't try to steal 'Our Correspondent' who covers the Post Oak beat for me. While it may be true that only God can make a tree, only Post Oak can make those sentences. I went over half her stuff and then quit. Kind of like taking a chisel and trying to edit an Epstein statue.

Again thanks for the watch.

LINDSAY McLOUGHLIN

WHEN he had finished the letter, he turned to Miss Fosbinder, who was standing behind him with a proof sheet. She handed it to him. "This," she said, "is an example of what I mean." Lindsay read the paragraph:

August Johns, 60, retired farmer, was released Saturday from the State Institution for the Insane at Walbridge. Mr. Johns, who is said to be completely recovered, will make his home with his son, Amos Johns, 208 East Market Street.

Lindsay laughed. "Are you referring to Bingo's cautious 'is said to be'?" he asked.

"No," Vivian Fosbinder said. "The item. I would leave it out. Everybody knows that when he lost his farm it put Mr. J. a little off his base.

Everybody knows he's back. Why point it out in cold print?"

Lindsay knew she was right but he put it to a vote of the staff. Bingo, torn between pride and pity, was dubious. Archie Bottom was assailed by no such doubts. "He was put there, wasn't he?" he asked. "Then they let him out. It's a news item. I'd run it."

Bingo finally decided against running it. Lindsay cut the story out.

All that day he felt a warm glow. He had done what Vivian had wanted him to do and it had been right. He still felt fine and generous about it when he drove her out to look at a house that was for sale. And while they were in the house, walking through the bare rooms, discussing what he would need, he got a deep feeling of content from listening to Vivian Fosbinder tell him how he could fix the house. It was, almost, as if she herself were moving in.

"You seem to have a very solid interest in my little nest-to-be," he said as lightly as he could.

Miss Fosbinder's face flooded with slow color. "I do indeed," she said, looking at him and smiling.

Lindsay felt his own face flushing. "Well," he said, "I surely do appreciate it. Your interest and all."

"It's a darling house," she said.

IT WAS ALMOST NIGHT when he drove Miss Fosbinder home. It was quietly dark in front of her house and the street was deserted. Lindsay was trying to think of something romantic to say. Instead he said, "This is a fine town. I am really contented, almost. There are two things. One of them is …" he paused, looking up. "Well," he said, "what's all this?"

"I can't imagine," Vivian said, a shade too quickly.

Seven cars were rolling down the street. They were all filled with men.

Lindsay started his motor. "I don't get it," he said puzzledly.

Vivian reached for the handle of the door. "Thank you for bringing me home," she said. "Maybe it's some people going to surprise someone at a party or something. I think you are going to like that house, if you take it. It's got a fine garden."

Something in her tone made Lindsay glance obliquely at her. Her face was slightly pale in the dim light. Lindsay reached over and took her hand from the door. "Uh, uh," he said, suddenly hard. "There's something funny about this and you know what it is." He started the engine. "After all," he concluded, "you work for me."

She started to say something, then stopped. Lindsay followed the cars, some sixth sense warning him to leave his lights off.

LINDSAY PULLED Vivian closer under the heavy bush from where they were watching the silver-hooded figures string a washtub full of tar across the fire. He had a pencil in his hand and a pad of paper.

Under the tree and near the fire was a bound and gagged figure.

"This is kind of new for me," Lindsay said, "but I guess they are going to tar and feather that man. You ought to be able to recognize them. Give me their names."

Miss Fosbinder, still breathless from their swampy walk, said, pleading, "Let's go home."

"Honey," Lindsay said, "this is a big story. We've got to get their names. We won't try to stop them but we've got to get the story. Who is the victim?" He gripped her arm.

"They call themselves the Silver Sentinels," she said. "Some of them are important people in Sassoon; they're your biggest advertisers. If you printed a story about them you'd go broke in a week."

Lindsay waited grimly. "Just give me the names," he said.

"The man who is tied up is Elijah Hale," Vivian said, her voice cold with disapproval. "I'm only telling you this because I'm in your employ. He's got some kids that go to school. The kids wouldn't salute the flag in the exercises. They belong to a religious sect which doesn't believe in saluting any flag. The Sentinels told him he'd have to salute the flag and his kids would, too. I guess he wouldn't."

Lindsay didn't say anything but his face was set in lines of sad resolve.

"Why don't you just skip it?" the woman said.

"You said you wouldn't crusade. It won't hurt that man to salute our flag."

Lindsay didn't answer for a moment. "The *Democrat*," he muttered. "Lindsay McLoughlin, Editor and Publisher. The *Democrat* ... 'In all criminal prosecutions the accused shall enjoy the right to a speedy and public trial by an impartial jury ... to be informed of the nature and cause of the accusation ... and to have the assistance of counsel for his defense.' That's in the Bill of Rights. And my paper is named the *Democrat*." He reached out and took Vivian's arm. "Tell me the names of those men," he said.

She looked up, tears in her eyes. The fire was brighter now, and the bound figure on the ground tried to roll away from it. A passing wood-gatherer kicked him.

"I'll scream. Those men will come and get you too!"

"'Congress shall make no law respecting an establishment of religion or prohibiting the exercise thereof; or abridging the freedom of speech or the press,'" Lindsay quoted. "You work for the *Democrat*. And that's what it stands for. If you want to scream, go ahead and scream!"

Vivian looked at the man beside her. In a level voice, she said, "That big one by the tree is John Atkins, the grocer, and there's Morris Jones."

"What does he do?"

"He's a feed-store clerk."

Lindsay McLoughlin's hand on the woman's arm was gentle now. "Tell me everything you can about each one. Name, age, occupation, address. We — I — go to press tomorrow."

Vivian's voice was still level. "That stringy one with the dirty mask, that's Archie Bottom."

Lindsay was writing down the names. "All right," he said finally. "Let's get the hell out of here."

LINDSAY got into his office at one o'clock in the morning. Vivian was home. He was grinning mirthlessly to himself as he sat down and put the thermos bottle, half whiskey, half strong coffee, between his feet. He reeled in a long sheet of copy paper and started slugging out his lead.

"In a dismal swamp four miles southwest of Sassoon, Elijah Hale, sharecropper, was tarred and feathered, warned to leave Coldwater County last night...."

Suddenly he paused, swinging his mind back to the scene out in the swamp, sluicing the picture through his mind, searching for the colorful phrase he wanted. But it didn't come back so well, sharp and drama-laden as it had been. Instead he thought of Vivian Fosbinder, wet with dew, disheveled, breathless. But pretty, still pretty....

Lindsay jerked his mind reluctantly from Vivian, leaned down and took a drink from the thermos bottle. The colorful phrase wasn't there, but the scene was. "To hell with it," he said dispiritedly. "I can still tell what happened. To hell with the jeweled prose." He started banging away.

Finally, after a long time, he set the margin in, glanced at his watch.

"The following members of the Silver Sentinels were participants in the affair," he wrote. Then he listed the twenty-six names that Vivian had given him....

Vivian opened the office the next morning. The thermos jug was empty but the copy was neatly stacked beside the typewriter. Lindsay slumped in his chair, sleeping with his mouth open. He looked old and Vivian's eyes softened for a moment looking at him.

She went quietly to her desk. Archie Bottom, appearing sleepy-eyed, was noisier. Lindsay awakened.

"Hello, Archie," he said.

"Mornin'," Archie Bottom said.

"I got a story here," Lindsay said. "I want you to set it right up. We'll have to pull out the front page."

Archie's eyes opened wide. "Yeah?"

"Fellow got tarred and feathered here last night," Lindsay said. "Big story for the *Democrat*. I was working on it all night, pretty near."

Archie Bottom's eyes got small and venomous. "Yeah," he said again but his inflection was vastly different.

"Yeah," Lindsay mimicked. "You're in it."

Archie Bottom walked over and picked up the copy paper. He glanced down it. "You think you're pretty smart," he said finally, "comin' down here from the city and pokin' your nose in stuff ain't any of your business. But you can't do that."

"You won't set it up?"

"No."

"All right," Lindsay said, "here's your check. You're fired."

Archie Bottom grunted. "Ain't nobody else in this town can set up type nor run a Linotype," he said. 'I'll go back and get my stuff." He moved off to the back room.

Bingo Gannett appeared. "Can you run a Linotype?" Lindsay asked.

"I — I dunno. Maybe," Bingo said.

"A lot depends on it," Lindsay said. "A lot. We've got a big story here, about the Silver Sentinels. We've got to get it in the paper. By the way, are you afraid of the Silver Sentinels?"

"Are you?" Bingo asked.

"Yes," Lindsay said slowly. "I am. But I've got to print the news."

"Sure," Bingo said importantly, "we gotta go to press." He paused and his voice sounded pleased. "Gettin' kinda like a city paper around here. Remember Cary Grant in …."

ARCHIE BOTTOM reappeared in the room. He had a little kit under his arm. He walked out the door, not saying anything.

Bingo retired to the rear. Lindsay looked at Vivian Fosbinder. "Miss Fos —" he began.

A man came in the front door. He was a big man, genial.

"Hello, Mac," the man said. "You know me. I'm John Atkins. Run ads in your paper. Bottom was tellin' me about a story you stumbled onto last night." The man paused. "I wouldn't run it if I was you. 'Course you can't run it anyway, but I wouldn't try. Just make hard feelins' all around."

"Oh. I can't run it, eh?"

"Why, no," Atkins said, "as a matter of fact, you can't. But that's not the point. Point is we're doin' a duty to the community. Clear this trash out. We don't want nothing but Americans around Sassoon."

"Elijah Hale's an American. Born in this country. His ancestors came over here the same as yours."

Atkins frowned. "Archie says you got all our names. You may wind up without any advertisers. I'd go easy if I was you, Mac."

"If you are performing a public benefaction," Lindsay said, "I should think you would be proud to have the facts about it printed."

"Listen, Mac," Atkins said belligerently. "I'm not going to argue with you. I'm just warnin' you."

Lindsay stood up. "So you are just warning me? Well, I'm warning you. You better get the hell out of here before I come around there and punch you in the nose. I may wind up without any advertisers but I'll have a paper worthy to call itself the *Democrat.*" He moved toward the little gate. "You haven't got a mask on today and you haven't got a bunch of yellow-bellied bums with you. You'd better take *my* advice!"

"You've done it now," Vivian said grimly when the grocer was gone. "This will cost you your paper."

Bingo Gannett burst back into the office. "Gee whiz," he said. "The big press's ruint. The roller's all broke."

Lindsay walked back into the press room. Presently he reappeared. He sat down. "Take us days to get that part in here," he said. His face had great lines in it. "Archie wrecked it."

VIVIAN came over and stood beside his desk. "You could have avoided all this," she said.

" 'The Truth shall make us free,' " Lindsay said sardonically. Then he added, "No, I couldn't have avoided it. I've got to print the news."

"But you *can't* print it now," she said. "Nobody can say you didn't try, didn't do your very best."

He took out his watch and looked at it. "It's getting late."

"I wonder what Lee Tracy'd do?" Bingo muttered.

"I'm sorry," Vivian said coolly, "but it's really a blessing in disguise. If you'd simply realize that the —"

"Bingo," Lindsay said, "Cary Grant would get his paper out, wouldn't he? And so would Lee Tracy. What have those guys got that I haven't got?"

The lines were going from his face and his eyes were brighter. He reached over and picked up the phone. "Long distance," he said. Then: "I want Walter Garand at the River City *Free Press.*" He winked at Bingo.

"Hello, Walt. This is Lindsay. I'm in a jam. My

press is ruined…. Yes, yes. You'll understand, all right … yes, Walt. I want you to set my whole paper up and ship it here in your plane. I'll give it to you over the phone from front to back."

After a pause he went on: "Give me a layout man and a guy can take shorthand."

Vivian picked up her purse and walked out of the door.

Lindsay watched her, his mouth an even line. Setting his teeth, he said into the phone: "Leave me room for a three-column head on page one." He started dictating.

Occasionally Bingo would come up from the back with proofs. Lindsay talked on steadily.

"All right, page two. Get this masthead right. The Sassoon *Democrat* — Lindsay McLoughlin, Editor and Publisher." He talked on.

When he had finished he heard Bingo's admiring whisper. "Lee Tracy never done nothin' like that."

"But he got the girl," Lindsay said, half to himself. Then he straightened up and looked at Bingo. "Well, kid," he said, "we went to press, didn't we?"

"We sure did. And I hope you ordered lots of extras. Gonna be a lot of people want to read this issue."

story that got stirred up by a man not saluting the flag."

Lindsay put his arms around her and kissed her gently. Then he picked up the phone. When he got the connection, he said, "Change the masthead on my sheet. Have 'em make that Vivian McLoughlin, Advertising Manager."

Bingo Gannett heard the squeaky voice come back over the wire: "Lindsay, we're about to roll. Okay about the masthead change. I'll fake a little story on the wedding and stick it on page two. But what's your head on the big yarn on page one?"

"That?" Lindsay said. 'Why for that, just call it — slug it across there big and black — just one line. Just call it *A Salute to Old Glory*."

"When I was in that nice furniture store about a bigger ad," Vivian said, "I saw some stuff for the house …."

Bingo watched a moment, then turned his head, and Lindsay heard him mutter … "No, nor Gary Grant."

LINDSAY SWUNG in the swivel chair, looked for a long moment at the lettering that adorned the glass front of the building, then put his head in his hands. He didn't hear the door open.

Vivian Fosbinder tapped him on the shoulder. "All in?" she asked.

Lindsay looked up and grinned crookedly. "All in. Walt's pilot will drop 'em on the golf course."

"I saw some people," Vivian said.

"Maybe you'd like to buy the paper yourself."

"It's not for sale." She was having trouble with her voice. "I didn't realize some things."

"No?"

"It's still the only paper in the county. We've got our legal advertising and our national accounts. I got promises from most of your local people to keep right on."

"You what?" Lindsay stood up.

"I didn't understand some things," she said again, frank tears in her eyes now. "Every ex-service man in town is strong for you. Funny … on a

Narrowing her eyes, she read the inscription aloud, her voice filling with surprise and wonder.

"THAT WYNNE GIRL"

They were saying things about her — and Christmas was just ahead. Swifty grumbled to himself — but did a lot of thinking ....

THEY CALLED HIM SWIFTY. He being one of the couriers that the rain or something kept not from the swift completion of appointed rounds. He knew the quotation and secretly was proud. He came into the Post Office and pulled off his woolen gloves. Small icicles hung from the rim of his walrus mustache.

"Good Mornin', Swifty." said Edie Adams, the widowed postmistress.

"Cold in here," he said. That danged boy's supposed to build the f'ar at six o'clock — give it time to warm up."

"Guess the storm held him up."

"I got twenty miles of it," Swifty said bitterly. "Car broke down and I got to do her in the buggy. Just as well," he went on mutteringly. "Snowplow probably ain't out yit, and I'd bog in the car." His voice rose, petulant, though he was inwardly glad he had to use the buggy; it would remind him of older, kinder days.

- 15 -

Edie Adams went on sorting mail with brisk inattention.

"The U.S. mail's going through," Swifty fumed, "but that danged boy can't get down here to build up the f'ar." He walked over to the cannonball stove, stepping around the cat. "Consarned animal," he said. "Place for animals is outside."

"You leave that cat be," Edie told him.

"Women, too," he grumbled, stamping his foot at the cat. The cat looked at him with mild interest, not moving. He rubbed his gnarled hands, blue with cold. When they were warm he picked up the limp sack and went to the table where the letters and packages lay. The cat watched him affectionately, its eyes opening and closing in sleepy awareness.

Swifty cast a guilty glance at Edie's back and brought up a package from the bag. He vigorously canceled the stamps. The ink smudged dark and illegible on the clean brown paper. "Tsk, tsk," he clucked.

"What?" Edie Adams turned around.

"Nothin' woman, nothin'." He peered at another package. "Looks like it's for Alf Taylor, but you'd never know it. Folks write worse ever' year, seems like." Carefully he stowed the letters and parcels.

"GO TO MEETIN' last night?" the postmistress asked.

"Nope."

"That Wynne girl was there." She paused expectantly.

"Hmmm …" Swifty, the new cud bulging in his cheek, eyed the stove, looked at the postmistress, decided against it.

"It's downright disgraceful."

"Hmmm …."

"Been here six months. You can't tell me she's got a husband. He'd be writin' to her with her in *her* condition."

Swifty went to the door and spat skillfully, scarring the clean snow, lying over two feet deep on the level. "Get back in, dang ye," he whispered to the cat, which had followed him and was peering out. "Seems like I heard she had a husband," he said mildly, "in one of them veterans' hospitals somewheres'."

"That's *her* story," Edie said scornfully.

Swifty bound the muffler high around his neck and shouldered the heavy bag. "Women," he said bitingly. He hesitated at the door, reluctant to face the cold, then trudged to the buggy, his old body inclining against the weight of the bag. He shoved the bag up in the buggy and climbed in after it. The snow made a flurry when he shook out the canvas shield, and the mare moved her ears as she set out with no word from the man.

The cold was seeping into him by the time he reached Alf Taylor's farm. Alf was standing on his porch, fifty feet from the road. Swifty reached in the bag, extracted two packages, a letter.

"COME AND GET 'EM," he called, holding the mail aloft. "I ain't got all day."

"Any one registered?" Alf yelled back.

"Yeah," said Swifty. "The letter."

"Well, bring it up. I gotta sign for it — and besides my woman's out tendin' the chickens in my overshoes."

Grumbling, Swifty wormed from behind the canvas shield and trudged to the house through the snow. "Better re-wrap this'n," Swifty said. "Your young un'd sure know it was a pair of skates from his Uncle Bill."

Alf Taylor was inspecting the address on the other package.

"Anything the matter with it?" Swifty asked belligerently.

"Huh… yeah. It don't belong to us."

"Let's see." Swifty looked at the parcel with his sharp blue eyes. "Danged folks can't write no more so's a man can read. Danged country's goin' plumb to hell." Still muttering, he struggled back to the buggy.

Two miles farther along, he made the same mistake again. It was Mrs. Sunders, of the Five Corners' Quilting Club, to whom he gave the package this time. Mrs. Sunders had seen his buggy and was waiting for him at her box. He was back in his buggy before she called to him.

"Now what?" Swifty yelled crossly.

"This," Mrs. Saunders said shrilly. "It ain't ours."

SWIFTY climbed laboriously out of the buggy and took the package. "Taken you long enough to find out," he said bitterly.

"I'm sorry."

"Hmmmph."

It was almost dark, with the early night of December, when he came to the small house that stood close by the side of the road.

Newcomb's tenant house it had been before that Wynne girl had rented it. Swifty felt the jolt when his chilled feet touched the ground, felt it clear up to his knees. He took the only parcel left and plowed through the deep unbroken snow.

The girl came and answered the door. She had nice clear eyes like he'd remembered. Swifty held out the package. "Your'n," he said.

"You didn't need to bring it up. I could have gone to the box." Then, narrowing her eyes against the failing light, she read aloud, her voice filling with wonder. "To Mrs. George Wynne. From Sergeant George Wynne."

"I know I ain't *required* to fetch 'em to the door," Swifty said testily. Then more mildly, "Your husband, I guess." He paused, spat. "Had the durnedest time with that package. Give it by mistake to a couple o' the dangest gossips in the county. Young folks don't seem to write writin' a man can read."

She looked at him and smiled a slow sweet smile, full of sadness and understanding. "Thank you," she said. "Thank you very much. Shall I open it now?"

"I gotta be goin'," Swifty said hastily. "A man can't dally carryin' the U.S. mail." He turned and went back to his waiting buggy. The bootees would be nice, the diapers, the little shirts, the wrapping blanket. "Whole durn outfit only cost me nine dollars," he chortled to the horse. "Women!" he snorted.

HE HEARD THE GIRL call "Merry Christmas!" and then he thought of something and gnawed another icicle from his mustache, smiling.

I'll get me a telegram form along 'bout groundhog day and let him die, he thought. But by golly, I believe 'fore I do, I'll promote him second Lootenant.

The mare raised her ears, waggled them, and went into a trot. The buggy wheels sang in the cold snow.

NIGHTMARE

His honeymoon was over. To Richard Trailkill all that remained
of his brief paradise was a womanless house,
and a stranger son who was not his own.

*There was a crash, then silence.
Trembling, Joe looked down the stair well*

RICHARD TRAILKILL stood by the grave and felt the sleet biting through his thin hair. The preacher was hurrying now, so that there were no spaces between his words, and the cold wind took the jumbled words and tossed them playfully away.

The preacher finished with a little rush and there was an instant's deep silence; then the little company turned away. Joe Gordon, the boy, put on his stocking cap and rubbed his cold and moist nose with his mitten. There were tears standing in his eyes, but he wasn't crying. A few of the people shook hands with Richard, patted Joe Gordon on the head; the women eyed him tenderly. Then they walked down to the road and climbed into their buggies and their little cars and drove away, and Richard Trailkill heard with numb and bitter rage one man say, "An' now he's got him a fair-la-yin' piece of land and a young'un pret' near big enough to work it."

Richard Trailkill took five steps toward the voice, felt the boy's hand on his forearm. He stopped, took the boy roughly, jerked his arm, walked with him toward the road, and turned up it toward their house. He walked in silence, stifling rage, and the boy walked beside him.

Inside the house, the boy replenished the fires, and Richard Trailkill went to the barn. The boy followed him warily. The stock was up, looking well cared for.

"Mr. Barnes looked after the stuff," the boy said. Mr. Barnes was the one who had made the remark Richard had overheard.

The man looked at the boy, hate under his eyes. "Can you milk the cow?" he asked.

"Yeah, but the cow's dry." The boy paused. "Her name's Ruby," he added.

"Gather the eggs, then."

"Hens ain't layin' — they ain't finished moltin'."

"Well, do something!"

The boy's eyes were wet, and two tears got away from them and ran a little way. He rubbed them off with his mitten, leaving his face smudged. "I was fixin' to throw down some hay, feed the chickens, and pump up some water. That's about all the chorin' there is." He turned his back on the man and climbed into the loft. In a moment hay cascaded into the mangers, and there was a pleased excitement among the mules, and the cow mooed softly.

It was still in the barn, and the mules' chewing made a warm sound. The boy could be heard moving in the loft, and the man leaned against a wall, his head against his forearm, and stopped a sob in his throat.

THE BOY climbed down and, moving across the barn lot, threw grain to the chickens from a bucket looped over his arm. He spoke to one of them, a big, baleful-eyed rooster, with warm affectionate scorn. Then the man heard him pumping water into the tank, the sheet ice cracking as the warmer water from the well hit it. The mules came out and drank; a little later the cow went out to drink from her side of the barn. The man still leaned against the wall.

This was the farm near which his camp had been in that unreal, distant summer, five years before. He had been a private in a company stationed there. And this was the farm where the girl named Margaret lived; Margaret Gordon, the widow of twenty-five with a six-year-old boy. Joe was a little boy, then, going sleepily to bed soon after Richard would arrive to sit in the parlor with his mother. Joe's father had been dead since he was three months old, and the neighbors farmed Margaret Gordon's fair-lying quarter section on shares and did the heavy chores.

"I can't imagine you being alone so long," he'd said one night.

"I'm not alone — you're here. And Joe —"

"I mean, why you never remarried," he said.

She told him very simply, "No man has asked me that I love."

Richard Trailkill's hair had not been thin, then, but thick and curly, and he had felt it tighten on his scalp. "I'm a bookkeeper," he'd said. "An imitation soldier. But I could farm."

She made her eyes round, mocking, but so soft.

"Do you love *me*?" he asked.

She had told him.

They were married late in the fall, when he had a leave. The frost was on the shocked corn, the wheat nestled dormant, waiting for the spring.

Five years later, the spring came again, as the

spring always comes, and the wheat was bravely spearing toward the sun, soft green, unserried ranks of matchstick height, a young and haunting green.

Joe was almost twelve, carrying water for the threshers, driving the mules to the bull rake in the haying, but his mother and his new father weren't there. He stayed with Mr. Barnes while they had their honeymoon. She loved Richard just as well with his left elbow shattered; she thought the ribbons pretty on his blouse.

They came home in the fall.

THE WIND that slanted the sandlike sleet against the barn carried the boy's call: "Mr. Trailkill! Mr. Trailkill! Supper's ready." The voice was faint, in it a note of sad pleading.

Richard Trailkill straightened, pushing himself from the wall. He looked blindly toward the house through the open barn door.

They had come home. Home to the bare hill, with the sleet, turning now to rain, slanting blindly down upon it, making little rivulets in the mounds of clods. And he was home with a boy. A boy who wasn't his.

They had been happy, so very happy. Happy in a breathless way. And suddenly she was sick, and he sat in the hospital, numbly faithful to the thought that pneumonia now wasn't much. With the new drugs it wasn't much. But it had been enough. He walked, stumbling a little, toward the house.

It was a good farm, fair-lying land. The house was warm, and the lamps glowed on the windows lightly beaten by the rain and sleet. In the big kitchen, plates were on the table, and on the plates rested slices of too thick bacon, congealing eggs.

Richard Trailkill sat down and picked up his fork. The boy watched him through his eyelashes until he cut a bite, and then they both tried silently to eat.

The man poked at his eggs, looked up. "Why are you looking at me?"

The boy dropped his eyes. "I didn't mean to."

"Oh, it's all right," Richard Trailkill said. "I just wondered."

Tears formed quickly in Joe's eyes and he wept. "I don't know," he said.

Richard looked at him. "What would you like to do, Joe?" he asked.

"I don't know," he said again. "I got no kin."

It was true, Richard Trailkill reflected; he had no one. HIs father had been an orphan, his mother an only child, her parents dead.

"I have no relatives, either, Joe," the man said. He wanted to say something more, but he didn't know what to say.

"You — you think you'll sell the farm, Mr. Trailkill?" the boy asked finally.

"I guess so," the man said.

"What'll become of me?"

Richard Trailkill almost laughed. "Oh, Joe," he said. "It's your farm."

"Didn't Mamma give it to you?"

"Oh, no. If I sold it you'd get the money. It would be enough, I expect, to put you in a good school, clear through college."

"A better school than Pleasant Valley?"

"What's Pleasant Valley?"

"Where I go. It's just two miles from here." The boy paused. "Gonna have a baseball team next year."

"Oh."

"My mom was gonna get me a glove for my birthday —" Tears started again in the boy's eyes.

"They'd have teams where you went. You'd probably get to wear a uniform."

"Would it let out summers?" the boy asked, drying his eyes. "I get to come home summers?"

"Oh, yes," the man said. He felt sorry for Joe in an impersonal sort of way. It was rough. He remembered vaguely when his own mother had died. He'd been about Joe's age.

"Where'd I come home to?"

The man looked at the boy, seeing him clearly. Small, freckled, smudge-faced, grieving for his mother. "Here we sit, grieving for the same thing," he thought; "differently, but the same."

"You couldn't farm the farm, Joe," the man said softly.

"I guess not," the boy said. He gave up his pretense of eating, took his dishes to the sink, poured hot water in the pan. He came back, a question in his eyes, and the man nodded. He picked up Richard's dishes and put them with his own. He poured in soap, washed the dishes carefully, standing them on edge in a rack by the sink. Richard

Trailkill found a towel and stood there drying them.

"You don't need to go to school tomorrow."

They finished the dishes in silence. "Let's go to bed, Joe," the man said. He reached clumsily for the boy, but Joe pulled back, then stood. His shoulder was tense under Richard Trailkill's hand.

They walked up the steep stairwell into the cold, big room, the boy carrying a turned-down lamp. He put it on a table and turned it up, moved to the door of his own room.

"Can I leave my door open?" he asked.

"Sure, Joe. And I'm sorry, kid, sorry about it all. I'd like to cry, too."

"You would?" The boy's voice was eager.

"Sure, Joe."

"But you can't, can you, bein' a hero and all?"

"I'm not a hero, Joe."

Later, he heard the boy getting under the cold covers, felt his sharp, intaken breath. "Did you ever play baseball, Mr. Trailkill?"

"Yes. I played shortstop in college."

"Gee, that's what I'm tryin' out for at Pleasant Val —" The voice stopped.

"Don't cry, Joe." Richard Trailkill climbed numbly into the cold bed, got up, blew out the light, and felt his way back. It took him a long time to get warm, and perhaps that helped him sleep, getting warm after being cold and up so long, wracked so long with fear and grief....

IT WAS COLD and dark. Only the patter of sleet swishing on the window broke the black silence. But Richard Trailkill was up, moving on cold, cat feet. He was whispering. Sharp, unintelligible commands issued from his lips, and Joe Gordon woke and heard him.

Joe went damp all over, lying tense and still, hearing the man moving almost silently on his bare feet. "Lob it," Richard Trailkill said, his voice quiet and tight. "Lob it barely beyond the wall."

Joe Gordon heard three slow-taken breaths, then: "Cover me and I'll go around." Quickly slithering bare feet, a grunt, a crash. There was silence. Utter and complete.

Joe Gordon lay quite still for fifteen seconds, and then he got up. He walked out into the room, scratched a match lying on the table, and lit the lamp. He walked to the stairwell and looked down. Richard Trailkill's bare feet were in sight, his legs.

Joe Gordon took the blankets and pillow from the bed and, dragging them, holding the light high, he made his way carefully down the steps and around the pajamaed, recumbent form of Richard Trailkill.

Joe Gordon looked at him, put down the lamp, and leaned down and listened. Richard Trailkill breathed. With infinite care, Joe inched the man's body down the last step until he lay flat on the kitchen floor. He raised Richard Trailkill's head and put it on the pillow, worked a blanket under and around him, laid another blanket on him. He walked to the stove, opened it, and put chunks of wood on the coals. He looked at the alarm clock by the cookie jar. It was quarter of two.

He walked to the phone on the wall beside the parlor door, took down the receiver, and spun the crank. He listened. The phone was dead.

Joe Gordon knew what had happened, all right. The sleet, wet and freezing, had built and snapped the line.

HE MOVED BACK and stood beside the man, listening to his breathing. It was rough and loud. He rearranged the blankets, climbed the stairs, dressed quickly in the dark. He came down, jammed on his cap, pulled his coat and overshoes on, took out his mittens from his pocket, then put them on the table. Couldn't harness mules except barehanded, couldn't light a lantern except barehanded.

He got the mules harnessed. They were sleepy and surprised, reluctant to go out, but he got them out, hitched to the spring wagon. He'd propped the barnyard gate open when he came from the house. He thought briefly of going back and looking at the supine figure once more, decided against it, slapped the mules with the lines. They were annoyed and shook their heads, and the off mule broke into a canter briefly; then they shook their heads again, making a great clatter against the swishing quiet of the night with their bits, and settled to a hard trot.

There was an inch of sleet, and where the road was smooth the white was unbroken.

The doctor was middle-aged and fat. He wore

glasses and his color wasn't good and he smelled of tobacco. But he was all awake when Joe Gordon pounded him down to his door.

He pulled the boy in, listened silently, dressing as he listened. With his coat on, he walked to the door. The sleet was heavier now, whistling in the bare limbs of the trees.

"I'll get the car and go on, Joe," he said. "He'll be all right."

Joe went out and climbed into the wagon. He turned the mules for home. They smelled sweaty, even in the cold. He let them go, and they went for home, trotting doggedly, evenly now, not shaking their heads.

The doctor's car passed him, and the doctor hit his horn in salutation. The mules saw the twilight of his car and snorted and moved back to the tracks of the car, heads down, their harness jingling. Joe made them walk a hundred yards.

He brought them into the barnyard, unhitched them, led them into the barn. He unharnessed them and rubbed them and tossed them each three ears of corn. He patted them on their heads, and they threw their big ears up and looked at him, chewing their corn.

Joe Gordon took the lantern from where he'd hung it and moved slowly toward the house. He had to loop the lantern over his arm. He couldn't hold it with his hands.

RICHARD TRAILKILL lay on a single bed against the wall of the big kitchen. His eyes were open, and he chatted idly with the doctor, in slow sentences. The doctor sat at the kitchen table, taking measured nips from a half-filled bottle of whiskey.

"Hello, Joe," the doctor said. "I told you he'd be all right."

Richard Trailkill looked at the boy, white and sleety, his eyebrows white with frost. "You made me plenty comfortable, kid," he said. He closed his eyes. "Thanks!"

The doctor looked at the whisky bottle and put it down. He looked at Joe trying to take his coat off. "Joe!" he said. "Get those hands in cold water. Leave the coat alone." The doctor walked over and pumped cold water in the sink, took the boy's hands, looked at them, and put them in the water.

He turned to Richard Trailkill. Richard's eyes were wide with fear. "Very slight," the doctor said. "They'll be all right."

Joe Gordon held his hands in the water and felt the hurt and felt two tears form on his cheeks. It made him ashamed.

But at last they didn't hurt very much, then hardly at all, and the doctor helped him with his clothes and he was very sleepy. He noticed, then, that his bed was down in the kitchen, too, under the far window, neatly made. The doctor rolled him into it in his underwear. He was very drowsy; it hurt, almost, to try to stay awake.

Richard Trailkill's voice came slowly. "So you think the kid could teach me how to farm?" he said.

"Why not?"

Richard Trailkill breathed carefully four times. "His mother used to wake me when I had those dreams," he said.

"You took quite a crack. Stay down for a couple of days," the doctor said. "He could do that, too."

"Wake me up?" Richard said dreamily.

The doctor took a measured swallow from the bottle. "Sure," he said; "and your head's hard enough. You only got a mild concussion. What happened to your arm? You got a good job on it."

"German bit it — hadn't cleaned his teeth," Richard Trailkilll said softly. "My head hurts."

"Want a shot of morphine?"

"In a minute. Wire a guy for me when you get to town, Doc?"

"Okay; tell me."

"Slim Duffy."

Joe Gordon moved his ear, squinched his eyes tight shut to keep awake.

"Plays shortstop for the Sluggers. I know him a little. Ask him to send me a glove he's used — for little Joe. He wants to do some shortstopping for the Pleasant Valley team next spring."

"You're all right, fellow," the doctor said.

"A kid oughta get a kind of special birthday present," Richard Trailkill said slowly, "from his dad."

The doctor stood up and squinted at the needle against the lamp and moved toward Richard Trailkill.

Richard looked up and smiled. "Skip the needle, Doc," he said. "I'll sleep — I'll sleep fine."

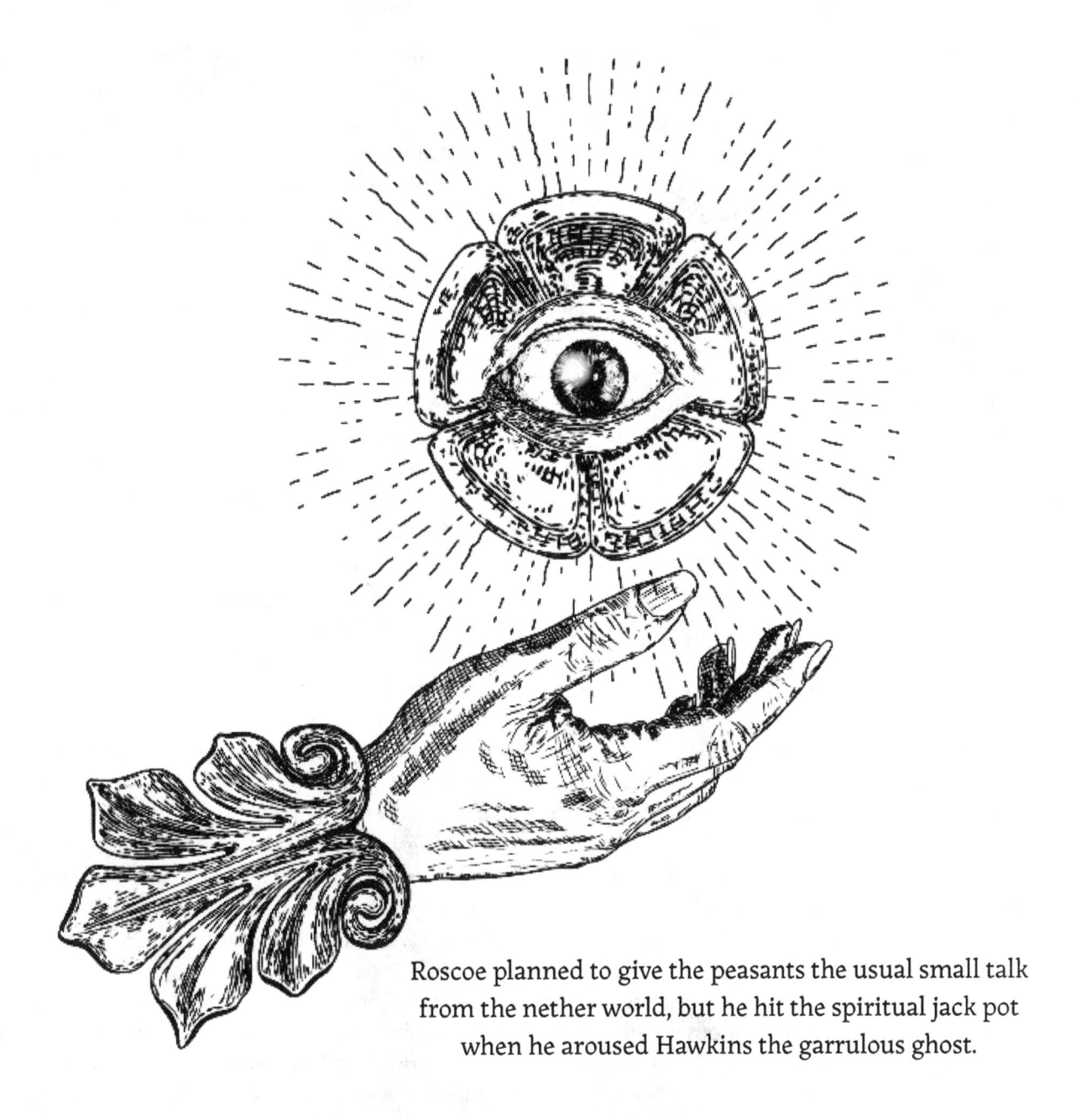

Roscoe planned to give the peasants the usual small talk
from the nether world, but he hit the spiritual jack pot
when he aroused Hawkins the garrulous ghost.

NO REST FOR THE MEDIUM

I AM INTO L.A. from Vegas after a run of unluck, and I got markers here and markers there with guys touchy about letting their markers get yellow with age. In a word I am at the point where not only has the landlady nailed down my truck, but if I go back to my room she will doubtless nail me down also. The beetles are going at Santa Anita and I have not got the streetcar fare to even get out there and try and tout me a sitting peasant for a deuce for a tip.

I am thus. Sitting in a bar gnawing a small beer with my last dime and almost desperate enough to go to work when a cadaver in hand-built Scottish tweeds comes in and sets down beside me. He pulls out a large roll of bills, lays them on the bar and downs three double cognacs. This brings enough color back to his face so that he now only looks like he has been dead three days instead of a week.

I study him in the mirror, trying to figure a pitch, and also I am eying the head of greens lying in front of him upon the bar, when suddenly I recognize him. Or rather I recognize the half of him that is left, for he is so thin he could stand in for a clothes tree by putting on some weight. He is Roscoe Killian.

Now when I last seen Roscoe he weighed two hundred and was doing mind reading with a carnival with which I was connected as a shill. And now he would have to give weight to a midget. But his clothes talked money, the cognac was money, and that big wad of green stuff laying in front of him wasn't run off by no job printer.

"Roscoe," I says, with understandable cordiality, "how's the boy? Don't you remember me, Old Wheelhorse Harry?"

He turned to me and his eyes were wild. In his haggard face they looked like a couple of burnt-out taillights in a dish of cottage cheese. I tell you the guy didn't look well. He looked at his watch then, and groaned. "Yeah," he says enthusiastic as a turnkey. "I know you, Harry. You're right on time."

I did a take. If he was a refugee from a strait jacket, the pitch would have to be very delicate. "Ha ha," I says. "You mean you are right on time, Roscoe."

"Go ahead," he says wearily. "Go ahead with what?" I asked, a little startled.

"Go ahead with the bite." "What makes you think I'm going to …" I caught myself. If this was a standoff it was the most novel and effective I had seen in forty years man and boy fanging people. He'd like to have me denying I was angling or a touch. But as I say, I caught myself. "Now that you mention," I say lamely.

"I know I look prosperous," he says. "You have cased the raiment and are debating between fifty and a hundred. Well, Wheelhorse," he goes on, "take the weight off your head. I will stand for the yard." And with that he hands me a C-note.

To say that I am taken in a heap is a sad understatement. But I get my mouth closed, finally, and Roscoe pours another slug from the brandy bottle and moodily inhales it.

"Gee, Roscoe," I says, "I always thought … well, you know how it is … I didn't *really* think you could read minds."

"Give the gentleman a drink," he says to the bartender. He turns to me. "Worse than that," he says. Then he grabs me by the shoulders and holds me. "Wheelhorse," he says, "have you got a few minutes?"

Not being able to tell time by a pawn ticket I am forced to bend my head around and look at Roscoe's wrist watch. It is such a fancy affair, cluttered up with stuff that will doubtless give the phase of the moon and the barometric pressure and what time it is in Sweden, that it takes me a minute to read the time. However, I finally figure out that it is eleven a.m. "Well," I says, "I have a date with a overlay out at the track …"

"You'll have time," Roscoe says. "And not only that, I'll give you eight winners, if you'll listen — and," he goes on, dropping his voice to a hoarse whisper, "*believe me*."

"For the lend of a yard," I says truthfully, "I will believe anything."

And this is the story Roscoe told me.

You will remember (he begins), when I was with the carnival, I was doing a straight mind-reading act, working palms, heads, cards, whatever looked would pay the best. Well (he continues), I am with the carnival for a time after you leave, playing little towns, the wheels still fixed, and in one the grease goes in wrong and the owner gets arrested and us help are at loose ends. So we are near L.A. and I finally drift on in and am looking around for a casual date — as they call club dates out here, or anything for that matter — and as I am casing the local bladders I see that there is a staggering total of operators making their cakes in some very strange ways. There are astrologers, palmists, psychics of all descriptions. In fact, the town is medium-happy.

So being a man to roam when in Rome, I catch a couple of the smaller advertisers' routines and find they are running to capacity; at a buck to five clams a throw.

Generally the setup is a ring of peasants holding hands in a dark room and the medium fetching up a dear departed, who says things are okay and not to let the children play in the street as they hear terrible things in the spirit world about L.A. traffic.

Now I am a fair ventriloquist myself, and I figure this dodge is tailored for my talents, and to make a long story short and not get into no marathon about the housing shortage, I finally get me a bungalow and hang out a sign. "Roscoe Killian," it reads, "Lunologist and Medium." And before you ask me what a lunologist is, I do not know.

Roscoe shudders violently at this point and pours a dollar and a quarter's worth of brandy on a hundred and seventy-five dollars' worth of lapel, trying to get his drink into his mouth. "I don't see nothing so ..." I begin, but he stops me.

No, nothing so much (he goes on), yet. But wait. Anyway, I get set up, run an ad and set back. The first night I get six squirrels; youngest working guys with their wives, half-stiff and kinda for the lark — I forgot to tell you I had the sign in neon; anyway, I gloom the crib where I work and get them to hold hands and I hold their hands and ask what they'd like to know ....

Oh, another thing I forgot to tell you. I decided my contact with the spirit world would be an old Indian chief, back about ninety years, not too bright and not speaking much English; then when I get stumped out of it on the ground of no savvy.

Well, these squirrels, they would like to know how Cousin Elmer is doing who fell off the scaffolding last year, and I catch this for a rib and have Horsenhalf give them a couple of five-way answers and then shuts up and I herd them out and I got six clams fresh money in my kick. It looks like I blundered into a vein that'll assay out pure wealth.

At this point Roscoe clutches his hair and gives a faint moan.

"I can't see nothing yet," I says, "except that you have found your proper medium, no puns intended. Why the tragic ...?"

"It was the next night. My God, that there next night!"

I go out at the regular time, he goes on, and switch on the neon light. There in front is a convertible that sells for a lien on the mint. And from it stumble three couples whose youth and beauty is a byword on the silver screen. They come up to the porch, kid me a little bit, and we go into the room. I darken her down and we get hold of each others' hands and one of the dolls — you'd know her if I called her name — says, "Tell me what *Beauts and Siedels*," that being the picture she has just finished, "is going to gross?"

Roscoe at this point clean broke down. He put his head on the bar and sobbed. "Roscoe," I says, "don't you think you need air?"

"Don't leave me, Wheelhorse," he pleads.

"Okay," I says, "but get on with the story. I have a date at Santa Anita ...."

He grits his teeth and goes on thus: I start to give her the Horsenhalf routine when this voice, this horrible Brooklyn voice comes in sharp and clear. "This ain't Horsenhalf," it grates.

I jump a foot. Then I am thinking that one of these kids is giving me the big rib. I am about to say as much when this voice goes on. "*Beauts and Siedels* is gonna make like it's Thanksgiving every day. Whew, what a turkey. And you know why too, don't you, sister? Yes, indeed. You can't drive up to Santa Barbara every night and act in no picture in the daytime, too. Not when ..."

"Turn on the light!" the girl screams. I switch on the lights and one of the dolls is white as a sheet. Every one of them is right there where I can see them and still this voice goes on. *And nobody is moving their lips.* The voice is coming from everywhere and there ain't a ventriloquist in the trade can do that.

"Hell, baby," the voice says, "I can talk as good in the light. And take it easy, sugar. I just give Santa Barbara routine to show you I was up. It wasn't your fault. It was the script. It oughta be screen play by Gobble and Gobble."

I am ankle-deep in cold sweat at this point and one of the guys hands me twenty and thanks me.

"Don't thank me," I says. "Honest, I never ..."

"Who shall I thank?" he asks.

"Thank me," this voice grates. "Who else, chump? Thank me, Hardway Hawkins, of the nether world, now operating in pasts and futures, care of Roscoe Killian, a phony and a faker who pulled one fake too many."

I give Roscoe a hard look. This is really tough to believe, but there is evidence right there before me that Roscoe has suffered some kind of horrible strain and has also glommed onto a serious wad of scratch. He has got a watch that is encrusted with diamonds and extra hands, he has got a suit, hand-loomed and hand-built, he has got a roll of bills — from which I see him peel my C-note — which could never bypass the tonsils of no Percheron. He also has the world's greatest reducing system, having dropped from two hundred to ninety-eight pounds, give or take a ounce.

"Well," I says cautiously, "could Mr. Hawkins really foretell the future? And if so what's the beef? I would venture that the act was the uniquest in the trade."

"The next night all the movie colonists in town was out to my place. I raised my price to a hundred clams a clip and was taking circles of ten. Three nights after Hardway contacted me, half the Bunco Squad was out there."

I pricked up my ears. "What gives with the cops?" I ask, being a man loves a uncomfortable cop.

"What Hardway told them cops," Roscoe says, "shouldn't happen to a cop. Not no graft or nothing, but little personal stuff — and I mean personal. They left me be."

"But I don't see what's wrong," I says. "Knowin' what's gonna happen. My God, Roscoe, you got the world by the tail."

"No!" he screams. "Don't you see? It's murder. He's driving me crazy. Nuts, stark staring. If I don't call the so-and-so in, he comes in anyway. I know how the election's comin' out in forty-eight! My God, the odds I could get. I know ... oh, my God!"

I begin to get it, I mean I begin to get it if this thing ain't a thing and Roscoe ain't balmy — but there's the clothes, the cabbage. The thing is that if you know what's gonna happen to you, you are whipped. There can't be any fun then. Then I get the big If. He's liable to tell Roscoe when and how he's gonna die.

I am feeling cold and sick. I got to cop a sneak or I'll be as bad as Roscoe. I give him the small farewell and scram. He collars me at the door, borrows the bartender's *Racing Form* and writes me down eight horses. "Parlay 'em," he says. "You'll win a half a million. Hawkins was playful this morin'. He woke me up at four-thirty and give me the whole card."

Well, I get out to Santa Anita and am beginning to think I been having a bad dream, but I got a C-note that's mint quality. I got that list of horses.

I start easy and Hardway's horse canters in the first. I have ten on his schnozzle and collect forty-eight ... but why go on? I am twenty-thousand winner with the eighth coming up (I hadn't had the guts to parlay 'em, and anyway there practically ain't that much money as I would have won) and the horse on my list goes on the board at ninety-nine to one. Of course if I chuck it all in, it will pull him down probably near evens in the machines, aside from giving the stewards heart failure and probably getting me a escort of a squad of Pinkerton men.

But damn it, I'm a horse player. What does this spirit know I don't know? Sure he has swept the card, but mostly favorites, and Mayer has got a filly going in this heat that stands out like a Christmas tree and Longden up. I put it all on the Mayer filly. To hell with Hardway Hawkins!

I do not see Roscoe Killian for quite some time. Why should I? With the stake I am holding, I am beating them beetles to death. Right out of the form, no tips from the sport world, nothing but form and my intelligence.

But finally I see him at a bar gnawing a small beer. His clothes don't half go around him and he is back to two hundred. I start to duck, remembering the C-note, but he hails me like I really had the hundred. I can't get away. I come over and set down beside him. "I haven't got the yard, Roscoe," I says. "I get so I can't pick my nose after winning forty thousand bucks that day you give me the eight horses. I hunted for you," I lied, "to give it to you. But you didn't look like you needed it, and frankly," I adds, "you didn't look like you would be able to take it with you as the saying goes."

"Forget the money," Roscoe says, "for, my boy, you was instrumental in doing me the greatest favor a man ever had done for him. It comes about like this. After you leave, I sit here and I am drinking brandy trying to get insensible so I cannot hear that Hawkins and it gets to be maybe five, about say the eighth race coming up, and he comes.

"Now ever since that first night he loves to come in on the line '*this ain't Horsenhalf.*' He thought it was cute or something. And sure enough, here I am not quite passed out and in he comes on that line." Roscoe stops to laugh. It is the laugh of a fat and jolly man who don't know what'll happen tomorrow. "After he says that line I hear some kind of sounds like a fight, and then I hear Hawkins' voice kind of desperate. He is yelling for the horse that he give me and I give you."

"Well," I says, "it was some horse race. I had twenty G's riding on it. I know."

"Sure," Roscoe says. "I know, too. But let me tell you. Old Hardway is yelling for this horse, this one he picked. *But there is somebody else yelling, too!* This other voice is plainly up with Longden on the Mayer filly. "The race is over, the photo comes down, and here I am laying in a stupor hoping to die.

"Well, the Mayer filly won it," Roscoe says. "And I hear a scream and a gurgle. Then silence." He orders two beers and fishes two dimes out of his watch pocket.

"Good God, Roscoe ...!" I say. "The silence," he says, grinning. "And then the words: '*This IS Horsenhalf, Mr. Killiam,*' the voice says. "*Hardway Hawkins won't bother you anymore.*'"

"What happened?" I babbled.

"That's what I managed to ask this new voice. The one that said he was Horesenhalf," Roscoe said. "He answered me. '*When one of us go into the predicting business,*' this voice says, '*we ain't allowed to miss. When Hardway give you the wrong horse he was what we call medium done — so I scalped him!*'"

Roscoe signed hoarsely. "Then he told me that never again would I know from nothin' ..." Roscoe fetched himself back to now. A fat guy, happy in his ignorance of things to come.

I sit there feeling very funny. He nods abstractedly.

"What are you doin' now?"

Roscoe laughs that big happy laugh. "Truck farmin'," he says. "I just dump a load of oblongs known in the trade as squash at the wholesalers. I just happened to come by here to give thanks for a day I seen you here and Horsenhalf scalped Hardway." He gets up then and slaps me on the back and gives me the big goodbye and goes on out. I sit there and wonder. Of course I tab the whole thing as a large economy-size lie and that really Roscoe had figured out a wonderful gimmick for taking off the old suet and that he had used hisself as a example while peddling the system. A method like that would be worth a fortune in Hollywood.

Like the sign of wind from a swinging door there is a whisper: "*Wanna shoo-in at Hollywood Park at sixties?*"

I sit there and finally I get my shoe off and get the insole pried up and take out my bedrock ten and get it on the bar. "Brandy," I says. "The bottle."

I spilled some of it on my lapel trying to get down the first drink. But anybody knows this town's full of wise-guy ventriloquists, don't they? Sure it is, ain't it? Please, ain't it?

She came in, all dusty, with hollows under her eyes.
"Where you got him? she yelled.

"You go on home now, Miss," somebody said.
"We'll take care of him.

He wasn't her man, but she done him wrong anyway..

CODE OF THE WEST

GRANDPA was living down on Coronado Island in San Diego a hundred or a hundred and fifty years old — well, old as hell. He's asked me to come down and see him. I've been a writer all my life and I've got grown kids but it seemed Grandpa had found it out — about me being a writer — just a couple of days before. Came as a surprise to him but a pleasant one, he said. Because he had a story. And he wanted it set down, official.

I went down in the morning and he met me at the door and shook my hand. He noticed me dropping his hand gently — it felt like a worn-out cloth bag full of little sticks — and he grinned at me. He said, "That ain't much of a hand, is it?"

He took me around his house — he had a big house with a nurse and a couple of servants — and we sat down in the sun.

"Reason I asked you down," he said, "was that yesterday I found out I was officially dead. Insurance people called up and asked me did I want 'em to pay off now or wait for formal interment. I told 'em to pay off, so you'll be gettin' some money one of these days, soon."

I started to say something, but he stopped me.

"To hell with that!" he said. "I want to get this down, or leastways, told. You don't have to do nothing with it. I just want to tell it."

He sat there a minute and then all at once he started beating his hand on the arm of the chair. "Ain't that it?" he cried. "Damnedest thing, fulla guts and passion and low comedy and now it ain't anything. I put it away too long. Oh, I can remember it all right. Clear. But there's nothing to it. It's like somebody else and of course it *was* somebody else. There ain't no more relation to me and the kid this happened to than me and the man acrost the street. Hell, this kid, this Amos Sanders, shut up in a cubbyhole in Bill McCauley's Oroport Saloon with fear and lust and the drizzlin' sweats, that was me, but it wasn't me and —"

"Look," I said. I knew what it was, the losing it. "I know what you mean, Grandpop, but go ahead and say it off and I'll put it down like you say it and maybe it'll be all right; you can't tell about that."

He thought about that for a minute and then he told me the story.

I WAS BORN in Brooklyn (he said) and I was twenty and I decided to come West.

I went to Kansas City and later to St. Joe and there I practiced playin' poker and I had some money and some patience and never drank when I played — hell, that was enough, just stayin' sober when you played, to make you wages. But I was good. I knew percentages and I got to know people pretty good and I never played a hand nor a game like it was to be my last on earth, which is a failin' of many poker players.

I won money in Kansas City and St. Joe and Dodge City and I was twenty-two years old and I rode into this town, set down in a bowl of mountains, a played-out mining town, just a place to stop.

There was big saloon left there, the Oroport, and in the boom days there was a stage at the back where I guess the girls danced — back when the ore was coming out like, they say a hundred dollars a wheelbarrow.

But the girls was gone, the stage was boarded up, and up over it was a little room made out of heavy timbers and set up on railroad iron stilts. Bill McCauley, who owned the Oroport, had put his safe up there and cut a couple of slits in the timbers. On big nights, when there was gambling and money being spent, he had an old man — an old gunfighter named Willis Anderson — who set up there and looked out the slits with a carbine in his hands.

Bill McCauley figured fights inside a place was bad for trade, and old Willis had orders to shoot anybody who went for his gun or knife whilst inside. You got up there by a ladder that could be pulled up, and even when old Willis was dozin' he'd prop a gun through one of them slots and it had the effect of makin' the trade right meek. It was a well-run saloon and gambling hall if you didn't care what you drank.

I'd been in the town two-three weeks and that was because there was ranchers around had the fiercest curiosity ever I saw. You draw one card and chunk a big bet at 'em and there they'd come. They'd call with baby threes and they thought aces up was cash in hand. They called it "keepin' the kid honest." It was like shootin' sheep with a scatter-gun.

But still and all I wouldn't have lingered there if

it hadn't been for the girl. Sydney Johnson was her name. Her paw had a pretty good cattle spread near the town. She was seventeen years old and got into town right frequent being close by, and she was ripe and frisky and eye-rolling and any man who had enough blood in him to support as many as two corpuscles would have had trouble not rolling his eyes back at her.

SHE made it to meet me on the street and talk to me and it was her paw himself that introduced us. She'd ask me things, questions, but it was the things she didn't ask that was bothering her; me too.

I remember once I met her on the street and we stopped and talked.

"Amos," she says, "I'm going to call you Amos if it's all right."

"It's all right."

"Amos, how come you wear low-heeled boots like you do? I thought everybody wore high-heeled boots."

"Well," I said, "it was told to me that high-heeled boots was a help in holding a horse you had roped in the corral and also if you got throwed you could leave the boot in the stirrup and not go bouncing your head along the ground if your horse run off."

She nodded.

"Well, I don't intend to rope no horse in a corral and I don't aim to buy no horse to ride that ain't gentle as a kitten. I can't ride a horse very well and I don't much want to know how. I am aiming to get to Los Angeles before the railroad gets there and go into the real-estate business."

"How fascinatin'," Sydney said.

"What?"

"The real-estate business."

"It'll fascinate me," I said, "if I can get out there and buy some ground before the railroads get there and if it goes up after they reach there."

"I'll bet Los Angeles is some place. I'll bet you'll be lonesome there."

WELL, I'D NEVER been lonesome except riding from place to place — never being one to consider a horse much company in spite of the songs. But Sydney *had* kind of grown on me and I got to thinking I would be lonesome for her.

"You suppose I could hire a rig at the livery stable and you and me could go buggy ridin'?" Soon as I said it I knew there wasn't a chance of that. Her paw was awful strict and he'd been so savage with the few young fellows that had pined around their place that they'd give up.

"Oh, Amos," she said, "there isn't anything …"and then she stopped and tears got in her eyes and she turned and walked away.

You know, it's funny about the men of the Old West. Willis Anderson give me an idea about why they acted like they did. Like their attitude about women, there being bad women and decent women and not none in between. And their kind of unnatural gallantry. I think that it wasn't that way at first, but it was like elsewhere, but then fellows back East wrote books about 'em being like that and they read these books finally, or heard about 'em and got to acting like the fellows had 'em in the books. Kind of life follows art, though I don't suppose those books was much for art.

And that's important because it caused a lot of what happened.

And what happened was that I stood rendering in that hot sun and watched Sydney walk away from me, kind of stumbling like she was blind, and I decided it was time for me to go.

I went over to the hotel and got my stuff packed and went down to the livery stable and told them to get my horse ready and then I went to the Oroport to tell Bill McCauley and Old Man Willis Anderson goodbye.

I bought drinks for them that was around, including Mr. Bigelow Johnson, and when they heard I was going on they complained about my leaving a winner from them and so I set down with them for a last two hours and won seven hundred dollars more. There is nothing like having people trying desperately to beat you to make them easy to beat.

Then I went away from there. I went down to the Wells Fargo place, give them all but movement money to send along for me, and got my horse at the livery stable and headed toward the settin' sun, like they say. Only the sun wasn't settin' very fast and was up where it'd fry your brains out like it had them that lived there, I guess.

My horse poked along and I set up on him and thought about Miss Sydney Johnson, and I thought about her bottom bouncin' off up the street under them long skirts and her cryin' and it made me sad in an amorous sort of way. I didn't look up, hadn't looked up for a long time. I just set there bobbin' gently on my horse, feelin' kind of piny and terrible virile.

"Oh, Amos."

I looked up. I knew Mr. Johnson lived out this way and I was goin' by his place and on the porch of the adobe house was standin' Miss Sydney Johnson, yo-hooin' and wavin' her hand.

I rode up to the porch but I didn't get off my horse. I was scared to.

"Amos," she says, "are you leaving?"

"Yes, ma'am."

"Oh." She stood there and I set there. "I came on home," she said. "Paw ain't coming till late tonight."

I didn't say anything. I was scared of my own feelings. Also Mr. Bigelow Johnson.

"Wouldn't you like to step down and get a glass of cold water?" Sydney asks. "And water your horse and let him have a little bite to eat? It's thirty-some miles to the next town."

"I aimed to ride while it's cool," I said. "I really ain't got the time."

Funny thing, I was standin' on the ground. The horse kinda edged into the shade and I kinda edged into the house.

She was handin' me a gourd full of water and I spilt it on my front and then I taken her around the waist and kissed her, with her helpin'.

"Oh, Amos."

I had sense for just a flash. I knew if things proceeded and Mr. Bigelow Johnson came on us, he would nail my hide to his barn door and cure it with salt with me still in it. I bolted from the room and jumped my horse and give him the quirt. I run him for several miles through that sun and finally I slowed him down. I was in a turmoil. I'd have turned and gone back and married her if her paw would have let me. But I knew he wouldn't — me a Easterner, a gambler, in low-heeled boots. He wouldn't never let me.

IT CAME ON NIGHT and started gettin' cool and then cold like it does in that foolish country and I figured that by the time the sun come up hot I'd be in the next town. I had decided by then to sell my horse and go on to Los Angeles by stagecoach. I had more money than I had figured I'd have.

Well, I struck a match to look at my watch and I heard the man say, "Don't make a move or I'll blow you in two."

I never made a move and I don't know yet what time it was.

"Stand down."

I stood down.

He come into closer range, then, holdin' a double-barrel scatter-gun and a-breathin' hard. He wasn't wearing no mask and for a minute it didn't figure.

Then I seen it was Mr. Bigelow Johnson.

"Mr. Johnson," I says.

"Don't you open your sweet-talkin' mouth," he says and he sounds like he's stranglin', "or I'll blow you plumb to pieces and stake down the remainders for the ants."

I never opened my mouth.

He put my hands behind me and tied 'em tight and put me up on my horse and taken a runnin' loop around my neck, snugged it up and got on his horse. "It'd be a pleasure," he said, "for you to run off."

He sounded like he was clean crazy so I didn't tell him he'd still have my head and half my neck did I try.

"Where you takin' me?" I risked finally.

"Back," he says. "And don't say nothin'. Not a syllable or I'll blow you in two."

Well, I was scared all right, and mystified too. He seemed so hipped on havin' me divided up I didn't say nothin'. I didn't even agree with him when he told me he rode a short cut — "like a madman" — to head me off.

He hustled me along at a good trot, makin' me quite sore for I don't jibe with a trottin' horse, and we passed his place about ten o'clock and got to the Oroport about one, I judge, for it was still lit up and they was three tables of poker and some fellows at the bar. It was Saturday night.

Old Man Johnson herded me in, punchin' with his shotgun. We attracted some attention.

He went and spoke to Bill McCauley, and then

he came back and herded me over to the safe room up on stilts, got old Willis Anderson to lower the ladder, and drove me up. He come up after me and taken an old pair of handcuffs from the wall and put one around the safe handle and the other around my right wrist though I was still tied up.

"Watch him, Willis," Mr. Bigelow Johnson said and then he climbed down again and went to the bar.

I INCHED over and looked down through a slit. Mr. Bigelow Johnson had quite a audience then and he taken a drink and turned.

"I brought this skunk back," he says, "to hang him official. He ruint my innocent daughter and rode off."

"Why, he's a big liar," I says to Willis Anderson who was watchin' out his slit. "I never done any such thing. And anyway how's anybody going to hang anybody official? They ain't even a justice of the peace here."

Old Man Johnson had taken another drink and he was hollering now, workin' himself up. He was workin' up some others, too. Mostly ones I'd won money from playin' poker.

"That snake in the grass with them city boots and them lucky draws and them sweet-talkin' ways, comin' through here and winnin' our money — cheatin' —"

"I never has to cheat them morons," I said. I was plenty scared but I was kind of sore, too, by then.

"...Then rides out to my ranch and ruins my daughter, leavin' her a ravaged bundle of tears..."

Old Man Willis Anderson looks at me and he looks right interested, but not sore at me.

"...Ruinin' decent girls, rapin' helpless motherless females —"

"Let's hang him now!" somebody hollered.

I really got scared then. And I felt the cold sweat start on me and the handcuff cut my wrist, numb as it was from the rope.

Old Willis Anderson looked real interested at me.

"The murderin' drunken fools," I said and I guess I sobbed a little, thinkin' of Wells Fargo holdin' my money for me in Los Angeles and me only twenty-two years old.

"Funny thing about the West," Willis Anderson said. "Ain't got anything in it but trollops and angels. I'm a Kentuckian myself, been out here fifty years but it wasn't like that at home."

"You suppose they'll hang me?"

"I guess," Willis Anderson said. "They kind of got to."

I didn't understand that then but he went on.

"They'll get really drunk and probably hang you at sunup. Make it kind of official."

"I didn't do nothing to that girl," I said.

"You didn't?" He seemed disappointed. He climbed down the ladder, and through my slit I seen him go over to the bar and talk to Mr. Bigelow Johnson. Mr. Bigelow Johnson was red and his neck was a-throbbin' but I couldn't hear what he said.

Willis Anderson come back up the ladder.

"The girl was layin' in tears when Bigelow came home early. She give you full credit for her condition, which she allowed was changed." Willis Anderson rolled a cigarette. "Or so says her paw."

"She's a big liar," I said and I was cryin' then. "And you'll let 'em hang me."

"I can't stop 'em, son," he says. "They got to hang you. You ain't only violated a girl, son. You've violated a code of the West."

I sat up there numb and watched them get drunk and the clock over the bar crept around and crept around and they got drunker — even Bill McCauley who owned the bar—and they talked low now it was decided and every once in a while they looked up at where I was, though they couldn't see me and licked their lips and turned and drank some more.

They was bums or they'd have been home — bloodthirsty stupid bums plannin' to hang me when it got light.

I prayed some and begged Willis Anderson to do something but he said he couldn't.

I told him to fetch the girl. He said they wouldn't expose her to the shame. "Lettin' people see her right soon like this after the talk...."

I looked down, and Bill McCauley's bald head was shining in the lamplight, and Mr. Bigelow Johnson's neck was gettin' redder, wattlin' up, and those others were lookin' up toward me, lickin' their lips.

She come in then, all dusty, dust clean up to her waist where she'd been in weeds with dew and then walkin' in the dust, and hollows under her eyes.

"Where you got him?" she yelled.

"You go on home now, Miss," somebody said. "We'll take care of him."

Her cheeks was red as apples and she looked at her paw. "If you'd left me a horse to ride, hadn't turned 'em out, I'd have been here sooner."

"Daughter, spare me —"

"You bring that weasel-mouthed rascal down here right now," she said, seein' everybody lookin' up at where I was. "And marry him to me." She stopped and taken a deep breath. "I'm going to have a baby!"

My mouth fell open and the hangin' bee started fallin' apart. I guess that's quite a line and it numbs folks better'n most any other there is. Miss Sydney went over and put her arms around her paw and kissed that repulsive face of his and said, still loud, "You're going to be a grandpa."

Fellow named DeWitt Tyler, a hanger-on around there, he said, "How do you know?" And Mr. Bigelow Johnson went over and hit him, and knocked him down. "That's for you," he says. "Of course she knows."

I didn't know whether I was wakin' or dreamin'. They taken me down and untied me and give me four-five drinks, and Bill McCauley give me the loan of a ring—had it in the cashbox; somebody had put it up for drinks years ago—and Willis Anderson got up and said that by the power vested in him as a former town marshal of Amarillo, Texas, he pronounced us, if we would both nod, man and wife.

I nodded, glad to have a neck to nod and a head with it and I guess that girl did, too.

She took her paw's horse and we rode out away from the rising sun. Headed west for Los Angeles. Last thing I heard was Bigelow Johnson buying DeWitt Tyler a drink.

She was pretty in the dawn, there, even the way she was, dusty and all.

"I told Paw that lie thinkin' he'd fetch you back and make you marry me," she said. "And then I heard you trottin' by the place and I hollered but you didn't hear and I tried to catch up a horse and couldn't. Paw had turned 'em all out. I had to walk and run to town."

"I see," I said.

"You take me along with you to Los Angeles," she says, "and I'll be good to you and take care of you and I can sell Paw's horse and saddle for enough to pay my share. I won't be bad." She blushed but she didn't stop talkin'. "I'm quite a girl when you get to know me."

"Damned if you ain't," I said.

"WELL," GRANDPA SAID, "that's about all. I thought it was kind of interestin' though it come out flat. Sydney was your grandmaw — we had a hell of a time for sixty years. And she never had no baby 'til we was living in Los Angeles and had been for five years. She had your mother. And I guess Willis Anderson wasn't no official marrier at all and I guess all your descendants is really not quite legitimate, but they'll leave you the money. We never got married again. Didn't think we could improve on Willis."

I didn't say anything. Looking at this wizened old man, trying to see him seventy years or more ago.

"Some code," he said, "some West!" He grinned. "I never did no good playin' poker after that. Always impatient to get back to my wife or whatever you call her and you know there is nothing like an impatient man to be easy to beat."

The kid said, "I think the bicycle fell off this way about twenty feet."

FOR DIVERS REASONS

THE KID walked out on the pier and then stood a little distance away, watching the man beside the air compressor. The man was short and swarthy, maybe sixty years old. It was a warm day but he wore a stocking cap.

He said to the kid, noticing his ragged pants, his clean face, "Good evening, son, the top of the evening to you; also any other part of the afternoon you would care to have."

The kid said, suppressed excitement in his voice, "Watcha doin'?"

The swarthy man put his head down to the cone of the speaker and the tassel of his stocking cap bobbed brightly. "We got a kid up here wants to know what we're doing. What *are* you doing down there, Matty?"

There was an annoyed grunt from the speaker that sat on a box by the compressor. Two lines trailed off into the water. They were lashed together, the air hose and the smaller lifeline.

"I could get me a paper route," the kid said.

The man in the stocking cap said, puzzled, "You lost me, pal."

"There ain't many jobs around in the summer. Deliverin' papers is about the only one and the man promised me a job if I had a bicycle."

The man in the stocking cap made a minute adjustment on the compressor. "In other words," he said seriously, "you need a bicycle."

The boy said patiently, "A rich summer kid lost his bicycle over the pier last season. I thought if your guy down there saw it he might not mind tyin' a rope on it for me."

"Oh." The man said into the speaker, "Seen any bicycles, Matty?"

"I'm ridin' one now," the diver's voice said.

The boy said, "Aw, he's kiddin'."

The man in the stocking cap looked at the boy, noticing him. "H'm," he said, "why don't you get somebody to —"

"I don't take no charity," the boy said, flushing.

"He don't take no charity," the man in the

- 35 -

stocking cap said into the speaker's cone. "So if you see a good bicycle —"

"I can hear you and him, too," the diver's voice said. "You don't have to say it all twice."

"What's he doin'?" the kid asked.

"Inspectin' the pilin'," the man said. "For an insurance company. But about that bicycle. Man ain't got the money to buy one, and needs one to make any money and won't take no charity, he's in kind of a fix. You doubtless also have strong feelings against buying on time?"

The kid grinned. "Naw, but the man runs the bicycle shop has."

"A jerk," the man in the stocking cap said carefully.

The kid said, "I think it fell off up this way about twenty feet."

A few yards out from the pier, the little circle of seething bubbles moved seaward, hovering above the diver. The man in the stocking cap considered the bubbles and the run of the lines. "About there, Matty," he said.

There was a steady and constant burbling noise coming out of the speaker, Matty grunted and started to say something, changed his mind and said, "Hell."

The kid said, "He gettin' mad?"

The man said, "He's always like that."

The diver said, "While you sit in the sun and gab." The small voice came out of the speaker in clipped words, precisely spaced from habit. "And if it ain't a kid wants a bicycle, it's some dame wants to know can I find her wedding ring she dropped in this very spot only forty years ago. I'm in mud up to my neck. I can't see my hand in front of the face plate, and you want me to find a bicycle."

"I guess," the kid said uncomfortably, "it's time I was gettin' towards home. He comin' up soon?"

"Naw. It'll be quite some time — if ever. I'm fixin' to cut his lines."

The kid looked at him attentively, then said, "You're foolin' — well, so long — an' thanks." He walked down the pier.

"Hey, kid! If I were you, I'd come down in the morning. The light is better then."

The kid said, "All right. I'll be down —" The man in the stocking cap lifted the helmet expertly, without scraping the diver's nose.

"It was a nice kid," he said, "needed a bike to get a job. Wouldn't of hurt you none."

Matty said coldly, "I should crawl around in the mud looking for a bike."

"He was proud," the man in the stocking cap said thoughtfully. "A nice clean kid, and proud." Tugging sharply, he unbuckled a lead-soled shoe.

Matty kicked and the shoe clumped heavily some five feet away. "Let his old man buy him a bike."

"He looked to me like a kid didn't have an old man," the man said.

MATTY was just swinging down the ladder the next day when the kid came out on the pier.

The man in the stocking cap winked at the kid, and kept paying out the lines. When he stopped, Matty said, impatiently, "Give me more slack." Then soon: "Got a bike down here."

The man shoved back his stocking cap, looked sideways at the kid. "You ever seen this bicycle?"

"Never did." The boy moved to the edge of the pier and considered the diver's bubbles in happy anticipation.

The swarthy man said into the speaker, "Hang on. I'm haulin' you up," and when the shining red bike broke water, he said, with the proper wonder in his voice, "Salt water beats all for preservin' things. That bike looks as good as new."

"Don'tcha think it's his?" the boy asked. "He found it."

The diver said, "Hurry up with the helmet."

"Get goin', kid. He never would have found it if you hadn't of known where it was."

"Yeah, I guess." The kid moved down the pier, pushing the bike. "Thanks."

Turning his thin, pale face toward the swarthy man as he raised the helmet, Matty said bitterly, "Wasn't that bicycle red?"

The man lighted a cigarette and placed it between the diver's lips with a smooth, backhanded motion.

"Yes, it was, Matty."

"Which you bought and thrower in there last night?"

The man in the stocking cap blushed, stammered, but said no word.

"I had a coupla drinks and bought a *blue* one

and eased her offa there about midnight," the diver said, abashed. "What the hell we gonna do with it?"

"Yeah," the man in the stocking cap said, "Now we got one bicycle too many. What we really need, I guess, is another kid."

A thin boy with great dark eyes walked up the pier and stood at a distance. "What're you doing?" he asked.

The man in the stocking took one look at the boy's clean clothes, his bare feet, and snatched the cigarette out of the diver's mouth and picked up the helmet.

"Waitin' for you," he said.

*I heard snatches of what he said
when I listened stealthily before the keyhole.*

As her boss said, "Now how could a nice girl like Kathleen
do a thing like that?"

THE KEYHOLE ARTIST

August 1st, 1948

MR. BRIAN MORIARITY,
THE EYE IN THE SKY DETECTIVE
AGENCY, NEW YORK CITY.

DEAR CHIEF:
  Pursuant to your directive I have obtained work in the household of subject (M. Donnelly) as maid. This first step was easily accomplished by bribing former maid with week's pay and appearing next day at door with story she had sent me to substitute for her until further notice. It may be germane that subject accepted this rather obvious device in perfect good faith revealing a truly bucolic naiveté.

Now, as I understand this assignment, I am to make a general character analysis of subject, determine former social stratum, if any, family background and acquire any other data that a man with the enormous wealth of Mr. Horace Cavendish (our employer) might find of interest about the man affianced to his daughter Gertrude. In brief, I am to find out if the guy is a fortune hunter.

KATHLEEN O'BRIEN (Agent No. 14)

P.S. I enclose receipted bill for three maid's uniforms. Please remit.

August 7th, 1948

DEAR CHIEF:

This is discouraging. I have yet to find anything wrong with this character. Subject was born in a small town in the Middle West, second son of a minister, regularly sends substantial sums of money home to his mother (father deceased). Worked his way through College and Law School, admitted to bar in 1937 and practiced in Kansas City until outbreak of war. Enlisted in Marine Corps December 11th, 1941, discharged October 14th, 1945. Rank, Major. (Silver Star.) Thirty-two months overseas. This is confirmed by perusal of home-town paper to which subject subscribes and reading of subject's old mail. Credit and professional rating AA. Was spoken of — off the record — by Judge Linshaw as "most brilliant young attorney in New York."

Personally I find him modest, jolly, a fine sense of humor. He is kind (will make more detailed report in person on splinter in finger and burnt asparagus incidents), and why did Mr. Horace Cavendish hire us anyway?

Entertained daughter of employer, Miss Gertrude Cavendish, last night here at dinner. Personally, I thought Miss Cavendish rather cold and superficial and unduly snoopy about subject's background, though subject seemed to evince no reticence in discussing same.

K. O'B, (Agt. No. 14)

P.S. Did you get receipted bill for three maid's uniforms? If so please remit.

August 8th, 1948

DEAR CHIEF:

Miss Cavendish appeared today and questioned me exhaustively as to subject's personal habits, outside interests in general. I gave guardedly favorable replies to questions but naturally refused specific information on basis of domestic ethics. Subject's well-ordered life caused Miss Cavendish some distress and in course of conversation she spoke wistfully of indigent polo player named Sonny McGuire. I found Miss Cavendish less cold and superficial after show of emotion resulting from mention of Mr. Sonny McGuire. But seems parental pressure favors subject.

I waited in (subject had outside dinner engagement and had told me to go home early), suspecting of him of having cold and fixed him some hot lemonade. Had interesting discussion of economic theories of Mr. Thorstein Veblen. Subject very sound on works of Mr. V.

K. O'B. (Agt. No. 14)

August 13th, 1948

DEAR CHIEF:

Subject had cold which turned into alarming case of grippe (temp. almost 100) and I am *very* busy. Have arranged to sleep down the hall with Mrs. Gibbon's maid so can give full attention to subject without causing gossip.

K. O'B. (Agt. No. 14)

August 14th, 1948

DEAR CHIEF:

Subject's temperature now 100.2! And *I* am in shock. Subject underwent violent moral disintegration with mounting temperature.

A true case of schiz ... Dr. Jekyll and Mr. Hyde and Mr. Hyde has been in ascendancy ever since our discussion about Mr. Thorstein Veblen (whoever Mr. V. is). This morning subject felt hotter to touch and also felt badly. Apparently was enough to cause reversion to true character.

First thing he did was call office to say he would not be in, then after crafty closing of bedroom door (I listened at keyhole), subject phoned one he called Muscles McGill.

I report these snatches of conversation:

"… have hooks in rich broad …"

"… old man's bankroll thick as his head …"

"… quick wedding before Horace tumbles …"

"… richer than Ernestine in Kaysee and you remember what we took her for …"

Also additional random words and phrases. "Old man's blood pressure. Won't be long … gilt edged … fronting for this mob …."

Took subject breakfast, subject snarled, cursed and threatened me with bodily injury due to condition of egg. Subject refused to shave.

The next morning subject's apartment was littered with empty highball glasses, lipstick smudges, cigarettes. For man in subject's weakened physical condition feel that subject's keeping late hours (pardon pun) shows definite schiz … definite irrational behavior.

K. O'B. (Agt. No. 14)

P.S. Due to startling nature of this report have sent report in triplicate to Mr. Horace Cavendish and daughter Gertrude.

THE EYE IN THE SKY
DETECTIVE AGENCY
NEW YORK CITY

August 16th, 1948

KATHLEEN:

Case closed this a.m. With elopement of Miss Gertrude Cavendish and Sonny McGuire. Please report this a.m. To explain:

1. *Your* "violent moral disintegration," evidenced by unethical, dishonest, shysterish trick of sending fantastic reports to our ex-employer, Horace Cavendish and daughter.

2. Why contents of said report are at strict variance with all preliminary investigations, including your own?

3. How a nice young girl with your up-bringing could do such a thing?

BRYAN MORIARITY

August 16th, 1948

BRYAN MORIARITY, Esq.
THE EYE IN THE SKY DETECTIVE
AGENCY, NEW YORK CITY.

Dear Sir:

I herewith submit resignation effective this date. I am being married in the morning.

Yours truly,

KATHLEEN O'BRIEN

P.S. Please make check for three maid's uniforms payable to Mrs. Marshall H. Donnelly.

*With the aid of the guard's gun he got a suit of clothes.
He also got a car with it.*

"You want to be a hero, Billy?" Max Stanton asked.
"I'm wanted five grand's worth.
Turn me in and it's all yours!"

HOT PILOT

THE KID in the next bed was dying. He had started dying very nicely but his performance was getting steadily worse. The prison doctor had told him that morning he probably wouldn't last the night and the kid had said, "So what?" "Max," the kid said huskily, "tell the guys I took it good."

"Sure," Max Stanton said, thinking: *But I'll bet he goes out like Little Eva in a third-rate stock company.*

Max had seen a lot of them go before he'd begun to fly dope into the country — and quite a few since then.

Now it was late and the kid was dying with the prison doctor beside his bed and one guard had gone for a priest. Max Stanton lay in his bed, his face tight with contempt. The kid was delirious, muttering of his father and mother and occasionally of how he had lost his nerve when the plane caught fire over the desert and how brave, good Max had tried to save him.

Max Stanton told the doctor, slowly and precisely, so the doctor would be sure and understand, that he hadn't been trying to save the kid but the kid had been between him and the cargo of narcotics. That he had known the kid was no good when the trouble started, but in order to unload the dope from the burning plane, Max had first to move the kid. It was the kid's first try and he was yellow and.... The kid was as good as dead already and when he heard Max say these words it snapped the tenuous thread that held him to this world and he half sat up in bed and when he fell back, he was dead.

The priest, young, drawn with fatigue, hurried in too late. Max was amused. "Tough luck, father," he said. "I guess he couldn't wait." The young priest looked at the boy on the bed, then at Max, with bitter pity.

Max Stanton closed his eyes and started working on the problem of his escape. He wanted to get back in time to start with the new syndicate which was forming to fly the stuff in by the carload. They had promised him the job, and the setup was right, down to maintenance crews on either end of the run and two emergency landing fields, one on either side of the border. He dropped off to sleep hoping that his reputation for close-mouthed sobriety and his skill in handling an aircraft would be enough to prevent them from taking a chance on an unknown pilot before he got back.

THE MAN they put in the kid's bed next day was almost fifty. He was a three-time loser who had been somewhat slow in departing from a bank with a sub-machine gun and a canvas bag full of money. A furious burst from a squad car had killed his young companion, but the old boy had prudently dropped his gun, lowered the sack and raised his hands. Now he was in the prison hospital with only a bullet hole, a small one, in his leg. Max said he wished he were out of there, that today's prices were such that a man could fly in ten loads and retire.

The bank robber scratched himself and said that a man who would transport, sell or use dope was either a hop-head or fool.

Max sat up in bed. "We can't all be smart," he said coldly.

"I never was," said the other.

Max quit talking to him and lay back, trying to remember all the escapes he had read of. Several came to mind: riding out in a dead man's coffin, digging a tunnel over the years with a teaspoon and disposing of the dirt by scattering it in the yard. He gave these up. The one great advantage he had was that he spoke like an educated man and didn't look like a convict. Also, he was feeling very well. He had been put in the hospital for observation, in case he had been injured internally when the plane's gas tank exploded. The doctor changed the bank robber's bandage, looked at Max's chart and told him he'd be out of the place by tomorrow. It was a prophetic statement. Max got out of his bed that night, slugged a careless guard with a bedpan wrapped in a sheet and, with the guard bound, gagged and naked in a linen closet, walked away in his uniform. He took his time about leaving the prison grounds and layover through the day. That night he got a suit of clothes. The guard's gun assisted him mightily.

He held up a filling station and stole a car. His goal was Mexico, but some place in California the fever came upon him and he was sick.

He was sitting beside a little road, dirty, unshaven, and the memory of his long flight was vague in his mind. He remembered the nights when it was cold and the days when it was hot, and the fat police in the little towns, and the frequent planes in the sky. And all night long the whistle of the trains on the mountain grades, and the fever was coming back upon him and he was sick.

He sat there, and the trees danced before him as they should not dance. He had been afraid to try the border at Juarez. He had planned to go through at Caliente with the race-track crowd some Sunday. But no, he was sick. San Diego was only forty miles but that was far, far away.

He stood up with an effort. The trees still danced, but he held his head down, looking at the rolling ground, and the sweat came coldly down his face. He turned away from the road and started up a little lane into the mountains. Finally he saw a house. It was white and he made toward it though it wavered and was far away. The sunlight was heavy on his back. And he carried it, hot and heavy, on his back toward the house.

The house moved, grew and shrank and moved away, but finally it waited for him and he got on the porch and to the door and rapped upon it as hard as he could. He heard some movement inside the house and a dog barked. He wrapped his mind tightly around the thought that he must not think in case he fainted and was delirious, and he remembered the kid in the bed next to him back in the pen, calling for a priest.

The girl opened the door and drew back, instinctively. Max Stanton looked at her and remembered a mirror in a place called Electric Park, in Kansas City, where his father had taken him once. And the girl looked as his reflection had looked in a mirror there. Now constricted, short and wide. Now ridiculously, grotesquely, tall and thin. Behind her was the smaller figure of a boy. He said to the boy, "Have you ever been to Electric Park in Kansas City?" And that was all he said.

HE WAS LYING on a couch and it was cool. The girl said, "How do you feel?"

The perspiration on his face was dry and he felt nothing but weakness. "Better, now," he said.

The boy, looking wide-eyed around the girl's skirts, said, "You ain't very heavy. Me'n Sis lifted you."

"Thank you very much," Max Stanton said. "I'm sorry I caused you so much trouble."

"You have a fever," the girl said. "I'll send Billy for the doctor." The girl was young and tanned and very earnest. She wasn't frightened, just concerned.

There was the sound of planes overhead and the boy disappeared out of the door. He came back in a moment. "Trainers," he said disdainfully.

"Do you like airplanes?" Max asked. "I was going to San Diego," he added slowly, "to try and get a job in one of the factories."

"Billy," the girl said, "you ride down to the store and call Dr. Dave."

"I'm sure that won't be necessary," Max said quickly. "I had the-the flu a little while back and I guess I got up too soon. I'll be all right in a little while."

"I like to watch the hot pursuit jobs and the bombers go over," Billy said. "I betcha I could fly a trainer."

Max smiled. "I expect you could," he said. To the girl he added, "I feel better now. I believe I'll go along."

The girl said, making a womanly gesture, "You'll do nothing of the sort. You are much too sick. If you won't let me call the doctor, you must at least stay here and rest."

"Won't your husband —" "I haven't any husband," the girl said. "This is my little brother. I had another brother, but he went down and joined the Navy after Pearl Harbor. He didn't come back. If you'll go in there," the girl went on, "and go to bed, I'll fix you some milk toast."

Max was suddenly very hungry. He went docilely, leaning on Bill's shoulder. Billy helped him off with his clothes and he got into the bed. "I'll getcha my brother's old straight edge tomorrow," Billy said, "and you can get you a shave."

Max Stanton put a hand to his face and it was trembling. "Thank you," he said. He lay there a moment, very tired. Then he asked, "Do you and your sister live up here all by yourselves?"

"That's right," Billy said. "Pa, he died; then there was Sis and me and John. John went off to the Navy, so there's just Sis and me. We're runnin' a few head of cattle up here and you purely can't go off and leave no cow solo."

"What's your name, Billy?" Max asked. They haven't a telephone, he thought, and it must be a long way to a neighbor. I could stay here, perhaps, until I'm fit again.

"Brock," the boy said with profound disgust. "Ain't that a hell of a name? Billy Brock. Sayin' William don't help it none, either."

The girl came in then with the bowl of milk toast. There was the sound of a plane overhead and Billy Brock disappeared out of the door to take a look.

Max looked up at the girl. She was clean and sturdy looking, and her legs were brown and straight below her faded cotton dress. "Here," she said, smiling. "This will make you feel better." She put a cool hand on Max's brow. "You still have a fever," she said. "But I think you're better."

The next day his fever was gone. He found his clothes all clean, on the foot of his bed, and the sun high in the sky. Billy came in with a bowl of water and the razor. "Do you know anything about airplanes?" he asked.

"Why, no," Max said. "No, I don't."

"You seen landing fields, ain't you?"

"Yes, I've seen landing fields."

"Well, when you get up, I want you to walk up to the big pasture and see if it ain't big enough for a landing field. It's near level, a mesa like, a hundred and fifty acres."

"I'm sure that's big enough," Max said, lathering his face and sitting up in bed.

"That's what I been tellin' the Army and the Navy …"

"Have you really been in touch with the authorities?" Max asked quickly. "Naw, not really."

Max Stanton kept the relief out of his voice. "Who have you seen?" he asked.

"Well," Billy said, "it's like this. Most of this country around is Indian reservation. Our neighbors is mostly Indians." Billy paused, looking out of the window. "Did you ever tell an Indian anything?" he asked finally.

"Why, no, I never did," Max said. "Well," Billy said, "don't."

"Why not?"

"Tellin' an Indian somethin' is just one step better'n tellin' it to a tree. I like Indians fine but they're sure poor to tell stuff to."

"Why do you tell them?" Max asked, puzzled.

"I ain't got anybody else to tell," Billy said. "I told Sam Torres about the landing field and you know what he said?"

"What did he say?"

"Nothin'. So I told him again and that time he said, 'Damn fine pasture,' and rode off."

"What's your sister's name?" Max asked, working under his chin.

Billy looked at him disgustedly. "Barbara," he said. There was the sound of a plane overhead and he disappeared through the door.

BARBARA BROCK came in the room. She looked at Max a long time, then came over and sat down on the edge of the bed. "Max," she said slowly, "are you in trouble?"

Max Stanton looked up, startled. He rubbed his clean chin. "No," he said, mustering a smile. "I'm not in trouble."

"Not about the Army, or the draft or anything?"

"No," he said. "No, I wasn't eligible for the Army." He tapped his chest.

"Is it your heart?"

"Yes," Max said quickly, "my heart."

Barbara Brock came over and put her hand on Max Stanton's brow. "Your fever is gone," she said.

"I feel quite fit," he said. "I really should be getting along."

"No," the girl said. "You mustn't. Not for a few days; if your heart is bad the after-effects of the flu can be very serious."

"You are very kind," Max murmured.

A week passed quickly. Max was up and about and he helped with the work and walked with Billy and his sister up to the big pasture. It was a lovely spot, an enormous flat indentation on the slope of the mountain, green with grass and spotted with black Aberdeen cattle.

Billy rode the fence on a pony. Barbara and Max sat in the sun and watched him. They said very little, but Max Stanton felt her presence as he had felt the presence of the federal officers behind him the day the plane had burned. But this was a sweet weight upon his heart. He cursed himself.

Billy rode up and climbed down from his pony and watched a plane go overhead. "That's the hottest pursuit job in the world," he said.

Max watched the plane disappear. "Why are you so interested in planes? he asked. "I thought you'd like this — being a cowboy!"

"Cowboy!" Billy snorted. "I'm some cowboy. Ridin' around with steeples and a hammer. I wanna be an Ace."

"Let's go back," Barbara said. She stood up suddenly, and her face was grave.

Max stood up and stretched his arms and looked away across the pasture at the cattle and up into the warm blue sky and took a deep breath. He smiled when he noticed Barbara was watching him.

The week slid into another week, and Max was well now. Tanned and gaining weight.

In the cool night he sat with Barbara before a tiny fire in the fireplace and that was the world.

"Barbara," he said finally, "I must go on. I'm well now. I can't stay on."

"Must you?" Barbara Brock said, and her face was very lovely, turned to him in the firelight.

"Yes," he said, and he twisted his mind back to its old channels. Only suckers work.... "Yes," he said again, more harshly, "I must." He moved quickly from his chair to the sofa beside her, and he took her in his arms and she was warm and sweet.

"No, Max," she said, and he saw the tears in her eyes.

"Darling," he said.

Barbara Brock pushed him away. "Poor Max," she said and stood up and moved toward her room. "Good-night," she said, and he heard the lock click and he heard the beating of his heart.

He sat there long, gazing into the fire, and as he sat his face changed and on it rode a look of tight contempt once more. He got up and went to bed.

Billy woke him the next morning. Billy, bursting with noise, the words tumbling. "There's a plane down! A plane in the big pasture. A trainer. Get up, Max. Get up! Barbara, Barbara!"

Barbara came out of the kitchen. She didn't look at Max. "Billy," she said, "calm down. Tell me —" "I'm tellin' you. Come on, Max. Let's go up there and see. There ain't anybody in it. I guess the pilot walked down to phone. Oh boy, I been tellin' 'em all along...."

Max Stanton kept his voice even. "Is the plane damaged?" he asked.

"No. Come on. Come on, Max. Let's get up there."

Barbara Brock said slowly. "You two go ahead, I'll be along in a minute."

Max followed Billy from the room. Billy raced ahead, came back, like a crazy puppy. Max followed him. *The phone is a long way away, even if the pilot knows the nearest one. He won't be back for an hour. Maybe I could fix it. Maybe I could.* Max was cool now, feeling a strange tightness. *If it had gasoline in it enough for a couple of hours....*

Billy shouted, "See — over there!" Max broke into a run.

There was nothing wrong with the plane. Nothing. Max climbed up, looked at the motor. The ignition, he thought. It must be the ignition.

He could see nothing wrong. Now he examined the motor more carefully. Maybe the pilot was afraid to try to take it back up from here. Maybe he'd fixed it already. Max climbed into the cockpit and pressed the starter. The motor caught.

Billy looked up at him, started climbing up. He saw Max's face and hesitated. "Beat it!" Max said harshly.

He taxied the plane around. To hell with them. He'd fly it out of here and set it down in Mexico.... He'd.... He stopped thinking. The old exhilaration was upon him and he forgot Billy, forgot everything but getting the plane off of the ground. "So long, chumps. Happy landings!"

The plane came off of the ground. Max knew the old godlike feeling. A kid could fly this plane. He looked out and down.

Down below, small now, pathetically small, he saw Barbara Brock. And he saw her stumble, straighten up, and look up at the plane; and she grew smaller.

He thought of the truck drivers and the sweet peace of afternoons in the big pasture and the fire in the fireplace and the oil fields and the planes and Billy and his pony and the Aberdeen cattle that couldn't be left alone. And he thought of Barbara. It was something that he knew existed but that he didn't admit. He thought of Barbara.

Small there among the frightened moving cattle. Still there, defenseless. Alone. There by itself, alone.

Max Stanton felt his heart constrict, and something flooded through him and something went away and the sweat was on his face and his hands were nerveless.

He shut his eyes to clear the tears from them and brought the plane around for the landing. The landing would be very tricky.

He climbed down from the plane, calm now, and happy, and he walked toward Barbara. Billy came behind him at a respectful distance.

He got to Barbara and he saw her face and he knew.

She stood away from him, not sobbing, but the tears coursed down her cheeks. "Max Stanton," she said.

"Yes," he said and smiled. "How long have you known?"

"A long time," she said. "From the first. I saw your picture in the paper ... and when you shaved —"

"I was going away," he said. "I knew I couldn't walk across the border. I was going away."

Billy came up cautiously and saw his sister's tears. He tried to speak but no words came.

Max Stanton turned to him. "Do you want to be a hero?" he asked softly.

"Awww ..." Billy began.

"I want you to take me down to San Diego," Max Stanton said. "You see, Billy. I was an Ace. But I'm no longer an Ace. I'm an escaped convict. You'll be a hero."

"Max," Billy said chokingly. He walked over and put his arms around Max Stanton and his wet face against his side.

"Max," he said.

Max turned and looked at Barbara and the contempt and the hardness were gone from his face and he looked young. "I'll start now," he said.

"Max, darling Max."

"But some day I'll be back. Always remember that. Some day I'll be back."

He took Billy by the hand and started down the hill. "I'm kinda hot," he said to Billy. "They wanted me five grand's worth. The reward — you give it to Barbara, will you?"

"We don't want the damned old money," Billy said then. "We'll keep it for you — sure, we'll keep it for you. For when you get back."

Football is supposed to be a man's sport. But women have feet, too—and Annie Thurston had given hers a college education.

BEAUTY AND THE DROP KICK

WHEN I HAD COME into the room, they had motioned me to silence and pointed to the telephone. No one was using it. They both just sat there watching it. I knew Jobbo Rourke, the coach, and I guessed that the florid-faced one at the desk was Swackhammer.

From where I saw and waited, I could see out of two windows. The east window disclosed a horseshoe drive, two small buildings and the little brown campus of Torgerson University. Three hundred and fifty students would crowd its classrooms to the limit, come the fall.

President Herman Swackhammer was still glaring tensely at the phone. I glanced at the stadium from the north window. Only a shade larger than the Yale Bowl, its great, gaunt unpaid-for bulk completely dwarfed the village of Torgerson, the meager buildings of the school. It fitted into the peaceful landscape like Carnera in a bassinet. The phone rang and Swackhammer grabbed it. "Yes?"

Conciliatory squeaks emanated from the receiver. President Swackhammer gave an anguished bark and hung up.

"Parole board turned him down," he said bitterly. "They think maybe they can schedule Sing Sing and they can't spare him."

Rourke sighed. "I saw him complete seven out of eight against the State Troopers, and ran for four touchdowns against the Deputy Sheriffs."

I took out my telegram. "I'm the guy you telegraphed about coming down here and doing some publicity," I said. "John Lindsay —"

"Okay, Lindsay," Swackhammer cut me short. "I'm prexy — Swackhammer's the name. That is Rourke, coach." He jammed out his cigar. "We're here for one purpose: save Torgerson University. Need money. Got to fill stadium four home games three thirty top or Torgerson goes under. Horrible indebtedness. Back in thirties Torgerson had couple great teams. Beat Yale, beat Notre Dame, beat Minnesota. Don't ask me how they scheduled 'em. Don't ask me why they built stadium. Fever, fervor and a great cement salesman —"

Jobbo Rourke said, "He's sent so many telegrams he talks like one. If he goes too fast for you, I can tell you what he means."

"Shut up," Swackhammer barked. "Gotta fight. Gotta get them. Great team. Publicity, fill stadium. Tell Lindsay budget, Jobbo."

Jobbo Rourke took a piece of paper out of his pocket. "We've scheduled some big teams," he said. "And we've still got four-year eligibility down here. But we are awful short of money." He looked at his sheet of paper. "We can't go better than a hundred and fifty a month for first-string tackles and guards — maybe a little more for ends. We figure we might squeeze out two twenty-five for a breakaway runner and if he could kick and pass, say two seventy-five; of course that includes room and board, laundry, and tutoring."

"That sounds pretty good to me," I said.

ROURKE said, "Well, you just ain't up on the market. If we had got that guy down at the pen paroled, of course, he would probably have stayed with us a year out of gratitude."

"Yeah," I said. "I hear they got a forger at Sing Sing could make any team in the country."

"What a spot for a coach," Jobbo Rourke sighed. "No alumni trouble."

"Get back to subject," Swackhammer barked.

"What we want you to do," Jobbo explained, "is to dream up some guff about Torgerson that might attract some players. Also, beat the back bushes this summer and try to sign prospects. You'll have to go back in the hills —"

"Beyond grasping tentacles of unethical rivals," Swackhammer said.

There was a lot more to it. Swackhammer was a professional college president. He was at Torgerson on a percentage of the gate. Jobbo Rourke was a good run-of-the-mill coach to whom Swackhammer owed money. I sent out a couple of releases about how Jobbo planned to use the intentional fumble as his chief offensive weapon and a three-man line with seven backers-up on defense; you know the stuff you read every year. Then I got in my car, clutched my budget in my fist and went out in search of talent…. It was discouraging, all right. I showed one kid, a good high-school back, what he could do at Torgerson and he laughed in my face until he damned near had hysterics. He had already picked up two grand for agreeing to go to Bay Root Poly, and as soon as he got eligible, they would buy his old lady a house and give him a convertible. He showed me the contract. As Jobbo said, I wasn't up on the market. Inflation had really hit the college footballing dodge.

But as I retreated farther into the back country, I did manage to pick up a package here and there. At Coon Track Corners I got two twins out of the seventh grade weighed a lean hard 214 apiece. Coon Track Corners was so far back in the hills that they spoke Elizabethan English, but I figured Jobbo wouldn't care. As long as they used Arabic numerals he had him a pair of tackles.

It went like that. I got some right handy boys

that might make linemen but nothing looked like a passer, a punter; a pay-off back.

I pulled past Coon Track and went on back into the hills. I hung my differential on rocks fording the same stream time and again and was shot at twice — once for being a Yankee and once for being a revenuer. Of course, it turned out they were just shooting to scare me — which they did. But I couldn't turn around and I was hunting for a wide place in the road when I came on this field.

It was a large spot, with mowed grass on it, marked back thirty yards with lime lines. And on the last line stood a goal post! I stopped my car and sat there looking at it, trying to figure what it was doing there when a man and a boy came out of a little opening in the woods.

The man was carrying a big sack over his back and a pail of water. He took the pail of water and set it down over at the side of the field and emptied the sack. About fifteen footballs rolled out of it.

He got down over one of the balls like a center and passed back to the kid. From over there at the edge, the kid booted it through the uprights with the quickest drop kick I ever saw!

I sat there afraid to move. The old man dipped one of the balls into the water and fed the kid a bad pass. The kid recovered like a ballet dancer and *plink*! Right down the slot.

Well, to get on with it, he popped forty or fifty straight through the uprights and then damned if he didn't start kicking 'em the same with his *left* foot. Bad passes, soaking wet balls, everything. He'd jump aside as if a blocker was surging through, give that little quick hop, and bingo. In there!

I was afraid they'd fly off like a convoy of quail if I moved but I had to, finally. I climbed out of the car and went over.

The kid looked awful small, but Swackhammer and Jobbo would guarantee a lifetime pension to an orangutan for this kind of thing.

The old man saw me coming and kind of bristled. I came on, though, until I got in close enough to talk.

"I just happened to see that performance," I said. "It was really something."

"We worked pretty long today. Missed one a couple weeks back."

"Your son going to school this fall …?" I began.
"What son?"

The kid turned around then and came up to us, shy as a gazelle.

It was a girl!

IT WAS a girl in a pair of tight-fitting jeans and a faded jersey, with a face and figure like — but what's the use?

I tried to get my mouth closed, but I didn't succeed until after I had made a number of strangling sounds.

"Yep," the old man said with a grim satisfaction in his voice. "She's goin' to Peabody Poly, by gum, and she's gonna make her letter."

"Peabody," I croaked. Peabody was Torgerson's last game, a rich and large school where they hired high-school football captains by the gross.

"Yep. I went there, thirty year ago. I sweated and toiled and never made the team. I swore I'd send me a son there that would."

"But —"

"But fate tricked me — or tried to. I just had one young'un. A girl. But I figured to trick fate right back. I looked it up and there ain't any rule says what gender a footballer must be and so, by gum, I been readyin' this'n for fifteen years. This year she goes."

It was soaking in. Here was the press agent's dream. If I could get this girl to come to Torgerson we could get beat eighty-eight to nothing every Saturday, and the stadium would still be full. I said, "Did you ever think of Torgerson …?" But I knew it was useless.

The old man was right nice; he invited me up to the little house. We had a drink of local origin and the countryside swam around. He lived there alone with his daughter, I learned. His wife was dead.

I kept looking at the girl and she kept looking at me. She was the most gorgeous thing I had ever seen. If she couldn't kick a volley ball off of a brick she would be gorgeous.

My mind was racing around and around. The branch water and nuclear fission that passed for whisky in those parts had me dizzy. I still sat there talking to the old man, looking at the daughter. It came up dusk.

The old man went somewhere to milk a cow or something and I made my play. I went over and sat down by Annie — that was her name, Annie Thurston — and started my routine. She took it all in like it was absolutely off of the top of the deck. Just then a great big moon peeked over the mountain and I got my arm around her, and kissed her.

Oh! *OH!*

That made the whiskey insipid.

I scrambled away as the old man came up with the bucket. My mind was a great, passionate void. I started staggering toward my car.

The girl ran after me. "I'll come to Torgerson," she said, "if you'll be there."

I kissed her fiercely again, unable to articulate, and stepped back and fell in some brambles. I heard her father calling her. She ran.

BY THE TIME enrollment was due to start I had lost eight pounds; I jumped at sounds. Jobbo and Swackhammer were fairly well pleased with the talent I'd sent in. Still no hot breakaway runner, but we figured we could get some pretty fair publicity releases out on the forward wall. "Seven heads of granite"; "pledged to mass mutual suicide if they were scored on" — Just the usual stuff, but it goes in the fall.

I hung around the registrar's office so much that they tried to enroll me three times, though my college football days ended back in thirty-nine. They just weren't taking any chances.

The second day, she came in. She had her suitcase in her hand.

She gave me a smile and came over to where I was trying to move from. "I convinced Poppa," she said. "I told him it would be so much better to get *revenge* on Peabody."

"Oh, darling —" I took her by the hand and grabbed her suitcase.

I hadn't tipped Jobbo, or Swacky or anyone. I took her hand and led her to the stadium. She was dressed just as she had been the first day I saw her — in jeans — which by fortunate coincidence was just like every other coed on the campus. I went down to the field house and got Jobbo and all the footballs I could find and led him out.

I told her what I wanted. She opened her suitcase and took out the ridiculous little square-toed shoes her old man had had made for her and put them on. She dropped the first one through from the twenty-five, kicked two with her left foot from the side line on the twenty, kicked two more — one with each foot — blind-folded.

I turned to Jobbo. He was down on the ground tearing great chunks of turf up with his teeth.

"It's no dream, Jobbo," I said.

"We'll charge ten dollars a seat and make every scalper in the state a millionaire," he gulped, trying to stand up.

"I don't see how you could possibly miss those great big goals," Annie said.

"What kind you used to?" Jobbo croaked.

"The ones Poppa built at home aren't but half that wide," she said.

"I never noticed. I didn't notice anything after I saw you," I said.

She blushed a lovely pink.

Jobbo must have tipped Swanky for I didn't get to talk to her again until the first game. They must have put her in a vault.

Jobbo had a good tight forward wall, big and rangy. His backs were only fair, and Torgerson came up to the first game playing to a thin ribbon of people on each fifty-yard line. But I was up in the press box with an open wire, waiting. I knew that this was the last time that stadium would be anything but bulging for a long time.

It was a standard football game, a little uneven like most first games. No score through the first half. Eight minutes had moved on the clock in the second half when a Torgerson end blocked a kick, and we recovered on the visiting firemen's eighteen. We mauled out two off guard, three through center. Third and five and they stopped an end run on the line of scrimmage. Fourth and five on the thirteen. I nodded at the telegrapher and he cleared his line. Here she came!

Swackhammer had her togged out in skin-light-fitting silver silk football pants, an iridescent purple silk jersey. Her shoes had been dyed silver. Her hair made a platinum halo for her face.

No padding was in her uniform but that which

Nature had so bounteously given her. The Torgerson band blared Annie Get Your Gun.

She reported to the referee, a man dashed out, and while the "crowd" stood with open mouths she dropped the ball through the slot. Lazy end over end, right down the center. She turned and trotted off the field.

It broke then. That crowd bayed! They whistled! They gave vent to every vocal leer in the range of human sound.

I turned and started dictating. "On the historic turf of Torgerson University stadium there was today a dream drop-kicking. Out of the ranks of all-time beauties came a demure lass clad in the colors of old Torgerson to put this great autumn classic in the realm of immortal epics. Not since Paris kicked the golden apple toward Aphrodite...." I went on like that. Two full columns. "Automatic Annie — Three-Point Thurston — The Conversion Queen — More fair than any in the land —"

It was page one in every paper in the country. Incidentally, and very incidentally, Torgerson won three to nothing.... Well I couldn't have seen her after that if I had wanted to. Torgerson became a trailer camp inhabited by reporters, motion picture producers, cosmetic manufacturers, et cetera, and then some.

Annie Thurston moved four out of four, beating somebody twelve to seven. The stadium sold out for the rest of the season and people camped all week in front of the box office to buy the general admission.

She got eighteen hundred proposals of marriage by mail and telegraph. In the Philippines four girls broke their toes trying to emulate her with coconuts.

She was offered ten thousand dollars to endorse a pedicure set.

I SAW HER after the seventh game. Torgerson and Annie had won then all and were coming up to Peabody, also undefeated. She must have pretended to be asleep and slipped away from her guards. She came to me in my room, clad in her jeans and jersey, the clothes she'd worn at Coon Track Corners. She came in and sat on the bed and cried.

I sat beside her and tried to comfort her. I didn't put my arm around her. You don't put your arm around a million-dollar property, somehow. You don't make love to a legend.

"Oh, John, it's all so awful!"

"What's so awful? You're the most famous girl in the country. The world is at your feet."

"My feet, how I *hate* my feet!"

"That's pretty good hating," I said. "Swacky's got 'em insured for a quarter of a million apiece."

"That night on the porch," she said. "Up in Coon Track —"

Just then the door flew open and her six bodyguards poured in. They sapped me out with a blackjack as their opening gambit. I don't know what happened after that. I didn't see her again until the game with Peabody.

Now Peabody had a big-time team, real class. They shoved us around for three quarters and only by the grace of pure luck did we keep them from scoring. And at the beginning of the fourth quarter they did score. They were down on our ten. They hit the line three times and only got six yards. Then they trotted out a place kicker and he shoved one through.

Peabody three.

Torgerson horse collar.

So what?

Well, this what. I was sitting down on the bench. Hell, the press coop was full to overflowing of the top men in the country doing my work for me and I couldn't get a seat in the stadium. Swackhammer comes over to me. He is white and groaning.

I asked him what was the matter.

He told me. It seems that Swacky, the great gambler, had signed a contact stipulating that if the stadium sold out half the home games he got paid an extra fifty grand. Ten of it went to me. Ten of it to Jobbo. *If we won every game.*

Ten grand! With ten grand I might have a chance. A chance with Annie. They'd changed the rules. She wouldn't get to play next year. Ten grand. I heard something and looked up. Peabody had fumbled and we had the ball on their ten.

"What about a tie?" I yelled at Swack above the roar.

"Yeah," he bellowed. "Just so's we're undefeated."

THERE WERE TWO minutes on the clock and we were on their ten. We lost two through the line, lost one around end. We made four off the strongside tackle.

Annie stood up down at the other end of the bench. Her bodyguard stood with her.

Fourth and goal!

I looked at her and she looked at me. She looked so helpless. I ran up to her. "Annie, darling, win this one for me!"

Jobbo hustled her out on the field. Torgerson went into the line of scrimmage. She stood back there, looking very small and very lonely.

She didn't look right. Something was wrong. I don't know what it was but there was something wrong. The center passed the ball back to her. There was a surge of bodies. And I heard the crack of the gun that ended the game.

But the play would be complete.

Nothing happened. Annie stood and held the ball.

And then she started to run! Carrying the ball in her two hands like a bowl of flowers, she started to run! She ran a little way to the left, then a little way to the right. It was so deathly quiet you could hear her tiny frightened squeals. It was like a horrible slow-motion nightmare. Everybody on both teams was so stunned they moved as if they were moving in deep water. All except Annie, who darted back and forth ineffectually.

Then suddenly she was on the goal line and a big Peabody halfback came to life and tackled her.

I was rushing out on the field, a red haze before my eyes.

They were untangling the players, the referee was signaling a touchdown but I didn't see that. I was heading for the Peabody halfback. Nobody was going to lay hands like that on the woman I loved! I measured him as I neared him and let go one from the ankles. I missed him, hit the field judge on the shoulder and then they had me.

But mostly somebody had me that was soft and wonderful.

"I won it for you, darling!" Annie said.

"Oh, yes, I told her to win the game. I had been excited; it had been a slip of the tongue.

"You slugged that cad because you care!" Her arms were around my neck, her lips against my ear.

"Care? I'm mad about you, darling. But you're the most famous woman in the country."

"Not in Coon Track Corners." So that's the way it is. We took down the goal posts in back of the house, and if we have a boy we're going to send him to Harvard. We don't take any papers up here at Coon Track and we haven't got a radio but we've heard it's a good school even though there has been some loose talk about one Herman Swackhammer as its next president.

*Eddie blew his horn and all his heart came through,
for the girl he fell in love with many years ago.*

NO ONE BUT YOU

EDDIE MUNRO came out into the hall, buttoning his shirt, and walked two steps down into the living-room. The phonograph and record cabinet looked huge in the little room. He stepped on what felt like a brittle sponge, a piece of toast the baby had thrown from his high chair in the dining alcove. He looked at the baby and grinned, and the baby grinned back. Eddie said, "Hi, Momma."

His wife was reading the Sunday paper, smoking a cigarette, leaning it against the saucer of her cup. "Hi, Pop. What happened to you last night?"

Eddie Munro looked at the clock on the big record cabinet. It said quarter of one. "Ah, I don't know. I sat around and talked to a bartender after they buckled up the joint. He knew some of the guys from the old days. Talked like he could tell a piano player from a player piano. We gabbed and had a few on the house."

"How's the new job?" Martha Munro put her cigarette out and looked up at him, smiling. For a moment she looked like the girl who used to look up at the bandstand, wide-eyed, her mouth a little open listening to the music, the wonderful music.

HE FELT HIS LOVE for her wash over him and he groped through his mind a word, any word. It wasn't there. He said at last, "All right. Mail-order arrangements and a Denture Boy up there showing his fangs and waving the stick a little outta time. But he'll get us work." He sat down a little heavily. "We got to talking about old times."

"Oh, my, the baby." Martha Munro got up. "That's the cutest middle-aged couple's baby ever was," she said. "If ever they have an event, 'The Soggy Toast throw' for kids under one, that lad's a cinch for the Olympics."

"The Old-Timers," Eddie Munro said. "Say, who was the guy started the Mound City Blue Blowers? We were tryin' to remember last night."

He didn't wait for an answer. "Remember in Chicago when we heard King Oliver, and Louis Armstrong was playing a second trumpet for him? And remember old Jelly Roll? Jelly Roll used to say he invented jazz, and some folks laughed at him, but Jelly Roll did a lot."

"Kids grow up now and it's here for them to listen to," Martha said. "We were the lucky ones; we had the fun of finding it." Her eyes went blank and far away. "Hearing fellows like you and Bix Beiderbecke for the first time …"

"Not me and Bix … even you can't put me in *his* class."

"Yes, I do. It was a great horn, Eddie — different maybe, but great, like Bix."

"What do you mean, *was*?" Eddie Munro bristled, feeling foolish but annoyed with the past tense.

"I don't get to hear you very often anymore," Martha said. "You remember, we got kids. A baby, and a daughter pretty near seventeen, and a couple of boys off at camp, but …"

"But this is the build-up to start turning the iron in me to go to work for the man that owns the record shop, and get up in the morning like a *respectable* family man."

"No, Pop," Martha said slowly. "Even if you can't blow your heart out every night any more, I didn't fall in love with a respectable family man."

"Sure," he said sullenly. "I know I'm only making crackers in a third-rate trap; workin' for a leader that's got nothing for the trade but a set of pretty teeth."

He wanted to say, *I love you,* like that, right out, with everything in it, with all the things that were in those words: two wonderful boys off to camp and a beautiful daughter and a gay little boy, and a wife. A wife prettier than any of the others of the old days. Way back yonder when she used to come and wait for him, and him thinking that

Eddie led with his clear, mellow horn, and the band swung in behind him.

she's in love with the music and not him, and the final wonderfulness of finding out he was wrong.

And now he couldn't even tell her on the horn any more. She couldn't come but once in a while to hear him, and it wasn't there anymore, anyway, just wasn't there. Mail-order arrangements and kids that talked jive but couldn't play, really. Making him feel as old-fashioned as ragtime. But because he was a musician he held the band together, such band as it was.

"Honey," he said lamely, "you look so tired; try to take care of yourself." He got up and walked into the kitchen and poured another cup of coffee. He heard the baby laugh...."

BUT MARTHA didn't take care of herself, or she couldn't, and the next week the boys were called back from camp; she was that sick in the hospital. And Sallie was acting like a grown woman around the home, and Eddie was down at his job every night, with his shiny horn, and he blew from nine 'til closing.

But it was different now. Denture Boy didn't say anything to him, because when he stood up and they let him go he went different. The tone had always been there, and the technical skill, also, these decades. But he said he loved his wife and that she mustn't die, and because he played a horn he said it on a horn. It got around. He didn't know it was different, because he was preoccupied. But out-of-work musicians started coming to the joint, sitting and listening, and some of the kids, even, they knew they were hearing something when he stood up with that horn and poured his music into the smoky room.

Denture Boy knew it, too. He said, real jolly, "Whenever you feel like takin' a break, Eddie, get up there and take it. That's a lot of horn you're blowing."

"Listen, Junior," Eddie Munro snarled, "I was blowing a lot when —" He stopped. "I'm sorry, kid," he said. "My wife's sick."

The young band leader smiled. "I'd like to give you some time off," he said, "but the truth is you hold this band together." He said it almost shyly.

The leader called a number, and they shuffled their music and the piano started chuckling, and Eddie Munro pushed the little valves down.

Martha, honey, remember all the love there is and remember me; don't die, honey. Not this time, not any time.

The musicians who crowded the tables close to the stand half closed their eyes and looked away at nothing. Here was a horn. The sound came out, no tricks, nothing but the horn, fluid and easy, all the heart that Eddie Munro possessed came out, and Eddie had a lot of heart, all down there at the hospital with a girl who had looked up at him a lot of years ago when he was young and handsome in a new tux. Mother of his four kids, beautiful kids who needed her. Eddie Munro didn't think it but he felt that God would hear him better if he played from where he lived.

The doctors told him it wasn't overwork, was just something that could happen to anybody. And Martha was a poor surgical risk, but they had to operate.

It was pretty wonderful, some of it. The boys home from camp and the house going along pretty good, with them trading off, taking turns to go to the hospital.

"The brave Munros," Eddie thought, "all brave but me and the baby, and us not brave at all. And every night I got to go downtown and blow my horn." The baby cried and called for his momma, and Eddie cried into his horn and called for Momma, too.

He'd played so long and was so good, in a way, that he played the horn like whistling through it, that effortless, and he didn't do anything in his mind but sieved his emotion from his heart to horn with nothing in the way.

They closed down the bar, but nobody left. The bartenders leaned against the bar, and the hat-room girl stood and listened.

The way the word got out was kind of mysterious — as if you could hear the horn for miles around, because working musicians came down from all over town, after they were off, and leaned around and listened. And a cop came in to see what went. The bar was closed all legal, and he stayed, and earned a reprimand. And gradually the band changed personnel, and grew, as the big-league guys sat in, the guys from the high-class joints.

But the horn of Eddie Munro was the all-pervading thing. And there was no envy from the others, only pleasure — only that is not the word.

Only a fermentation of emotion as such is very rare.

They shut down, petered out, the tired cohesion of the end in some ways better than the wild, sad improvisations of the first, about seven in the morning. And then Eddie Munro went over to the phone and stuck his nickel in and got the word.

Martha was all right, would be all right. He could see her that afternoon.

He got home in time to feed the baby in the morning, tell the kids, the brave young Munro kids, their mother was all right.

He went by to see her that afternoon, then went on down early to work, walking in the sunlight that made his worn suit shine as bravely as his horn.

The young leader nodded out at a bald man sitting alone at a table across the bare dance floor. Sadly he said to Eddie, "There's a guy here wants to see you."

Eddie walked over to the man, and the man stood up and laid a brief case on the table and held out his hand. Eddie sat down. They talked for quite a while, and finally the man left.

Eddie came back to the stand and the leader looked a big question at him.

Eddie Munro said pensively, "He said he'd heard of me, in the old days, and he heard us last night. Said he couldn't believe it."

The leader looked at him and bravely smiled.

"He can get us twenty-six weeks," Eddie said, "as a starter, at three times what we make here." He paused. "Eddie Munro and his band," he said finally. "And five hundred skins a week for me."

The young band leader, who knew that soon he would have no band to lead, said with kind impulsiveness, "You ought to call and tell your wife. That'll make her well." Then he turned his face away.

THE PLACE was filling, now, and the men were in their places, and they started out. The leader nodded, and Eddie Munro stood up and pointed his horn up toward the big money once again and blew. He blew seven bars. Then suddenly he sat down.

He sat with his horn across his knees and hung his head down and looked at it.

Once all it took was a pretty girl who bounced with provocation down the street, and you saw her when you were on your way to work and it made a feeling. It wasn't an important feeling, but it didn't matter because you didn't know what important was, and so the music came out true, anyhow.

And looking down at the horn, he saw it slowly come into focus, the golden horn that lay across his knees. He looked at is now, not as if it were a blood brother that had lied to him, but as an old, dear friend that he had finally recognized.

He stood up, and the horn dangled naked in his right hand as he walked between the crowded tables toward the phone booth.

They told him he could speak to her for two minutes. "Last night," he said, "I played real good — fine, I guess — and while I was playing I didn't think of anything but you." He stopped. "I love you," he said.

"Tonight," he went on, "I played a little bit, so bad you couldn't believe. In the old days a little thing could make me feel a big emotion and play it out. But now I gotta have a big emotion to play big —"

He didn't say anything about the guy with no hair and the big money — the money that he could no longer really earn. Instead, he said, "I'm closin' for the job with the Joe that has the music store first thing in the morning."

It was hot in the phone booth and Eddie Munro was sweating, afraid Martha would think he wasn't happy, like he really was for the first time in a long time; and so he put his horn to his mouth, the thing with which he was finally honest, and played it little, all that was in his heart.

Martha heard it, and knew it was all right. And she knew she'd never quite hear it again, and that was all right, too. She didn't say anything, just lay there in postoperative pain, happy as she wanted her kids to be, whomever they wound up with.

And the horn came muted through the phone; the heart-shaped tone of her man, who knew his trade so well he knew when to give it up.

Martha put her hand on his shoulder and he jumped up in the air. "What's the matter, Kibby?" she asked.

Max was a top rigger, but he needed a lot of vacations; and when trouble came, young Kibby was sure Max was in it.

HIS BROTHERS KEEPER

THE AIR has a flavor down around the piers: faint and teasing in the cool of the morning; sharp and pungent when the sun gets to it. It's a here-today-gone-tomorrow kind of atmosphere, and it makes the people who breathe it—well, not irresponsible exactly, but sort of easy-going. That is, all but Kibby McGowan.

Now Kibby worked for old man Hawkins, who owned the big marine supply house; and old man Hawkins wasn't half as earnest and careful

- 57 -

"We oughta send him up," Max said. *"He's such a pious one."*

as Kibby. Old man Hawkins, for instance, would leave dough in his desk — big serious heads of folding money in a desk anybody could open with a hairpin. Kibby was only a loft monkey working between terms of school, but earnestly he would chide his employer about his carelessness. Kibby thought old man Hawkins was the carelessest man he'd ever seen, outside of his brother Max McGowan, though Max had never had any of that kind of money to be careless with.

"Hell, Kibby," old man Hawkins would roar, "it ain't nothin' but money." And when Kibby tried to slant in an invidious comparison involving his brother Max, old man Hawkins would stand up for Max.

"But Max ain't gettin' anywheres," Kibby would argue.

"Shucks, Kibby, Max is the happiest guy on the waterfront. He may not wind up the richest stiff in the morgue, but so what?"

That kind of got Kibby, because he couldn't think of a real good answer. Max was a top rigger, and he could work for good money when he needed it. But Max needed lots of vacations. He worked like other guys took vacations, and it burnt Kibby up. Kibby wanted him to get married and settle down. He even had the wife picked out — Martha Jordan, whose father skippered a luxury liner. Martha was obviously awful fond of Max. But so were a lot of other girls.

KIBBY WAS HELPING take down a hawser on a platform one day when old man Hawkins called him into the office. Kibby couldn't hardly keep the disapproval off his face as he watched the old man jam a roll of bills into the desk drawer and snap the little lock. But the old man didn't seem to notice it today.

"Kibby," he said, "you reckon you could get Max to come to work for me for a few days?"

Kibby was young, and his face was a mirror for his thoughts. It lit up like range light. "I don't know," he said eagerly. "I could try."

"Well, get him over here, Kibby," the old man said, "and you might set him an example, and he'd stay on. Be a damn' shame if you didn't make something of that boy."

The fact that Max was ten years older than Kibby, and the old man made his voice sarcastic, didn't even get to Kibby. "I might at that, sir. I'll sure try. What do you want him for?"

"Well, a top rigger's always handy in this business. But right now I want him to renew the running rigging on a cargo ship. I just got the job this morning, and my top rigger quit. The apprentice can't cut it."

"Gee! I'll ask him, sir."

"Tell him I'll pay him scale and a quarter. I know he's a good man, even if he ain't exactly what you'd call steady."

So that's the way that Max McGowan happened to be working for old man Hawkins when somebody *did* open the desk and take a lot of money out of the drawer.

Kibby found out about it first. He came in the office one Monday morning after Max had been working for about a week or so, and caught the old man looking at the sprung lock. The old man didn't look sore — well, maybe a little. Mostly he looked kind of puzzled. Kibby didn't say anything, but he was scared because he thought of Max right off. He had a guilty conscience about Max.

"Kibby," the old man said, "looks like you couldn't teach me a thing."

"Is something gone?" Kibby knew something was gone, but he felt he had to speak.

"Yes," the old man said. "I didn't figure to let anyone know just yet. And I don't want you to tell *anybody*. Promise?"

"Promise," Kibby said automatically.

"Around two geesters," the old man said.

"Gee!"

"Oh, I'll get it back. I just want to be sure you keep quiet about it."

"I will, sir."

"I figured how to get it back."

"Who do you suppose took it?" Kibby asked miserably, afraid he'd get an answer.

"Somebody workin' for me," the old man said. "We got four guys on the floor, a couple on the truck, and Max and his helper. That's eight, not countin' you."

"One of them took it," Kibby said inanely.

Old Hawkins nodded.

"One of them."

"I promise I won't say anything."

"That's the kid!" The old man took a chew and reached in his pocket. "Go down to Al's and get me a couple plugs of twist," he said. He handed Kibby a dollar.

Kibby was glad to get out of there. But he cut down out of his way, going by the pier where Max was working. Max was up on the freighter's foremast. He had one leg hooked around a block and was reeling off a new topping lift. He was working quick and sure and casual. Kibby was partly relieved.

"Where you been?" he yelled up.

"Didn't you get my note? I went out o' town Saturday noon. Just got back in this morning," Max yelled. Max and Kibby shared a little flat.

"Well, I'm glad you got back," Kibby yelled lamely.

"I wasn't even tardy," Max laughed. "I'm sleepy, though."

Kibby didn't answer that; he only turned and went on down toward the drugstore. Max hadn't looked very guilty up there. He could stay up all night, and still was the best rigger in town. Look like a guy was real guilty, he'd fall off. Kibby knew Max wouldn't fall, but ….

Martha Jordan came up beside him and put her

Kibby looked in all their hiding places. When he got to the knob, he reached down and pulled out the wad of bills.

hand on his shoulder, and he jumped right up in the air.

"What's the matter, Kibby?" she asked. She was pretty, all right. Looked prettier than he'd ever seen her, and that was awful pretty.

"You scared me."

"Wait'll I tell you —"

"What?"

"I'll really scare you. Max and I are going to get married."

She flipped a finger through a hole in his jersey. "I'll be mending those for you."

Kibby didn't say anything. He felt an awful premonition in him, and it kept him from saying anything.

"Aren't you glad? I thought *you'd* be almost as glad as I am. Max said —"

"How come you just decided to get married?" Kibby asked. He was rude, but he couldn't help it.

"You won't tell anybody?"

"No."

"Max got hold of some money. Enough for a down payment on a house. He'd been waiting. He's going to stay on with Mr. Hawkins."

"Oh." *Sure, he got hold of some money, all right!* Kibby thought. He swallowed hard. "Oh," he said again.

"You're a funny boy."

"I got to hurry," Kibby said. He fled toward Al's drugstore.

But it was odd. Inside the drugstore, he couldn't think what he came for. He tried to think about what he'd come for, but his mind was all full of the other, and he couldn't. Miserably he called Mr. Hawkins on the phone.

"Two plugs of yardarm twist," old man Hawkins bellowed in the phone. "What the hell'd you think — taffy?"

Kibby got the plugs and dragged back. Old man Hawkins was just the same — just like somebody stole his money every day.

THERE WAS A MAN with a suitcase and a camera just leaving when Kibby came in late that afternoon. He'd had a bad afternoon of it, and it was worse now. Mr. Hawkins had told him to tell everybody to come into the office.

They all came into the office and sat around, and Kibby looked them over, feeling sick. None of them looked guilty, for a fact, except Max. But maybe he was just sleepy.

"Somebody — some one of you," old man Hawkins said, "stole some money out of the desk. My desk here." He pointed to it, and showed them the sprung lock.

There were little exclamations — just normal, though. Nobody blanched or anything like they were supposed to. They all seemed right sorry. They kind of looked at each other. All but Max. He yawned.

"You all are in and out of here all day, and I don't like to worry, and I still ain't worryin'. You're all good men, and that's a fact. One of you just give in to a quick impulse." The old man paused. "Also you made a mistake. The money was in a sack, a cloth sack, and I guess whoever has taken it figured a fingerprint wouldn't get on a sack."

'Well, I never knew that," Max said, real interested — and then he yawned again.

"Yeah. And we got that print, and we went around and got another print from here and there of every one of you, and got pictures of 'em. I had a man in here today." The old man chewed a moment on his plug and spit. "We ain't matched them up, 'cause I truly don't want to know who done it. I just want the man that took it to put it back."

Max yawned again and gave a little howl. Kibby felt himself sweating.

"I'm gonna give you each one a envelope," the old man said, "and I want the one that's taken it to put it back tomorrow. I want each of you to put your envelope back in the desk in the morning. I got some cut-up paper in each one, so it'll heft about right. Soon's I check over the envelopes in the morning and get the money, I'll burn up the pictures of the prints and everything will be just like it was. I ain't even gonna bother no more. I'm a easy-goin' man, and money ain't worth doin' time for, nor havin' no trouble about. I want you all to come in here one at a time when you come to work, and then nobody'll ever know nothing except the one that done it, and he'll have learnt his lesson.

The old man handed out the envelopes and then said good night to them all just like nothing had happened. Kibby couldn't help but like him awful well right then.

But then he remembered something. "You never gave me one," he said, panicky because he'd almost forgotten.

"Kibby? Why, son, you're too serious-minded to be a thief; takes a different cut of man from you —"

"No, sir. You gotta give me one. Why, I'm in here more'n anybody. I even warned you about the drawer."

Old man Hawkins grinned and made up an envelope and gave it to him. "I 'member when I was a kid," he said. "I hated to get left out of anything. Here's your envelope."

IT was pretty tough walking home with Max. Max was sleepy, but Kibby kept talking about what a wonderful guy old man Hawkins was to go about it like that and never gave Max a chance to say anything.

After supper they crawled into bed, and Kibby faked sleeping and gave Max a good chance to sneak up and put the money in the envelope, but Max just laid there and snored. Max must have figured old man Hawkins was throwing a bluff about the fingerprints on the cloth. But he sure snored innocent.

He snored so innocent that when Kibby got up and took the flashlight, he was just about convinced that Martha Jordan hadn't told him what she had told him. He looked in all their little hiding-places, though, and when he got to the knob that screwed off the brass bed, he was feeling pretty good.

He reached his fingers down and pulled out the wad of bills.

He got his envelope out of his coat pocket, and was crying so hard, trying to cry without making any noise, that he had a hard time getting his envelope fixed up with the money in it and getting the knob screwed back on the bed. And then he like to never got to sleep, praying and all.

MAX WAS CHIPPER as a lark in the morning, and they walked down to the office, and Max told Kibby about how he was going to get married, and wasn't he tickled, being such a matchmaker, and that maybe he was going to make something out of his older brother yet.

But Kibby couldn't take it, and he ran away from his brother and ran into the office and put the money in the drawer.

All the others struggled in, all of them looking self-conscious, and went in the office and then came out. It really went to show what they thought of old man Hawkins and each other for them all to do it, and Kibby thought about that; it helped a little.

Old man Hawkins came in and went into the office. They were all sitting around waiting for him, and finally he came back out.

He took the envelopes and some black-looking pictures and made a little fire with them and kicked the ashes all around after they burned up, not saying a word but grinning to himself, and then everybody started to stand up and go to work because that was the tip-off, all right.

But the old man stopped them. "Something went wrong," he said.

Kibby jumped right up in the air, and they all kind of looked at him; and old man Hawkins, he looked at him hardest of all.

"Somebody badly overdone it," old man Hawkins said then. "They was money in *two* envelopes: Twenty hundred fifty in one; seventeen hundred and ten in the other'n."

Well, now that was something! They looked at each other right good for sure then, and they all looked *real* good at Kibby, because Kibby was the one that had jumped.

And Max, he was looking the hardest of all. Right at Kibby.

"Kibby!"

Kibby jumped once more.

"You see Martha yesterday?"

"Yeah."

"And she told you…. Hell, I know what she told you. You been foolin' with that bed?"

Kibby hung his head way down.

Max stood up and went over toward the office. "Mr. Hawkins," he said, "I want you and Kibby to come in with me."

Mr. Hawkins waved the others on to work and he walked into the office behind Kibby, and Max was in front of Kibby.

Max didn't even look at Kibby when they got inside. "Mr. Hawkins," he said, "I aim to stay on with you indefinite if you'll keep me. I aim to get married."

Mr Hawkins allowed that was all right.

"I flew over to Nevada last Saturday noon, and I never got back 'til Monday morning. Next time I go, I am taking Miss Jordan, and we'll get married."

Mr. Hawkins said he wanted to be the first to offer his sincerest congratulations.

Max went on:

"But *this* time I taken a hot hand at a dice table, and I won a sum. When they cashed my checks, I had around seventeen hundred dollars."

"I'm gradually catchin' on," Mr. Hawkins admitted. "Looks like the honest and industrious loft monkey has practically got juvenilely delinquent overnight."

"We oughta send him up," Max said. "He's such a pious one!"

KIBBY HAD TO SIT down then; the tears were in his eyes before he could help it. But he looked up, and Max had tears in his eyes too.

"You was gonna keep me honest, wasn't you kid?"

Kibby couldn't even nod.

"You fire him," Max said, "and I'll buy him a flatty. I don't aim to have no little brother of mine workin' 'til he has to. ' Til he gets married."

"Reckon he can sail a flatty?" Mr. Hawkins asked.

"Sure. If he can't we'll teach him."

"You mean," Mr. Hawkins said, "take time off from work and lose money just to have some fun?"

Kibby looked up and saw the love for him they had under their talk, but he said anyway, because he was one of those: "I think it's fun *workin'*."

"Hell," Max said gruffly. "I guess we all do, a little bit."

Mr. Hawkins spit, and took the money out of his pocket and absently put it in the broken drawer, nodding in agreement.

Georgia had the right horse
and the right driver.
She could see herself standing
in the winner's circle.
Then, for the first time,
she took a long look at herself.

ROCKY'S ROSE

WHEN SHE WAS ASLEEP, or maybe half awake, or perhaps not asleep or awake but with her mind floating loose, she used to think she heard a sound. It was a drumming sound, like no other sound she had ever heard, and it would grow louder, and then under it would be a whine, and it, too, was like unto nothing that she knew. And the sounds would grow, and then diminish, the whining sound fading first. And sometimes she would will herself quickly awake — for no images went with these sounds — and try to capture and identify them, but she never could.

She wanted most desperately to know what they were and whence they sprang, for they were sounds — or was it a dream? — that were pleasant. Exciting and nice and pleasant; and, though exciting, still tied somehow to love and security.

This was the dream, the subconscious memory of Georgia Bresnahan, waitress in Joe's Place, right off Main on First. Georgia Bresnahan, nineteen, who took no hopes with her to work, but who couldn't help taking them to bed.

And so she awakened this morning, from the dream of the drumming; awakened blinking sullenly against the uncompromising light of day and swung from the bed, because if she did not she would go back to sleep again. And if she went back to sleep again Joe would make a scene. Some day she would tell him what to do with his job. Not today. Tomorrow — maybe.

The morning trade at Joe's Place was brisk and mostly surly. You could count the live ones, the ones who tipped, on your fingers with one hand in your pocket, and Georgia pegged the freckled man when he came in, not being immediately able to classify him. He was sunburned, all his face well weathered except for little white circles around his eyes. A riveter, maybe, or a guy that ran a jack-hammer. Anyway, he wore goggles.

He said, "Are you Georgia Bresnahan?"

"Yeah. What's yours?"

"Rock, Leonard Rock. They call me Rocky."

"Look, Buster," the girl said. "I don't care if they never call you. What do you want to eat?"

"Do you have coffee?"

"Black?"

The man nodded an absent assent. "I've got a horse for you," he said.

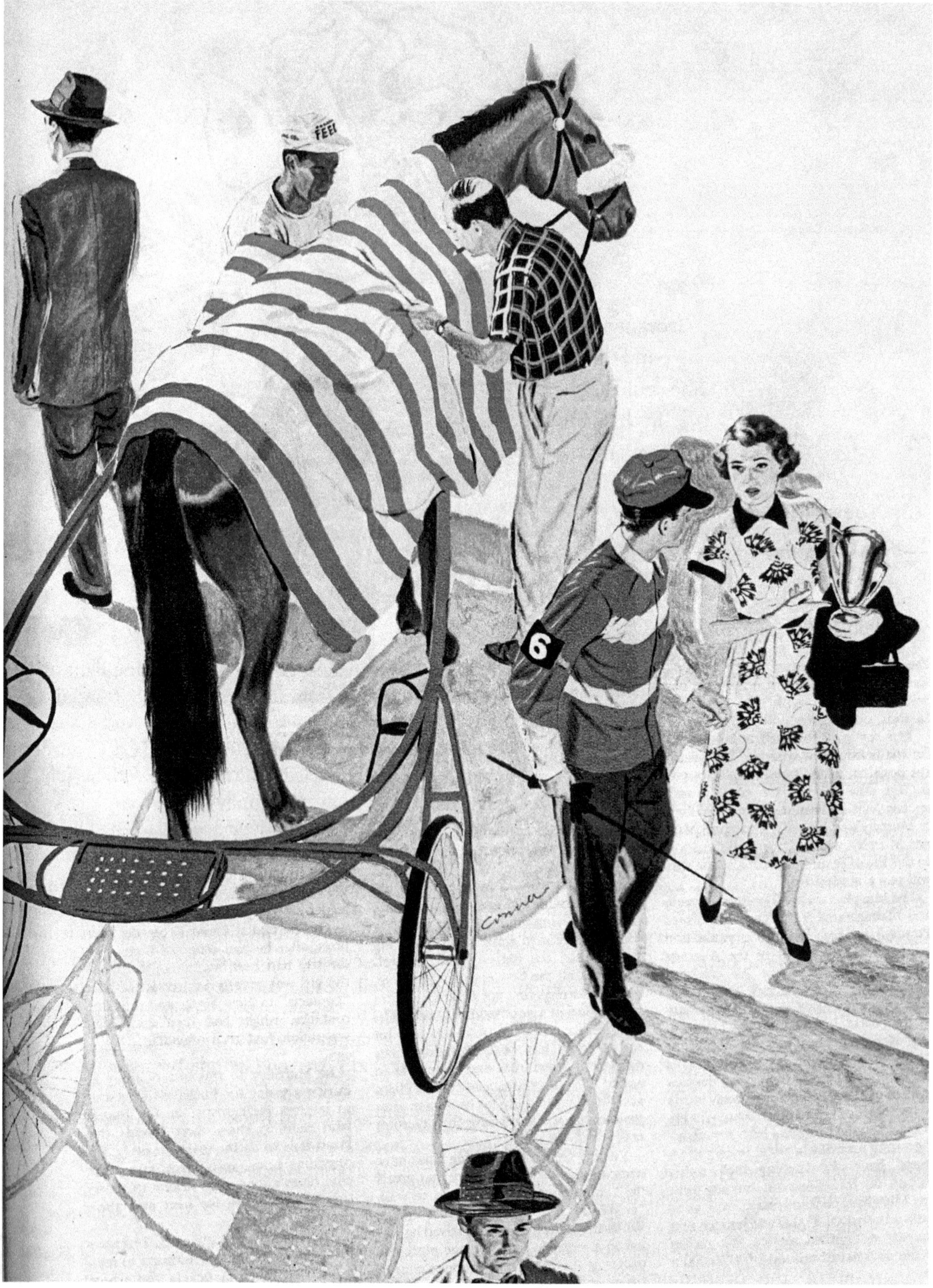
6

"Thanks. It's big of you Buster, but I never bet on the things."

"It's a handy virtue," Rocky said, and he grinned. "I mean I have a horse to give you. He's right outside. You want to look at him?"

Georgia looked at the man a long time. He didn't peg. "Get on to the funny part, mister. I got work to do."

ROCKY STOOD UP slowly, and she saw that he was lean and spare. He said, "No joke, miss. If your name is Georgia Bresnahan I've got a horse for you. Got him outside in a trailer. I'll unhitch and leave him there, or if you have other plans for him I'll help you carry them out. As long," he added, "as your plans don't take much time."

"Time?" the girl asked. "What's that?" It was some kind of a rib, all right, and she said words to stall, for jokes were cruel, always, down around First and Main, and especially at Joe's.

The man said patiently, "How about it?"

There was something about the guy. He had said it was no joke and she started believing him with a small, unwary bit of her mind that wanted to, and, anyway, time was what was going by. A man with small feet who walked like he wasn't used to it, and with big hands and a dark burned face with white around the eyes, and who wasn't in a hurry.

She said, at last, "I'll bite."

The man looked puzzled and a little hurt.

"Joe." The girl's voice rose in practiced stridency. "Back in a minute. Got to go see a man about a horse."

There was the trailer there, all right. A trailer hitched to a good medium-bracket car, and in the trailer was a horse. A horse of sleekness and beauty, a shining bay.

Rocky said, "This is Rocky's Rose, Miss Bresnahan."

The horse said nothing at all, but looked at her pink waitress's uniform and moved one hoof scrapingly against the boards.

Georgia looked at him a long time.

The man reached in his pocket and said, "Here are his papers."

The girl said then, finally, "I don't know about horses, but he isn't the kind of a plug somebody'd send around for a gag. Let's hear the story."

"I'll trim it down," Rocky told her, "skipping all the unpleasant things except to ask you your father's name."

"Mayo Bresnahan," the girl said.

The man handed her the papers. "He was killed in a stable fire trying to get his horses out. He didn't. But what I'm trying to say is that I was with him when he died."

"It doesn't make me sad," the girl said. "I was only three years old."

"It made *me* sad. I was thirteen, and Mayo Bresnahan had fished me out of an orphanage and took me with him on the circuit. I owed him a lot. And being with him when he was dying, I asked him what about you; his string had just burned up and he knew he was dying."

The girl didn't say anything.

"He did what he could, which was nothing, and you went to an orphanage. But he knew I'd do what I could, and so when I asked him what it was he whispered, 'If you ever get a good one, Rocky, and you figure you owe me anything, look her up and give the horse to her.' And so I'm doing that. I finally got me a good one."

"Thanks," Georgia said, and her eyes were bright and dry. "What do you figure he's worth?"

Rocky said noncommittally, "Twenty — twenty-five thousand."

"You're giving me twenty-five thousand?"

"If you want to sell him, you might do a little better than that."

"Where?"

"Out at the track."

"Let's go," the girl said.

"What about your job?"

"I'm unemployed as of from now. You might say I just retired." She disappeared into the restaurant, and a moment later returned, moved to the car, and plumped herself into the front seat.

"This horse," she said, as Rocky climbed in, "he's got a saddle and stuff?"

"No saddle. Rocky's Rose is a harness horse, a trotter. There's blankets and a sulky and all the other gear you'll need. They go with the horse."

"What are you going to do?"

HE DIDN'T ANSWER right away, and a funny, sad look came on his face. It was funny and sad because his face wasn't built to carry that expression, and it rode there for an instant like a mask a little bit askew and then it fell away. "I'm a good mechanic," he said proudly.

The girl said, "Oh."

"I've beat the sun up all my life," he said, "and mostly I have slept in barns." He paused as if he were through with talking about himself; then he said irrelevantly, "A horse will run back into his stall when the barn is burning and after you've got him out once."

The girl said, "Is Rocky's Rose the first good one? Didn't you ever have another one good enough to square off with Mayo's daughter?"

He didn't answer her, but turned his head and said, "They call a harness horse a jughead. You rig 'em with hopples to teach 'em to pace, and you rig 'em with blinders so they can't see the ground and jump shadows and gallop while the field goes by. You work your horses, feed them, groom them, warm them up, cool them out, and then they die when your insurance lapses."

"But Rocky's Rose?" the girl persisted.

"I never had a horse before that would trot under two minutes; the Rose has been crowding one fifty-eight a couple of times. That is a good trotter, if that's what you mean." He went on levelly after a moment: "Mayo had a good one once, too — Georgia's Rose. That was the horse he tried to save from the stable fire. And little guys who can't buy bread and haven't money, they hardly ever get two good ones. So I'm giving you this one quick. Now I know he's good, while he's all right."

The girl didn't say anything and finally Rocky spoke again. "I didn't do it on purpose," he said. "But, you see, I started the fire."

They parked the trailer on the backstretch side of the track and moved down through the barns. Georgia's eyes flicked about with the awareness that came from clawing her way from threatened extinction at the bottom of the heap. She measured the men who spoke to Rocky, trying to judge his standing by the way men spoke to him.

They moved across to the rail of the back stretch and leaned against the fence, their backs to the track. And suddenly the eyes of the girl turned deep and a little wet and she stood perfectly still.

For here was the sound of her dreams. The drumming sound, increasing, and in a moment the whine, the sound of rubber tires spinning smartly on the hard earth. She turned and watched the horse go by. The driver on the sulky, the horse's flashing haunches between his legs, was talking to the horse as they flashed by, and Georgia turned and watched and listened, and then she dropped her head.

"So that was it," she said at last. "So that was it." She looked up at the man and smiled tremulously. "I dreamed that sound a thousand times but never knew what it was. It was always nice in the dream."

Leonard Rock looked puzzled for a moment, and then he grinned. "Your old man used to hang you on the rail in a gunny sack, like a papoose, while he worked his horses in the morning. Yeah. I guess you'd remember a thing like that, wrapped up in blankets and hanging safe and warm watching the horses go by, and hearing them. I guess it would remember pretty good if you were a little-bitty girl."

"Funny," Georgia began, but Rocky cut her off: "Well, here's the guy we're looking for."

THE MAN in the narrow-brimmed Stetson and the worn, leather-reinforced driving pants was coming over.

She said uncertainty, "He don't look like big dough to me."

Rocky laughed. "How does big dough look?" Then he added to the man, "Matt, this is Georgia Bresnahan, Mayo's kid. She owns the Rose now and she figures she might want to sell."

"I'll still give you twenty thousand for the horse," the man said.

The girl's quick eyes moved from one man to the other. "Let me get this straight," she said. "You'll pay twenty grand for Rocky's Rose?"

The man called Matt nodded.

"Now tell me how much you can make with the horse."

Rocky shrugged. "Maybe nothing. Maybe a fortune. The Western is worth twenty thousand to the winner. He's entered in that."

"And you want me to *sell out* for twenty? What's a horse's life span — six months?"

"C.A. Harrison was out here last year winning regular. He was eighteen."

"And you jokers want me to sell out for one purse."

MATT SAID KINDLY, smiling, "Take the Western Free For All, miss. It's a big field. They'll probably go off in three tiers. Say you draw a back tier; but say you got so much horse and a driver who can get off and thread through. The horse thinks he sees a shadow and he jumps it, and all at once he's galloping, and by the time you pull him into stride, he's out of the race. Or say he breaks down and you have to destroy him. Oh, you got him insured, but you know what those premiums are?"

"Look, boys," Georgia said. "I got the horse. I don't know why Rocky gave me the horse. Why he had to, but he did, and now I don't see why I should peddle him back for what he can make in an afternoon."

"I told you —" Rocky began, and he looked puzzled.

"Oh, sure, you give me the scenario about the deathbed request of my old man, with the barn burning down in the background and catch installment seven next week." She paused in malicious pleasure at Rocky's look of consternation. "But I got the horse, bub, and I aim to pick up a couple of grand with him between now and the big race, and then I aim to pick up twenty grand with him, and I still got the horse."

Rocky said in a strangled voice, "We were winding him up for a mile and a quarter —"

The girl ignored him. She said to Matt, "Who's a good driver I can get?"

"Al Gore."

"But —" Rocky stopped.

"Peddle your papers, Buster. The deal smells any way you hold your nose, but it smells less with me hanging on to the horse. Go be a mechanic. If the heat wasn't on somewhere you wouldn't have given me the horse 'til he'd gone in the big race."

Rocky looked at her a long time, and then he looked at Matt and said, "So long, Matt." And then he walked away.

She watched his back for a moment and then she said to Matt, "Where do you find this Gore character? I got five hundred bucks saved up — and don't lift your eyebrow, I saved it the hard way."

Matt bowed formally. "Anyone can direct you to Mr. Gore," he said. And then he, too, was gone.

The remembered sound was almost obliterated now in the clamor from the stands. A week had gone since she'd straightened Rocky out, and Rocky's Rose was trotting third for Al Gore into the stretch turn and Rocky's Rose was finishing a desultory fifth.

Georgia found Al Gore in the stable area, and before she could berate him he said softly: "Never was one to talk my way out from behind a good horse, miss, but I'd try to get Rocky for the big one." He paused and thought a moment, and fifty years of driving went into the words he said: "Nobody but Rocky ever drove that horse. Them lines, they are kind like telephone lines. You can talk to a horse on 'em or you can't. And I reckon Rocky can and I can't."

"I never heard of such a thing."

"Well, miss, you saw it happen."

"Get this, Grandpaw. If you can't make a good horse win, there are other guys around."

"That's right, miss," Al Gore said placidly. "You can start huntin' at your earliest convenience." He walked away.

That was Al Gore — Peerless Al, they called him. The next one was Billy Durand, all right once, maybe, but now with many peers. He worked with the horse and he worked with the bottle, and Rocky's Rose tried to sit down in his lap the next time he went for cash and glory.

And so she fired Billy Durand.

IT WAS late afternoon and the stands were empty. The dust was deep in the stable area, powdery on her high-heeled shoes, and Billy Durand was gone.

The part of her, the little part of her blood and breeding, knew the Rose was a great horse, a beautiful horse, and, more than this, a magnificent machine. The other part, calloused and hardened by economic strife, was counting five dollars in the bottom of her purse and planning to liquidate this fortune on the hoof.

The man called Matt fitted into the plan by appearing.

"Hey!" Georgia Bresnahan yelled to him. "You still want to buy my horse?"

Matt raised his Stetson and scratched his head. "What're you asking now?"

"Your price. Same price — the one you named yourself." She was eager.

"Twenty thousand? That was a while back. I wouldn't go better than — say five thousand, now."

"Five — but why?" Georgia was aghast. "He hasn't been hurt or anything."

"He's way off. I wouldn't know why. He should cakewalk to the fields he's lost to. Maybe it was Rocky, but Rocky's gone."

"Yes," she thought, "he's gone."

"So you figure the horse is worth five thousand?" she said automatically.

"Losers go cheap," Matt said, and he didn't sound like a conspirator at all.

"Well," the girl said slowly, "I been working at this trade two weeks, and I'm out five hundred dollars of my own and I've got a horse that has depreciated fifteen thousand bucks. What I want to know is who's cheatin' who?" She said these things aloud to Matt, and to herself so she could hear herself say them, knowing all the while what she must do.

"Kind of funny," Matt said. "If you fool with them for money you never make it."

She groomed herself with calculating care the next morning and sought the man who knew a man who had heard where Rocky worked.

Rocky crawled from beneath a car to greet her, wiping off his greasy hands but not offering her one. "Miss Bresnahan," he said. "How's your horse?"

Georgia thought, "He gave me a twenty-thousand-dollar horse and went away, and the last thing he heard from me was that he was trying to cheat me." "You kidding?" she asked.

"I don't read the form."

"His health is fine," she said uncertainly. "You ought to see him tear into that forty-dollar hay." Georgia pleaded with slightly parted lips, with limpid eyes cast down: "I been around First and Main too long, I guess. Everything has got to have an angle. You give me twenty grand, and then I accuse you of cheating me."

Leonard Rock said nothing for a while, and then he prepared to crawl back under the car.

"We were wondering, me and the Rose, if you'd come out and drive him?" She was desperate now. "The Western Free For All's tomorrow."

Rocky stood up again and started asking questions: "How much had the horse been worked? By whom?"

Georgia answered as best she could, answered in manner most beguiling, still beseeching with those eyes, promising all she could without putting it into words. It had worked with other men. And now, watching Rocky's frown turn worried and thoughtful, she knew it was working with him; knew it for sure when he finally said, "I'll come and drive."

Reaching up, she patted his face with both palms and kissed him full on the lips. It wasn't the work she had thought it would be. It wasn't bad at all.

But she knew it paid to quit when you were ahead, and so she left him there. Bearing his promise, she went out into the sunlight.

SHE STAYED in the stands the next day, away from the stables, away from Rocky and the Rose. She watched as her silks went by, as Rocky breezed the Rose between the early races, and never once did the Rose break or sulk, but then Rocky hadn't asked him for anything.

When they went to the post it was as Matt had said it might be. Rocky had drawn the third tier back, and on the board in the infield Rocky's Rose was twenty-five to one.

That made her mad, somehow, and so she fought up to a two-dollar window and scrambled up loose change from the bottom of her purse and bought a ticket on her horse, and when she got back they were turning for the word.

Rocky was way back there, way back there in the third tier, and the assistant starters were yelling and cursing, and the crowd was still, and they were coming up to score. The starter let them go.

Twenty bicycle-wheeled silkies, twenty horses, twenty drivers, jumbled, scrambling for advantage, and they hit the clubhouse turn strung out. The Rose was laying next to last but trotting evenly.

They went into the back stretch, and three horses broke stride. And then Georgia finally found her colors and watched eight horses come back to them as Rocky took the Rose outside and asked him the big question.

But it was too much to ask, in a way, against the finest trotters and the finest drivers in the world. He collared two more at the far turn and was chewing up the daylight that lay between him and the leaders.

The announcer called him fifth by five lengths as they hit the stretch, and again Rocky went outside, the long way around.

GEORGIA CLOSED HER EYES, and then she opened them. Rocky's Rose seemed a good deal closer to the ground than she had ever seen him and he was reaching, never faltering, spurning the track with those big strides, on the outside, closing for the wire.

She elbowed her way to the rail then, and watched her horse go by. Rocky in his silks and goggles, his hands held sort of high, holding those two lines that old Al Gore had called telephone lines. And down those lines, and with his voice, too, Rocky was whispering endearments.

Rocky's Rose got up, or he didn't get up. It was a photo, and the wire that carried the box of developed film down from the camera to the judges swayed in the breeze a little as the picture slid down.

They posted Rocky's number, and Georgia Bresnehan went away from there and out down beyond the cashier's windows and sat down on a bench.

And then she heard them calling her name on the loud-speaker: "Will Miss Bresnahan please come to the winners' circle? Will Miss Bresnahan please come to the winners' circle?"

She stood up and started dazedly walking back through the tunnel from the paddock to the track. The winners' circle. She had, somehow, made the winners' circle. She'd never sling hash again.

She was still too dazed to hear the little speech, but she took the cup and put it under her arm, and she took the check and stuffed it in her purse, along with her papers on Rocky's Rose.

And then suddenly from her pinnacle of security she saw herself; through a dissolving veil of greed she looked up at Rocky's face, white around the eyes where the goggles had kept out the dust, and she said, "How can I thank you?"

He looked down at her a little pityingly. "Forget it, kid," he said.

She was inexplicably near tears. "But I want to thank you — to do something."

"Look, kid," he said; "I did it for the horse."

Georgia didn't answer. She turned, and stumbled a little, and then she heard Rocky walking beside her, talking quietly: "A horse likes to win. He's bred to win, and he wants to win for himself and for you, not for anything else. And when he loses to horses that he can beat, it gnaws at his heart. It messes him up inside. It shouldn't happen to the Rose; the Rose is lots of horse."

"I see," the girl said faintly.

"So I came down to try for him. Because, like Mayo, I kind of owed it to him." Suddenly he finished and was gone into the crowd.

Georgia turned and watched him until she could see him no longer, and then she turned, and the thoughts of a lifetime were spinning in her head. She walked to the man called Matt. She thrust out her handbag.

"Look," she said. "Give this to Leonard Rock. It's the papers on the Rose and the check." She held out the cup. "Give him this, too."

Matt took the handbag. "What happened?" he asked finally.

"Nothing. Nothing much. Only, I found out what kind of a guy he is. And I found out what I'm not."

"So," Matt said. Meaning nothing, meaning only that he had heard.

"I didn't ask him to come into Joe's. I was doing all right.... Tell him," the girl said slowly, carefully, "the next time he wants to give a horse away, to hunt him up another waitress —tell him we're even."

Matt said, looking at something above her head, "Mostly nowadays, every start is a race. That's for the betting, though some places they still race heats like in the old days." He paused. "Two out of three — so a horse could lose the first heat and still win."

The girl answered, half to herself, "I'm not a horse, Matt; I'm a hasher from First and Main."

IT WAS evening in Joe's Place, and Georgia Bresnahan was hearing a tirade on the subject of people who quit without notice. She said, "Save it, Joseph. What're we pushin' — the meat loaf?"

Blue eyes in a sunburned face looked up. Rocky said with satisfaction, "I figured I'd find you here."

"Go eat some place else."

"I'm not hungry. I came to bring you your stuff — the big check and your title to your horse. And to talk to you about what you said to Matt."

"Like what?"

"About me and what you're not, and all that kind of thing."

"Forget it, Rocky. We're even Stephen," the girl said. "What about some meat loaf?"

"I came to say the horse isn't mine. He's still yours, and the money, too." He paused. "You belong out at the track."

The girl said faintly, "Why?"

"Because when I looked in your purse that Matt gave me I saw not a dime — but a two-dollar ticket, worth fifty-five twenty, by the way. Well, I just *like* a girl who will chunk in her last deuce on the front end."

Georgia didn't say anything, but looked down at him, bemused, her eyes melting.

"Hell," Rocky said at last. "I ain't a mechanic."

"You loved Rocky's Rose, didn't you?" the girl said softly.

"My gosh, Georgia," Rocky said at last. "You don't see any horse in here, do you? When do you get off? I come *courtin'*, baby."

The girl looked at him and started to smile, tremulous at first, untying her apron. "Oh, Joe," she called politely.

Casey was a good guy, but tried to prove he wasn't.

IT'S ALWAYS THE WAY

YOU NEVER KNOW what will happen when you fool around with a typewriter, especially if it's a Chicago typewriter — or as it's shown on an invoice: *Thompson Submachine Gun (1)*. Casey Beaumont was the recipient of what once happened. Casey was walking home late one night, minding his own business; but because it was late, taking a shortcut down the alley behind Mark's Jewelry Store, when he saw two parties unknown emerge from the back door of the store carrying suitcases and start running.

Casey hollered and ran after them. It was a kind of reflex action, and like most such actions far over on the stupid side, because one of the parties stopped at the corner at the other end of the alley and wrote *"Now is the time for all good men to come to the aid of their party,"* with his typewriter, and some of it he wrote on the bottom of Casey's vest.

Nobody ever did figure out why a couple of petermen cracking a crib should be carrying that kind of armament, but that is beside the point. The point being, as they put it at the hospital early the next morning: "No hope is held for the recovery of Karl C. Beaumont."

The neighborhood grieved. Casey was a good guy. Casey was aces.

The old folks around the neighborhood said: "It's always the way." And they said it because of Johnny Grogan.

Johnny Grogan had been Casey's buddy. They'd buddied as little kids, then in the war, all through in the same outfit. Close as a dead heat they were until they came home from the war together and fell in love together — with the same girl!

Casey was steady and sober; Johnny was lazy and gay.

Casey went to work. Johnny didn't. And to live without visible means of support, you have to have invisible means of support and people figured they had caught up with Johnny Grogan's invisibly supporting himself.

The D.A. had a weak case against Johnny, really, largely circumstantial. Johnny was supposed to have stuck up a filling station and taken cash and checks. They never found any of the stuff that Johnny was supposed to have taken but they found someone who said it was Johnny that did it, they'd seen him. Johnny got one to five and had done a week when Casey headed off the Tommy-gun slugs.

The girl that Johnny and Casey had both fallen in love with was named Carolyn Miller, a comptometer operator for the gas company, with a luster to her that would light up a tenement hall, but not too bright in the head — in the judgment of the neighborhood — having fallen in love with Johnny Grogan when just as easy she could have had Casey, who even looked a great deal like Johnny, and was steady, and had a job besides.

Carolyn had cried when she told Casey she was engaged up with Johnny; perhaps knowing in the recesses of her heart that she had picked a wrong gee. She had cried and said she couldn't help it, and then kissed him on the brow. And then she cried again at Johnny's trial and vowed that she would wait for him forever.

And when she heard about Casey in the hospital, she really cried.

Casey Beaumont lay in the hospital with what felt like a blowtorch in his belly and half out of his head with dope. He lay there, and the two big things in his mind were Johnny Grogan — Carolyn Miller notwithstanding, for he'd loved Johnny all his life — and dying, for he'd loved life all his life too. And he knew for sure he was going to die, just as sure as he knew Carolyn Miller loved Johnny.

BUT LOVING JOHNNY became unimportant because he was dying; and loving life became unimportant too.

And then it occurred to him that he wasn't dead, and that until he died he had to live just as does everyone; that he just had a shorter time. And out of that thought grew another, and when the nurse came in with a needle, he shook her off and asked her to get him the D.A. "And a stenographer," he added, remembering just in time.

They came. They whispered with the Doctor in the hall, and then they came into the room, and the stenographer sat down, and the D.A. looked down at Casey and smiled. Casey was white, and his hair and eyes looked as if they were painted on his skin.

He said carefully: "The job you sent Johnny Grogan up for, it was mine."

The District Attorney said: "You are just making a play, kid. Johnny did it all right."

"No. I figured they would hang it on Johnny, and it worked out like I thought. Johnny and I went for the same girl, and I figured with Johnny away I could wind up with the girl. Well, I got Johnny away. But now I'm going away too."

Casey had figured it very carefully. He had been at the trail, Johnny's trail, all the way through and he knew what had gone on that night at the filling station and he answered very convincingly all the questions the D.A. tried to mix him up with.

And just as the thing was winding up, with the D.A. just leaving to set in motion wheels to right a miscarriage of justice, Carolyn Miller came over, to see if Casey Beaumont was still of the living.

They told her what had happened and she went into his room and knelt by his bed. He tried to reach out his hand and pat her head but he couldn't make it; and she knelt there and sobbed.

"Johnny'll be out in a few days," Casey whispered, for he was tired from the questioning. "Live happily ever after."

Carolyn looked up and her eyes were big and wet. "Oh, Casey!"

"Walk straightly with him in love," Casey said, feeling the moment called for a fairly high-flown sentence structure. "Name your first son Casey," he added, knowing instinctively any corn would go, in such a setting.

Carolyn said again, fighting with her sobs: "Oh, Casey!"

"You have your life to live, and Johnny has his life to live, and I have my little bit of life to live too. And never you wonder if I held up the station, for I did — hoping it would go like it did: that they'd put Johnny away for a crime."

"Oh, Casey, darling," Carolyn said at last, "*you* couldn't do a thing like that."

"The hell I couldn't," Casey whispered. "I love you, Carolyn."

THE NURSE CAME in then and ran Carolyn out, and it was just as well, for she could — save for that one line in which she doubted Casey's ability to hold up a filling station — manage very little contributory dialogue except an occasional, "Oh, Casey!"

Casey lived through the night on the nether edge of death, hopped up almost beyond hurting, and fairly pleased with himself, withal.

The Doctor who had issued the first bulletin came in and observed the slightly living Casey the following morning, and frowned and went away. The day went by, and again Casey didn't die.

The D.A. had moved fast, and when next came to Carolyn to the deathbed, Johnny Grogan came with her.

"Hello, Casey," Johnny said. "I hear *you* held up the filling station."

Casey looked at him meaningfully and then toward Carolyn Miller. He nodded.

"With a good job and all," Johnny Grogan asked, "what the hell did you want to do a thing like that for?"

"I needed the money," Casey said.

"He needed the money," Johnny said to Carolyn. Then he added: "I have known this guy all my life, and I don't get it."

Carolyn sobbed and went into her "Oh, Casey!" routine.

Johnny Grogan said embarrassedly: "How are you feeling, Casey?"

"He's dying," Carolyn wailed. "Don't you see he's dying?"

"Is he?" Johnny said. "He looks kid of peaked, but not *too* bad."

AND FOR A FACT Casey didn't look too bad. It took a minute for this to penetrate, but then Carolyn ran for the Doctor, and the Doctor came and looked at Casey, and then he took Carolyn into the hall.

"I stick to my original prognosis," the Doctor said, then added peevishly: "But if he gets well, it won't be the first time I've been double-crossed."

Carolyn rushed back into the room and knelt again beside the bed. "Oh, God," she howled, "let Casey get well!"

Johnny Grogan frowned. "They'd try Casey for the stick-up."

Carolyn hadn't thought of that. She whirled on Johnny Grogan.

"Why don't you admit you did it, you — you rat?"

"But honey, I didn't do it. It was like I said in court: I was down on the docks by myself at the time —"

"I'll die," Casey said lugubriously. "And you can walk hand in hand through life —"

"I wouldn't walk to the corner with that jerk," Carolyn said.

"I'll see you tomorrow," Johnny Grogan said, "when this silly broad ain't here. You'll probably get probation."

By the time Casey was released from the hospital, Carolyn was married to a widower who read meters for the gas company, for Casey's convalescence was very slow, and Johnny Grogan was running the filling station that he and Casey had gone partners to buy, and the police had caught the guys who had shot Casey after robbing Mark's Jewelry Store; and sure enough they found some of the checks from the filling station stick-up on one of them, and *his* confession stuck.

They say, the old folks around the neighborhood: "It's always the way," but then they say that about anything.

Strangely shaken, she turned her back to him—and she knew that she was in love with him.

Until a girl about town has met one particular kind of guy, her education is incomplete.

TAFFY'S TWO LOVES

SHE CALLED HERSELF TAFFY Taliaferro, explaining that it was pronounced "Tolliver" and that she was from the Tidewater country in Virginia; the lower tier of counties. Shandy Hall, just Shandy Hall, Virginia — though, of course, the Taliaferro's didn't have anything anymore. Just the big house and a little patch of ground. But who except the rich Yankees did have anything?

Actually, her name was Blanche Jones, and she came from near Florence, Alabama — but she had practically forgotten those facts and even when she'd had a good deal to drink and was a little tiddly she never slipped up, accent-wise or otherwise. She was one of those mystifying girls who hang around the East Side places in New York at night, sometimes with second- or third-string café-society escorts, sometimes with people nobody ever saw before. They seem to do all right; they look fine and pretty; they don't have jobs, but nobody keeps them; they know the angles and the score.

This Taffy was standing at a bar where she was well known with a man from Hartford. She heard somebody next to her, turned, and looked at the man who was complaining about a bottle of beer being a dollar and twenty-five cents.

He had red crinkly hair, and his suit, which Taffy, who could estimate the cost of men's clothes with accuracy, thought for a minute was from a knowing and expensive tailor, was really a cheap suit that rode his big frame in an expensive way because of his build and grace. Only his tie was wrong, just a little off.

He smiled at Taffy slowly, with nothing in the smile but friendliness, and she liked him right away, and she knew everybody liked him. As he looked at her, she blushed for the first time in a long time, the blush rising up from her breast to her hairline. She had on the kind of dress that made the blush take quite a long time.

Then she turned her back, but she was strangely shaken. Taffy had seen the girl he was with, and could tell she was in love with him. And the girl was the real article — with money — and rather beautiful.

The man from Hartford saw the redheaded man in the mirror. He put his arm around Taffy and leaned across her. "Where'd you get that tie, Red?" he asked.

"My mother sent it to me for my birthday," the red headed man said, and his smile didn't admit the possibility of malice in the question. "It's prettier in the daytime, but not much." He looked past Taffy, and went on, real interest in his inquiry, "You live around here?"

The man from Hartford admitted he lived in Hartford, and added, "Can I buy you a drink?"

The redheaded man turned to his girl. "This gentleman wants to buy us a drink," he said.

The girl looked angry but helpless, and she was trying to hide it. She was strong for the redhead.

So they learned each other's names. The man from Hartford was named Shackleton and Taffy Taliaferro stuck to that name, and the redheaded man was Guy Meadows and his girl was Lucile Grace. Lucile Grace's father had a lot of money, and Guy Meadows worked for him "downtown." Mr. Shackleton had a comfortable number of shoe stores in Hartford.

Taffy had a due bill at a hotel and some clothes.

Miss Grace seemed ashamed and proud of Guy Meadows all at the same time, and it made everybody a little uneasy. Everybody but Guy Meadows.

John Shackleton said to Lucile Grace, "Take it easy, honey, we won't teach him any bad words."

Everybody liked Guy Meadows — you couldn't help liking him — and everybody relaxed. After a while they all moved to a table, and John Shackleton was talking about the retail shoe business.

And Taffy fell in love with Guy Meadows. She did it much against her will, for Taffy knew that falling in love was the wrong thing to do. She knew it instinctively, because she had never been in love before. But she knew that the weapons she used to live by — her beauty, her agreeableness, and her knowledge of the angles — would be blunted beyond utility if she fell in love.

Nevertheless, Taffy, the smarty, fell in love.

John Shackleton of Hartford appeared not to notice it. He was a young man with a pleasant, bland face that told you nothing. Lucile Grace noticed it all right, and was frozenly correct and almost viciously animated by turns. Guy Meadows took it for granted.

Taffy made her play as best she could, handicapped as she was by the sense of overwhelming importance she attached to the maneuver. She indicated how it was possible to get in touch with her as subtly as she could, which wasn't very subtle because by now Miss Grace was putting the snaffle on Guy Meadows to get him away from there as subtly as she could — which wasn't very subtle, either.

Lucile Grace did manage to get Guy Meadows away, but by then it was too late, and pretty soon John Shakleton took Taffy home.

In the cab he put his arm around Taffy and laughed a little laugh. He didn't try to kiss her, but he gave her a fifty-dollar bill. "Take a deep breath, kid," he said. "He'll call you up."

Taffy asked, "Does it show that bad?"

John Shackleton said it did. "Put the fifty in your shoe," he added. "You'll need it."

Taffy gave back the fifty and kissed him on the cheek as the cab pulled up at her hotel. John Shackleton didn't get out of the cab. "Take it easy, kid," he said.

Taffy went to bed feeling good about not taking the fifty, even though John Shackleton had never been anything more than a friend — a friend with a lot of money.

But you couldn't be in love with a man like Guy Meadows and take money from people.

GUY MEADOWS called Taffy the next morning. She could feel his masculinity over the phone. He asked her out to dinner. Taffy gasped with relief and gulped a little saying yes. Tough, wise, beautiful little Taffy felt her heart beat hard and her head go soft.

Guy Meadows took her to a cheap little restaurant, and that was all right, too. He said he couldn't afford to take her anywhere better. During dinner he talked about being a poor nobody and working his way through a little fresh-water college, just as if it were all right to tell the truth — and of course it was.

It was a great love affair. All the silly lyrics became laden with poignant meaning. They rode on the Staten Island ferry and they had picnics in the park and they did the things that young lovers without funds are supposed to do so ecstatically in New York. Taffy didn't care for it, but she cared for Guy Meadows; she loved Guy Meadows so that nothing else mattered. She didn't have room in her heart for anything or anyone but Guy Meadows.

She hadn't ever seen anyone like him. He was honest, completely honest. He said he still went out with Lucile Grace because he had to keep his job. He said that they went nice places and sometimes she gave him money to pick up the tab. He admitted maybe it was wrong because he didn't love Lucile. He loved Taffy….

"Oh, darling," Taffy said. "Of course it isn't wrong." How could anything be wrong when he loves me, Taffy thought, and he tells me he does — and he never lies.

But it put a little pressure on Taffy. His utter candor was catching, and she told him her name was really Blanche Jones and that she wasn't from Virginia. And of course she couldn't live as she had been living — which was really off men, though she had never been a tramp. So, she went to work as a clerk in a department store after learning that modeling requires more than being pretty.

She knocked her brains out and the polish off her fingernails five and a half days a week. The due bill ran out at her hotel, and she moved into cheaper quarters.

But it was all fine. Guy Meadows loved her, and he showed his love every way there was that didn't cost over two dollars.

They never priced any chintz curtains or walk-ups, but it was lovely — they had each other. Or, rather, Taffy had Guy Meadows, big and handsome and wonderfully honest.

Frequently now, they didn't go out at all, but dined at Taffy's apartment; Taffy fixed steaks and other masculine and expensive fare. Guy Meadows always brought a bottle of wine, and they dined by candlelight. Love misted the grubbiness of the flat, and after Guy was gone Taffy did the dishes in a cloud of tired happiness.

They would sit and hold each other or listen to the radio or play Canasta. They didn't have much to talk about, for Guy Meadows never gossiped and Taffy no longer saw anybody to gossip about.

Taffy sold her evening dresses — including the one the man from Milwaukee had bought for her at sixty-six per cent off. It seemed to cost a hellish lot to work and live and feed a large and healthy man. Guy Meadows was honest about that, too. He liked steaks.

Taffy wasn't as pretty as she used to be — or maybe she just didn't work at it as she had before she met Guy Meadows.

THERE CAME A NIGHT when Taffy didn't feel good; she was tired. Guy came to dinner and brought a bottle of wine and two fresh candles and sat in the comfortable chair and watched her work over the salad — the picture of a contented man.

"I've got to go to Bermuda," he said. "Old man Grace wants me to go along with him on his boat."

Taffy said, "A yacht?" For it was an exciting word and her best day had never seen her in the yachting crowd. And then she added, "And Lucile?"

"Of course," Guy said matter of factly. "You know all about Lucile. I've never lied to you."

Taffy said, "It's just that I'm tired, and feel rotten."

"You oughta take a few days off and rest," Guy Meadows counseled. "You really don't look well."

"Maybe a nice ocean voyage," Taffy said.

"Oh, nothing like that," Guy said. "Just a few days of relaxation."

Taffy looked at him for quite a while. Then she laughed and went over and kissed him. "Sure," she said.

She felt wretched the next day, and feverish, and she staggered coming up the stairs. The following morning she fainted when she got out of bed. She came to on the floor, made it to the phone, and called Guy at his office.

He was in, but busy. He was patient, kind. He couldn't come because they were planning their trip. She must rest, drink liquids.

Taffy put the phone down, too weak to hold it.

Well, she thought, feeling clammy and sick and near tears, I have a lover but no friends. I used to have friends. Lots of friends, even if they were men. I wish I had the fifty in my shoe John Shackleton wanted to give me. I'd— She got to the phone again, a little delirious now, and told the operator she wanted John Shackleton in Hartford. He sold shoes.

JOHN SHACKLETON seemed to answer at once, though it must have taken time. During that time, Taffy sat and looked in the mirror over the telephone table. She looked awful, and she felt an errant guilt about calling John Shackleton when she looked so bad, for she had been beautiful and groomed when he had taken her around. That's why he'd taken her around, she guessed.

"Johnny," she said, "I'm sick."

He answered pleasantly, "Where are you living now, Taffy?"

She gave him the address. "Guy has to go to Bermuda, Johnny. I haven't any friends."

"Lie down and count your blessings kid," he said. "We'll see what we can do."

It all seemed to happen right together. She picked up the phone and John Shackleton answered, and then he came into her room with a doctor and then he left, and immediately he was back and they rolled her onto a stretcher and took her away from there, and she looked up at him and said, "I'm sorry to look so bad, Johnny."

"I'm sorry, too," he said.

The next she knew she was in a big room in a hospital. There were flowers around, and she felt much better — oh, a great deal better. John Shackleton was sitting in a corner of the room, reading a racing form. It made her feel good — at home, somehow. She hadn't seen a racing form in months.

Guy hated her to swear, but Guy was on a yacht going down to Bermuda. "I feel better," she said. "A whole hell of a lot better." It made her feel luxurious to swear.

John Shackleton looked up. "You had pneumonia, kid. But fancy drugs for fancy ladies."

"I'm no fancy lady. I've been punching a clock for months."

John Shackleton said, as if he hadn't heard her, "There's a Whitney colt going today. Want me to put fifty on him for you?"

"Do the horses still come out all bright and beautiful and does the guy blow the big gold bugle?" Taffy stopped and then she said slowly, "I'm not very honest, Johnny, letting you do all this."

John Shackleton said, "It's only money, Taffy." He added reluctantly, "Man that climbs a tree to tell the painful truth when he could stay on the ground and lie a little — well he's shooting an angle, too. Being a professional country boy, not putting up a front — that's putting up a front. Little different but all the same."

Taffy felt a wave of unutterable relief and then some warm tears came into her eyes. She tried to answer, but John Shackleton was talking on, at random. "You know," he said, "I've lied all my life, strictly speaking, telling women they had pretty feet whether they had or not. I got almost rich doing it." He paused. "I wanted to tell you that."

Taffy tried again, but John Shackleton picked up the phone and got the bookie. "I want fifty on the front end on Honest Guy in the second at Santa Anita," he said. "For Taffy Taliaferro."

He's said it all, Taffy thought. Wrapped up Guy Meadows and me and the whole business, left nothing more to say. She started crying.

John Shackleton didn't get up. He said, "Don't cry Taffy. You're a swell little girl. And if I can get you up out of this pesthouse and fatten you up a little and get you some gowns that'll show you off, I'd like to marry you."

She didn't know what to do or say, but she had to stop crying some time and so she stopped now. "Honest Guy going in a sprint or over a distance of ground?" she asked, and her eyes were pretty.

"Sprint," John Shackleton said, no surprise in his voice.

"I think we ought to back him up, John," she said. "Phone the book back and bet him to place, too."

"Well," John Shackleton said, "Okay, Taffy, honey."

THEY WERE IN A BAR in which she had been known in the old days. She looked better now — radiant in fact. Lucile Grace came in with Guy Meadows. As soon as there was a break in the conversation, John Shackleton said, "You should see Shandy Hall. Taffy and I were down there on our honeymoon. Damndest most beautiful mansion, pink brick with these white pillars —"

"Old Aunt Amanda was so glad to see me, she cried," Taffy added.

John Shackleton turned to the bartender. "What'd Honest Guy do today at Belmont?" he asked.

"Ran out."

"You know," Taffy said, "we've been following that *damned* horse every start, and he's never been in the money."

Guy Meadows smiled. "I don't know anything about horses," he said. "We had a mule on our farm. One mule...."

THE CAT AND THE CONSTITUTION

HE WENT TO THE CITY once in a while and today he was driving home. The air was still, it sat on the country, hot and heavy. Sat on the fine black land where on still nights you heard the growing corn.

His name was Taliaferro Davis and he thought of the land through which he drove and the people in it because it was a little bit his and he was of it.

He thought of a phrase: The trouble with the South is that the Republicans can't win it so they do nothing for it. The Democrats do nothing for it because they don't have to win it and the Independents do nothing for it because we don't deserve it.

He would like to pick up a hitchhiker to say that to him to see what the hitchhiker would say; and then he saw the figure far down the road, too well dressed to be a Negro, walking. He drew up the car, his nineteen-thirty-seven car that groaned a little as it slowed and the walker turned.

He was a Negro, quite dark, young, well dressed.

Taliaferro Davis thought first *I'll speed up and go on.* But Taliaferro wasn't rude and he made up a whole conversation with his wife. "Picked up a darky today, so dressed up, I thought he was white. Didn't know whether to put him in the back seat — but then people would think I was his chauffeur — (laughter) or the front. People'd think I thought he was as good as ...."

The boy got in the front seat as Taliaferro held open the door.

"Thank you, sir."

"Going far?"

"Home, other side of Griffithtown."

"Carry you there in a jiffy." Then Taliaferro said quickly, "Trouble with the South is the Democrats win whether they help it or not, the Republicans lose it whether they help it or not and the Independents won't help it because we don't deserve it."

The boy chuckled. "Colored folks live jammed up in Harlem, worst living in the world." He had some accent when he said that, familiar accent. "New York City, New York."

"Just what I say," Taliaferro said. "My name's Tol-ver Davis."

"T-a-l-i-a-f-e-r-r-o?" The boy spelt out.

"Yeah."

"So's mine, sir."

"Well, I'll be damned, named for the same folks, maybe? I been around here, us Davises, a long time."

Taliaferro Davis drove in silence and the boy beside him hummed a tune, a kind of happy bluesy tune.

Worry about money, your wife, about the kids, about the South; about everything but things you ought to worry about. Ought to hustle, ought to work more but hell, a lawyer … a little town. Ought to hum a tune, going down the road. Madgie was better than she got, deserved better — lots better. All screwed up in problems, but think about the wrong ones. House needed fixin', people needed payin', behind in the insurance and the schools for the kids weren't worth a damn.

"I live in Sassoon," Taliaferro Davis said. "Lawyer."

"Yes, sir." The boy hummed the tune. "I been going to school in the North, New York City, New York. I came back to see the folks. Live outside Griffithtown, other side. Didn't expect the ride; I'll surprise 'em."

"You like it up north?"

"It's different, sir."

"How do you feel? I mean, hell, I don't know what I mean. I ain't much, just a piddlin' poor lawyer. What you studyin'?"

"How to be an accountant, sir."

"You say *sir* to folks up north?"

The Negro boy hummed his little tune. "I try to be polite all over the country, Mister Davis."

Taliaferro looked down at the boy and grinned. "You're all right, but then, oh well, I wish I was young again, goin' to school … race problem, quite a race problem. Hard, hard problem. Colored folks are quite a … damn New Englanders fetched 'em … to start." He looked at the boy beside him.

The boy hummed his little tune, happy to be getting home before he expected to get home.

"Man's black or a man's white. I recognize there's a problem. I recognize it. There is, isn't there?"

"We got one, too, Mr. Davis. White folks is our problem."

Taliaferro Davis laughed. "Damned if they ain't, us too, that is us — too. Damn white people."

Taliaferro Davis looked down the hard road, into the setting sun and felt the exuberance of the ground around him, damp and fecund. Rich land. He said, "Say an old lady died and she didn't have chick nor child nor kith nor kin, nothin' but a cat. She left all her money to the cat. Ever' damn cent, a million dollars after taxes. Ever' red cent to that old cat. Now the Probate Court, they'd take care of that cat until he died and then they'd be a fight for that money or maybe they kill that cat. But say the cat, he came to court and he said right out, plain English, 'Reason that old lady left me that money was because I could talk and I kept her company. I want my money; that old lady bored hell out of me for years and I want my money.'"

The colored boy laughed, loudly. "Cat couldn't spend the money."

"Sure as hell could," Taliaferro Davis said. "Cat could talk, had a million, hire some man to carry his money. Cat goin' around, man followin' him with a croaker sack full of money. Drop into a butcher store, man followin' him. 'Order us up a ton of liver, gonna set up liver to every cat in the county. Count out the money.' Man say, 'Yes, Mr. Tom!'"

"Have to be a colored man," the negro boy said. "White man wouldn't work for a cat."

"Hell, he wouldn't. I'd be right respectful to a cat had a million dollars. I don't know why I think of those things. They come into my mind when I ought to be thinking about how to do better, hustle, make money."

"We're coming into Griffithtown. If you'll let me out, please, other side of that little lane, sir."

He let the boy out. I'd trade off black to be starting, yes, man, any damn color on the chart to be starting over, he thought. I'd like to owe me some different people and get me some fresh worries.

The sign said "Narrow Road" and he saw the concrete abutments of the culvert ahead of him as the sun lay horizontal rays upon the earth. He shoved down on the accelerator aware of the time going. Aware of his life going, aware for a long instant of himself and time and his failure. The car gathered itself and the right front tire, tired and swollen with the heat, let go with an unimportant pop and then there was the big crash, the smaller crash, the little settling groan.

The colored boy heard the sounds and turned and looked up the road and he stood an instant, hearing the silence. He started running.

THE DOCTOR was a very young and very blond man, with the fine impersonality of internship still upon him. He looked at Taliaferro Davis from behind his rimless glasses and smiled a smile he was practicing for later days and richer patients. In an accent strange from Tulane over Minnesota, he said, "Cut a big artery. Bled white, truly. Big transfusion. Man has five quarts of blood, say; we gave you three new ones."

"Right interestin'," Taliaferro said. "Feel all right, too, feel real good."

"Type O," the doctor said, "comparatively rare. Lucky. Found three ex-soldiers here that knew their type, said it was O. Didn't have time to check. Took their word. Just fooling around, old college try, ethics, et cetera. Actually thought you were dead."

"Feel right shiny," Taliaferro said and he hummed a tiny snatch of tune.

"They did it bigger on occasion in the army, I've heard. Four quarts. But I'm down here on fevers, malaria; kind of out of my line. Very interesting." The doctor smiled his smile again. "Here's your wife again, got the boy with her." He paused. "You can go home soon."

Taliaferro Davis said to his wife when she came and looked at him with anxious loving eyes, "Good as new, honey. I can go home real soon."

Bradford Davis, a large twelve, said: "Mess a people called about you, pop. A gang of 'em. You must know everybody in the county. They were worried, too."

"Honey," Madge Davis said, lowering her voice, nodding to the door the doctor had walked out of, "did he say, did he say how much?"

"He ain't worrin', honey. The blood donaters, they didn't take anything, didn't want anything...."

"Who?"

"Some soldiers around, ex-soldiers, knew what type they were, what type their blood was. Oh," he said, a little pride in his voice, "kinda rare. Hell, the Doc ain't worrin'. I told him about the insurance it being in arrears. Kitchen leak bad in that shower of rain last night?"

"Yeah, poppa," his son said, "run a regular *stream*."

"Guess we need a whole new roof."

"Was you unconscious, pop?"

"Didn't know straight up for two whole days."

"We're surely thankful," Madge Davis said. "Car's a total wreck."

"Total," his son said.

"Damn Northern insurance companies; all those insurance companies always up in New England. Seems funny to me."

"A mess of people called," his son said. "Phone ringing all day long."

"We *been* here, son. We got Negroes *named* for us, took the name when they came from Africa. Naturally everybody knows us."

"Before the war, your father's people ..." Madge Davis began.

"I can't imagine no war fought without no planes."

"Goodness gracious, Bradford!"

"That boy's a triple negative man; wonder where he picks it up!" Taliaferro said and sat up a little in his bed. "You know, Madge, I been thinking. I'm gonna run for solicitor, pays pretty good. Got to thinkin', all those people call us up, you I mean, about me. Poor but popular. And everybody knows I'm honest."

"Solicitor, pop. Hot dog, Mr. D.A."

"Shut up, Bradford. With no car I don't see ..."

"Hell, I'll campaign afoot. A little sympathy won't do any harm."

"Tol'ver," Madge Davis said, "seems like you've changed."

"I just been thinkin'." Taliaferro hummed the little tune then he whistled it some. "Just thinkin'," he said. "I'm gonna be happy. I'm gonna grin and hum. I got the prettiest wife and the best kids — how's little Madgie — owe a few rednecks and I ain't got any money. I'll make an A-1 solicitor, honest and fair and a good old name, fine old name, Negroes all over this part of the country named for me; wish they could vote. Yes, M'am, I'm gonna file, come the time, for people's attorney."

"Make speeches, Pop?"

"Sure."

"Well, Tol'ver Davis...."

"I ain't so damned old, give me a kiss, honey ... shut up, Bradford."

"Mark Cross's going to run again."

"Sure. I'll make him hunt the brush."

"He's a dirty campaigner."

"Made Mr. Dicey Brown leave the country, talked about him so last election."

"Mr. Dicey was a *Republican*," Taliaferro said contemptuously. "Didn't anybody contest Mark in the primary? Republicans run in Sassoon County just to hear the wind whistle in their ears."

"Republicans *never* win in Sassoon County?" Bradford Davis asked idly. "Can't feature no war without even no tanks."

"No, not since sixty-six. Son, lemme ask you a question ... you're always talkin' about studyin' the law; say a woman, an old woman with five million dollars, she died and left every red cent to a cat. Now the Probate Judge he .... Hush, Bradford, this cat could *talk*."

THEY SAT in the kitchen under where the leak was when it rained. Bradford, upstairs, splashed in the tub, sloshed water on the floor. Taliaferro Davis in his good seersucker suit, already wilted, looked across the clean kitchen table toward his wife.

"Little Madgie asleep?" he said heavily.

"Yes."

"Now let me tell it, tell it my own way."

"You saw them?"

"I was in Griffithtown, got to thinkin', thank those fellows, saved my life, pretty near a quart of blood apiece."

Bradford yelled down from the hall. "Why they have the primary first Tuesday after the first Monday in August, pop?"

"I don't know.... Yes, Madge, honey.... You go to bed, Bradford, you're gonna be busy haulin' voters tomorrow."

"Can't I come down for the speakin'?"

"Hush up. Yes." Taliaferro smiled at his wife but the muscles in his face felt tight, funny. "And I been so damn happy. Maybe that's why."

He looked at his shoes.

"They was Tol'ver Davis's two cousins, you know the Negro I told you about. Them and Tol'ver. Quart apiece."

Madge Davis sat still and looked at her husband. "Everybody that knows," she said, "says a man is a man."

"I ain't worryin' about that. Hell, three fifths darky blood, you think I'm worrying about that? I think Mark found out about it. I had him beat goin' into tonight, the speakin' tonight on the courthouse lawn, I had him barely beat."

"I guess everybody had plasma might be part anything with that foolish thinking."

"Foolish? Clear crazy. But there's stupid people in Sassoon. In the South," he said finally, bitterly.

"And the North, East and West."

"Well, we got to go on down there. Every county candidate speaks from the courthouse tonight." He leaned back looking up and trying to let some slackness into the muscles of his face. "See right through that hole," he said. "Star right exactly there."

They went out of the house and walked down the street between big spreading trees. Hot tonight, finishing the corn and opening the cotton. They didn't talk much, they knew each other very well, they loved each other very well. Their son galloped past them.

Taliaferro laughed. "All three of 'em," he said in a low voice, "black as the ace of spades."

Bradford galloped back, said, "Why don't they have the primary election on the third of August every time, why the first Tuesday after the first Monday?"

"I don't know," Taliaferro said and watched his son gallop away, his white shoes twinkling in the blackness.

"I thanked 'em," he said. "I thanked them politely and real, real grateful. Hell, Madge, I'm glad to be alive. I'm glad I got you and little Madge at home, and Bradford."

"Bradford loved it about the cat."

"Old Mark, he may say it. He was over there, they said, they didn't see him, but he was usin' around over there, talkin' to the doctor."

"That boy, that wonderful boy, that malaria-loving boy," Madge said.

"I didn't ask him did he tell Mark — hell, Mark found it out. I know that. Does he say it? That's the thing. He swing fifty votes he'll beat me. You can figure these little elections close when you campaign like I did."

"Oh, but he wouldn't."

They came into the square and Taliaferro squeezed his wife's arm and went away from her, walking up to the lighted platform where sat the candidates like children for diplomas in uniforms of white seersucker.

Mark Cross wore a large black bow tie and didn't look at Taliaferro.

The incumbent county clerk (unopposed) introduced a speaker.

Taliaferro took his speech out of his pocket and read a couple of familiar lines. He put it back in another pocket and sat and waited a long time, not hearing anything until Mark Cross was introduced.

Mark Cross was a fat jolly man who strangely didn't mind the heat.

He was fat and jolly and people liked him and Taliaferro Davis thought, *He's a symbol of a sickness, because people like him. He's what we don't deserve.*

Mark Cross made two rolling phrases roll and then he alluded to the supremacy of whites and got a cheer and then he stopped and said it right out about Taliaferro Davis being, well, he *had* blood, three fifths, roughly, Negro.

He made it funny. Just enough funny, not mean about it, quite. Just kind of funny. He was a man running hard for office.

Taliaferro looked up and saw his wife way out there and way way out there the colored folks, and closer, people he knew, laughing at him, they were, and he sat there and felt his face get tighter and tighter.

Finally Mark, he finished. He told them that it wasn't Taliaferro's fault. But then well … Taliaferro kept all through the campaign talkin' rights, rights for everybody. He hadn't seemed like that before.

Taliaferro sat there. The county clerk said his name and he got up and took his speech out of his pocket and threw it down. "Speech I was gonna make, had the word Constitution in it, had Democracy in it." He didn't know what to say and he looked out over the crowd and saw Taliaferro Davis way out yonder with his two black cousins and his black daddy. Taliaferro Davis said, "Us Davises *been* around here a long, long time. We got colored folks named for us all over the state, all over the South."

He looked out again and saw the people, and he thought they were good people, would do well to have him as their attorney. He said, "I figure every man named Davis, named Tol'ver Davis, ought to be able to vote. Black or white … and go to school." Some clapped. He remembered something.

He said loud as he could, suddenly grinning, hearing a tune in his head. "But that ain't the issue."

He took a deep breath. "Few years back Mark he had pneumonia, sent him to the city … before penicillin. They cured him up, give him a serum, a big dose of serum, to fit his *type* of pneumonia. Serum went right into his blood. Still there."

He looked out at them, laughing at them, "Serum made from blood of rabbits." The long pause, making up a fraction. "Issue is would you rather have a solicitor one fifth rabbit or would you rather have a Solicitor three fifths colored?"

They started laughing. They whooped and laughed and he held up his hand, finally.

"I want to ask Mr. Mark Cross a question. A make-believe case. An old woman dies, one million dollars, she leaves, million after taxes. And every red cent, she leaves to this Negro boy, right here in Sassoon. Now this Negro boy, he's a deaf mute."

Hell, he thought, I don't care whether I win tomorrow or not. I'm a well man, and if they stay this quiet at least they'll hear this story, the cat that could talk will be a Negro that can't and I'll make it lots longer and get the Constitution into it because they'll listen, now.

There are two kinds of fighters: gladiators and eagle birds.
(Champs and also-rans, to you.)
It was Lou Badzik's night to show the howling, hostile ring worms
which of the two he was.

Through the fog, he heard the referee: "Six .... Seven ...."
Lou thought: "I'm okay. Now I gotta get up and fight him."

THE EAGLEBIRD

HARRY FOX WAS GONE. He had said his piece matter-of-factly and gone away. He hadn't put on any pressure and he hadn't asked for anything. He hadn't looked prosperous, but he hadn't asked for anything.

Lou Badzik's pondered what Harry had said and he squirmed. Everything had been very orderly. Not going so good for dreams but going very good for life. Very, very good for life.

There was Joey, thought Lou. And thinking of Joey. Joey came in from the kitchen where Lou had sent him when Harry showed. Joey was his sister's kid. Joey was going on seven.

Joey pulled at his pants leg just the way kids did

in funny papers. "What's a gladiator, Lou?" he asked.

Lou Badzik's said, "Leave go my pants. Can't you ask a question without pullin' on my pants?"

"Sure," Joey said, turning loose. "I ain't got hold of your pants. What's a gladiator?"

"Leave me alone, Joey."

"Was that Uncle Harry? What'd he want? What's a gladiator?" Joey asked.

"An olden time fighter."

Joey had heard a good deal of reminiscence from Harry Fox. "Was Walker and Greb gladiators?" Joey asked. "Was Dempsey a gladiator?"

"Leave me alone, Joey," Lou said. "No, they wasn't. I mean way-back fighters, Roman times. They fought with iron gloves and swords and stuff and killed each other. Now leave me alone."

Joey lay down on the floor.

There was Ruth, thought Lou. And this was as good as a dream. Better than a dream. He loved her in a way that choked him. Soft and lovely and beautiful; but hard and wise-thinking for his good. Hard and wise for his welfare.

Joey said, "Where's Ruth?"

Lou looked down in annoyance. He knew Ruth would be coming by soon, but mixed with his love for her and wanting to see her was a faint dread. He didn't want to tell her Harry Fox had come by.

Joey said, not looking up. "What'd Uncle Harry want?"

"Nothin', nothin'." Lou was almost shouting. He checked himself. "He didn't want anything," he added lamely.

BUT RUTH came in anyway, as was her wont on her way home from work. She was a tall, blond girl, she worked in a cafeteria — "and will until we get married." The wedding date was set. Six weeks away.

She spoke to Joey, put her purse and a paper bag on the table.

Lou kissed her but she turned from him and sat down and said almost at once, "What's the matter, honey?"

"Nothin'."

Joey said, "Uncle Harry was by."

Ruth said quickly, "How was he, Lou?"

Lou Badzik shrugged. "Okay." Then he went on earnestly, looking at the floor. "Harry's a brave man. He's a real brave guy. He never made it big because he wouldn't play ball with the mob. But he stuck with me and made me a lot of money and then got me out before I got hurt."

"Sure," Ruth said. "He made a lot of money off of you, too."

"He ain't got it now," Lou said.

"What did he say?"

"He wants to buy a boy out in K.C. A young light-heavy. He can get his contract for twenty-five hundred. Says he'll be a fighter."

"But your money's all tied up in annuities."

"I know that," Lou said impatiently. "He was talkin' about a fight. His end would make it —"

"You?"

"You needn't sound so like it was jumpin' off the Chrysler building. I'm a fighter."

"Look, honey — Harry himself got you out." She paused. "Harry himself."

"Okay. I told him I wouldn't do it." He flexed his hands. "It was a TV shot," he added. "That's why it'd be such a good payday."

"If Harry'd stay away from the race track …" Ruth said.

"Sure. And if he hadn't found me gettin' my brains beat out as a preliminary boy."

"Lou, you're thirty-four."

"It ain't eighty," Lou said. "Marciano's thirty-three."

"But you told him you wouldn't do it."

"Well, no," Lou Badzik said. "But I will. He's comin' back later." He thought a moment, then he added, "I love you, darling."

"And I love you," Ruth said. "I like Harry. Harry is a good man. He was awful good to you. But you're out; you got your annuities coming up. You're not all beat up." She paused. "You're a wonderful man."

"Gladiators," Joey mused from the floor. "They killed each other. If you didn't win you were dead."

Ruth stood up. "I'll fix dinner for you all," she said. "I brought some stuff." She looked down at Joey. "What's this about gladiators?"

"Just heard," Joey said.

"The emperor sometimes let the loser live," Ruth said. "He turned his thumb up if he wanted the loser to live."

"Well, I'll be goin' to hell. I mean, that's very innarestin'," Joey said.

The girl looked down at the little boy and started to say something, then shrugged and walked into the kitchen.

LOU kept the conversation away from Harry Fox during dinner. He argued amiably with Ruth about the wedding. Only Joey mentioned Harry Fox. He asked when he was coming back.

"You'll be in bed," Lou told him. "Tomorrow's a school day."

Joey didn't answer.

Ruth washed the dishes and Joey went reluctantly to bed. Lou sat on the sofa. He wished Harry Fox wasn't coming back. He hated to say something Harry might not want to hear, but it was hard to worry about Harry. Of anybody Lou had ever known, Harry seemed the best able to take care of whatever needed taking care of. Including himself.

Ruth came in and sat down beside him and Lou put his arms around her and pulled her hard to him and kissed her, trying to get into it how much he loved her. Trying to communicate to her the inexpressible feeling he had for her.

Ruth squirmed. "You'll muss me up."

Lou Badzik said huskily, a little hurt, "I'm sorry."

Ruth smiled. "Don't be." Then she added, "When's Harry coming?"

Lou felt it then. She wanted him to tell Harry no dice. She wanted to wait and hear him tell Harry; then she would kiss him.

He felt vaguely that it wasn't fair. But then it was woman-fair, he guessed. It was for him. For his own good.

Harry rang the doorbell and Lou let him in and he came in and shook hands and spoke to Ruth and sat down in a straight chair. He looked at Ruth and spoke to Lou. Harry Fox was a bald, skinny man. He had always seemed exactly the same to Lou. But he must have changed some though the years. He must be sixty now.

Harry said, "Don't say it. You don't have to say it."

Lou Badzik shrugged. "I'm sorry, Harry. If you want the dough we could probably figure to borrow it around. The two of us."

Harry Fox laughed. "Three-horse parlay and all my worries are over."

Lou looked quickly at Ruth and frowned. She managed not to say anything about people who played the horses.

But Harry didn't leave. He sat and chatted and reminisced and told a couple of jokes and took a present out of his pocket for Joey. It was a knife you could set up housekeeping with in the woods.

"He'll cut himself," Ruth said.

And Harry said sure.

Ruth yawned.

Harry said, "Have you set the date? The wedding, I mean."

Ruth told him the day and Harry smiled wryly. "The date of the fight," he said. "That's the same day the fight's gonna be."

"There isn't going to be any fight," Ruth said.

"Oh, sure. There'll be a fight," Lou said. "It just won't be me bein' half of it." He paused. "This Cuban boy, Kid Gila. He's young. He'll be fightin' for a long time."

"He'll be champion," Harry said without feeling. "Lou woulda been," he added, "if he hadn't come along right when he did." He went off into a long story.

Ruth said with a little edge to her voice, "I believe I'll go on home. Will you call me a cab, Lou?"

"I'll take you," he said. "I'll —"

"No. Just call me a cab."

"I'll go down and whistle you up one," Harry Fox said and he got up and walked out of the apartment door.

Lou took the girl in his arms when she stood up. It was better than any dream he'd ever had. She kissed him back and whispered, laughing a little. "I wish Harry hadn't come. Tonight."

"There'll be a long, long time," Lou said. "All good."

Harry Fox came back. "Hack's downstairs," he said. He sat down.

Lou walked down with Ruth and paid the cabby and kissed her again shyly, standing in the street. The cab left.

When he came back to the apartment Harry Fox said, "She's a swell girl. You're a lucky fellow."

Sure, thought Lou, my sister and her husband were killed a long time ago and I got a little boy to raise, a real wonderful, ornery little boy, and I got money starting in pretty soon, and I got a wonderful girl that's going to marry me, and I got no bells in my head.

Lou said, "A lot of worry goes into livin'. You never know what's right. I'd like to write a letter to Joey sometime and maybe when I'm dead he could open it and see how much I wanted it good for him and how I never knew for sure what was good."

"You never know," Harry Fox said. "And words don't mean much. You pick up the paper and find a line in fine print and it says: *Joe Balloon beat Joe Doakes tko 8*. There's forty books, maybe, of words in that. Or you take a little old line like: *The war's over.*" Harry Fox paused. "You'll never write a letter to Joey and it won't matter. When he grows up he'll maybe know it or maybe he won't. Best you can do is live with yourself as clean as you can all day and try to forget the rest."

"I appreciate everything you've done," Lou began.

"Forget that," Harry Fox said. "I'm glad you didn't take the Gila go. They just wanted you on his record."

Lou said, bristling, "You mean they thought I'd get out of there; go four or five frames and get out of there for them."

Harry Fox looked at the floor. "They got to have a big indoor fight for Gila and there ain't anybody much but you. You never retired. Officially, you know. You're still ranked. You just haven't been working for a while, that's all."

"You didn't answer me, Harry," Lou said.

"You got a swell girl," Harry said. "You got a swell kid."

"Knock it off," Lou Badzik said. "Did they think I'd get out of there for this Cuban?"

Harry Fox looked around as he always did for something to do with his cigarette. "Maybe if Joey starts smokin'," he said, "you'll have an ash tray around here once in a while."

"Harry."

Harry Fox's smooth face didn't change. "Lou," he said. "I been around awhile. I never had a stable — just a boy or two I tried to do correct by. I also been playin' the horse races since a filly won the Kentucky Derby, and in the old days there used to be a boat race every once in a while. They'd fix a race — they wouldn't fix it exactly —" He stopped.

"What I mean," he went on, "was, say they was three horses figured to win it, they'd arrange for two of 'em not to. This was in the days of the legal books when a price would hold. The books would pay what they had chalked up." He pressed out the cigarette and put it in the cuff of his pants.

"What the hell you tellin' me about horses for?" Lou Badzik asked. "I don't know anything about horses. And from you and them I don't want to know anything about 'em."

"It's a great diversion," Harry Fox said. "But that wasn't what I was gettin' at. Like I say, they arrange for two horses not to win, where they figure three are in the contention. Then they chunk it on the third one." He paused and lit another cigarette. "But there's maybe ten horses in the race. So there's seven of 'em they don't bother with. They had a name for these horses. I never knew where they got it. They called them eaglebirds."

"Look," Lou Badzik said in irritation. "This is all nothin' to me. I don't know what you're talkin' about. I asked you a simple question."

HARRY FOX looked up. "I'm trying to answer you," Harry said. "They figured you an eaglebird, Lou."

"They knew they couldn't put in any fix with you and me," Lou Badzik said indignantly.

"They never bothered to try," Harry Fox said patiently.

"So I figured a cinch loser," Lou Badzik said levelly. "I've seen this kid a time or two on TV and —"

"You can't tell how rough he is on TV," Harry Fox said. "You are smart and you know your way around in there. I figured you could make us a good payday and not get hurt."

"*You* figured he'd beat me."

"Look," Harry said. "It's off."

"But you figured he'd beat me?" Lou Badzik said.

"Yes," Harry Fox said. Then in apology he added, "It would be your last fight. I didn't think it would —"

"You make me sore sometimes, Harry," Lou Badzik said. Then he muttered, almost to himself, "Eaglebird."

"This boy is young and very strong," Harry Fox said. "He's a gladiator, Lou."

Lou Badzik stood up, the word hanging hot in his mind. "Joey was askin' me …" he stopped. "What the hell do you mean by that? A gladiator."

"Drop it."

"You come up here to ask me could I fight on my wedding day. You're the busted horse, layin' one that's hustlin'. What do you mean: 'He's a gladiator?'"

"I should louse up your wedding, louse you up with your girl. I told you I was glad you turned it down." Harry Fox paused and lit a cigarette and knocked the ashes on the floor. "But I'll tell you what I mean. With Gila, fightin' ain't a trade. He comes to win, or else. That's why I said he was a gladiator."

"And I ain't?"

"Outside of Robinson, you're the sweetest in your division I ever saw."

"But I don't come to win — or else."

"This Cuban," Harry said, "if they don't get him out of there — and they won't — he won't be worth throwin' away ten years from now. But he's mean in there now. Nobody can beat him now."

Lou Badzik thought about Ruth, and his love for her was a wave of choking tenderness; and he thought about Joey and how he wanted it for him. And then, finally, he thought about himself. "Harry," he said at last, "we'll take it."

"But, Lou …"

"Call 'em now," he said. "Call Al now. Get him out of bed. Tell him we're going to take it."

"Not tonight."

"Yeah, tonight. Tell him we'll take it. I'll train up in the country."

He fixed for a woman to come and stay with Joey at the flat. And then there was Ruth. And finally he figured how to tell Ruth. He went to the cafeteria where she worked and got some stuff and pushed it around to the cash register and there she was. She looked up and smiled and then the smile went away. He said the speech he had rehearsed.

"I took the fight. I'm going up in the country to train. We'll get married just the same, the same day. I'll come out of the dressing room and you be there with Joey and we'll have Harry drive us down to Maryland and we'll make it so it's the same day, with luck. I took the fight for a reason."

The man behind him said, "Pay your check and get outta the way, Buster."

Nothing showed on Ruth's face. You could read shock or pity or nothing. Lou forgot the rest of what he meant to say. He put down three one-dollar bills and left the tray with the food on it and walked out, not looking back.

HE SAT IN HIS CORNER and looked around to find the camera. He'd never fought a TV shot before and he watched the floor after he found the camera. Joey would be watching, maybe Ruth. He hadn't heard from her. Harry had stopped by the cafeteria and she'd been nice but she hadn't sent any message.

Joey had come up week ends and he'd loved the camp as much as Lou had hated it. The cruel jokes, the boredom and the irritability and the work, and the drying out at last.

The fight was an anticlimax, something to get over with. He'd looked at Gila when they weighed in and now he looked across the ring at him again. A black and somber chunk of muscle.

Harry went out to the center of the ring with him, rubbing his shoulders. Nobody listened to the referee's instructions.

Lou thought, you can't stay mad six weeks. I took this for my pride, and it all seeped away up there in the camp. I want to get it over with.

Harry said over again, "Stab, and go to the right. Stay away; he's very strong in close." And the bell rang.

Lou saw the camera up above and then he felt a stiff left hand in his face and he slipped it partly and then he stabbed with his left and went to the right so he'd be going away from the left hooks. He stabbed and went to the right and Gila came after him and Lou let him come in and tried a long right that missed and then he tied up the black arms, but Gila tore loose and Lou felt his wonderful strength and vitality as the boy broke out fiercely; and then the left hook thudded under his heart and he felt sick; there was a tremor in his legs and a wave of nausea.

Lou Badzik stabbed and moved away, the picture fighter who knew his way around in there — just a little nauseated, a little wavery, but concealing it so well he was the only one who knew it.

Who else needs to know it? he thought. And then he thought: We will get paid. I'll get hurt tonight.

The bell sounded like a Christmas carol.

Harry snatched out his mouthpiece and said, "See what I meant?"

Lou nodded and looked up at the camera and then he remembered the commercial would be on. Joey would be watching the fight.

"I was awful brave when I told you to make this one for us," Lou said to Harry Fox.

The whistle sounded. Then the bell clanged.

You can stay away, but you can't go home until it's over. And you can't stay away so good when you are fenced in with ropes. Lou Badzik was working at his trade — the beautiful left — but what was a left in his opponent's face? Only an annoyance. He almost admired the speed with which Gila started the combination. And then he heard the referee say, "Three."

I got six seconds, he thought. He wasted one looking up at the camera. Joey would be watching back there some place. Back behind the camera. They didn't have television in Roman times. And there was nobody hereabouts to turn a thumb up for him.

The referee said, "Seven."

Lou thought: I'm all right. And now I gotta get up and fight him.

He got up and the referee wiped off his gloves and the Cuban came in savagely.

Lou stepped to his left and whistled the long right cross. Everything paused for a moment as Kid Gila stopped momentarily. Then he moved again and Lou moved toward him. Gila put his head down and hooked with both hands for the body.

Somebody grunted. The left hook caught Lou too high; all it did was peel his eyebrow back, but it made a great opening for a fighter who didn't mind getting hit, and Lou wheeled the right again, and Gila went down. He got right up, though, too stupid or too strong to take a count, and came in swinging.

He didn't have to come far, for Lou went there to meet him. Put your head in the way of that left hook, Lou thought, and you can hit him with a right. And bang him very hard and he'll bleed, too. It was a relief to learn that.

He took the left hook high on his head and crossed the right and Gila went down. This time he took a five count, with his corner screaming for him to take nine.

Lou looked at Gila's corner and tried to smile. They didn't even understand their own guy. He came to fight as long as he could get up. And he could get up. He got up with a spring and came in banging. He came to win — or else.

Lou dropped his right and asked for the left hook. Again it landed. Too high to kill me, Lou thought, and he threw his own right again from 'way back.

Gila went down again, this time on his hands and knees. He clawed his mouthpiece out with his right glove and spit out some blood and pushed himself up and came to the wars.

The referee grabbed him.

AND Harry Fox grabbed Lou. He held his mouth to his ear and yelled, "They had to stop it on three knockdowns."

Lou walked uncertainly toward the Gila corner where there was screaming in shrill Spanish. Gila threw his arms around Lou and said, "Fight again?"

Lou Badzik looked at him, a block of ferocity, and smiled. "No," he said. "Thank you very much — but not again."

On the rubbing table the house doctor sewed his eyebrow and then Lou Badzik walked out of the dressing room door and looked up.

"Sure, I'm here," Ruth said. "How did you think I loved you?"

Joey pulled at his pants leg, just the way kids always did in jokes and funny papers. "I saw it with Ruth from the ninth row."

Lou Badzik patted him abstractedly on the head.

"I didn't want to bother you," Ruth said, "until after the fight. I don't love you less because you think you are an ancient gladiator."

"Car's on the Ninth Avenue side," Harry Fox said. Then he looked at Ruth and saw her smile and he picked up Lou Badzik's right hand and handed it to her. "Some eaglebird," he said.

Charlie Hedges and Miss Wilson were quiet people,
but they nearly caused a riot when the suddenly left our town.

THE LONG WAY HOME

*Just then I heard an explosion, and an automobile came around the corner by the People's Bank.
It was a great big long thing, no like any I'd ever seen before.*

WHEN SAMUEL PHILLIPS DIED, Sassoon was sad and pleased at the same time: sad because Samuel had been everybody's friend, or at least nobody's enemy, and had lived in Sassoon for seventy-six years; pleased because his funeral provided the best occasion the town had known since the livery stable burned down.

I remember the funeral quite well. Everybody came. It was Saturday, and so school was out and we all came to see Samuel. A lot of the folks said later that he looked so peaceful, like he was sleeping; but my dad held me up as we passed the coffin, and I can tell you Samuel didn't look like he was sleeping at all. He just looked dead.

At that, though, he looked more peaceful than either Charlie Hedges or Miss Wilson. It was the first time I'd ever seen Mr. Hedges out of his store, and I'd hardly ever seen Miss Wilson except up in her shop by the window — but I don't think that's the reason I thought they looked so odd, as if they were grieving, only not for Samuel. Mostly it was the way they just stood staring down at the coffin, just standing there and staring, even after most of the rest of the others had left the church.

It was the same at burial, too. When I got back on my bicycle after the reading, Mr. Hedges was still there by the grave, and Miss Wilson not far behind him.

Later on I thought that it must have been this that made them do what they did. Samuel Phillips had run the George Washington Hotel for fifty-seven years, including when the quarry was in operation and the town hummed; and though he might not have made a great deal of money, he made some, and it naturally built up over the years. He salted away every penny, too. And all the time saying that he was just waiting to get enough, then he was going to retire and shake the dust of Sassoon off his boots and see what the rest of the world looked like. It was what he talked about day after day, year after year: New York, Paris, London, Germany — all the far places that he was aiming to see. He had travel folders, too, on every one of those places. Whenever anybody saw him they'd ask, "Well, Samuel, you still here? Thought you was leaving us!" And Samuel'd grin and answer, "Never mind, now. I'll be goin', just as soon as I get me enough to do it right."

But I guess he never did get quite enough, or else by the time he did he was out of the notion. Not counting the three months at the Brickville Hospital with a broken hip, he never set foot outside Sassoon. And then he died with close to $80,000 in the bank. I guess that's what decided Mr. Hedges and Miss Wilson.

Charlie Hedges had a grocery store. It had been old Mr. Middleton's, and Mr. Hedges had been a clerk there and had finally bought the store, a little at a time. He lived in the back in a little room, and I suppose that sometimes he did go up to the post office or across the street to the drugstore, but I never remember him except in the store.

His business was steady and good. Lots of people swore by him and wouldn't trade anywhere else. He opened at seven in the morning and closed at eight at night and never had a regular lunch, because he was always eating piecemeal out of the stock. His hair was a little thin. He seemed quite old and just the same always.

OVER HIS STORE Miss Wilson had her millinery shop, a little cubbyhole of a place you could make out through the window, though I never was inside. She lived by herself in the big old house at the edge of town, and now she was the only Wilson left. Her granddaddy had been a big lawyer and finally a judge and had built the house, but her daddy, I hear, didn't amount to much and kind of let it go down. Even so, it was the biggest house in Sassoon.

Sometimes Miss Wilson would stop in Mr. Hedges' store. I used to hang around there because it was next to the telegraph office where I was a delivery boy. "Hey, Charlie!" she'd call, coming into the store, making sure there weren't any customers. "Here's something for your dyspepsia." And she'd give him an ice-cream cone from the drugstore, always chocolate.

Mr. Hedges would walk up from the back, slow and calm, but like he was hurrying too. Then he'd see the cone and walk back to the cash drawer and take out a nickel and give it to her.

The morning after Samuel's funeral, though, this seemed to make Miss Wilson mad, for some reason. I was behind the cold Franklin stove in the back, reading. I saw Miss Wilson stamp her foot. "Darn it!" she said, in a voice I'd never heard. "Can't I even buy an ice-cream cone? I wanted to be nice, and now you've ruined it." She slammed the nickel down on the counter.

Mr. Hedges looked at her in a funny sort of way, and I knew that he'd forgot that I was around. He picked up the nickel and put it back in the drawer, softly, like something was hurting him. "I'm sorry," he said. 'I don't want to ruin anything for you."

She looked up quickly, and her eyes were wide. "I guess you don't," she said. Miss Wilson's face was all different — tight as wax, with the muscles jumping. "It's just that all of a sudden I believe it's got me," she said.

Mr. Hedges licked the ice cream cone thoughtfully; then he put it down on some wax paper, very precise, and moved over closer to her. I thought there for a minute that he was going to grab her and kiss her or something, but that was hard to believe. You couldn't see Mr. Hedges kissing anybody, not even his own mother. "What's got you?" he asked.

"Sassoon," she said. "Charlie — I'm thirty-three!" and her voice rose. I was afraid she'd drop her vanilla cone.

"You been thinking about Samuel?" Mr. Hedges asked.

Miss Wilson nodded.

"So've I."

"Have you, Charlie?"

Then Mr. Hedges nodded, too. They were quiet for a time. I didn't move. I saw him take the cone from Miss Wilson's hand and lay it next to his on the wax paper. "I'm almost forty," he said.

She looked at him. Her eyes were still wide, like she was about to cry.

He reached out and touched her hand but then got scared and drew away and coughed. "John Owens wants to buy my store," he said, "and I've got some money in the bank."

She smiled. "You ought to have," she said. "You never spend a dime."

"There's nothing in Sassoon I want to buy," he said.

I sat still. I wanted to leave now, because there was something about the way they were talking. I got a little farther behind the stove and hoped a customer would come in. In the light from the front window, Miss Wilson's face was pale. Then suddenly it started getting pink, and her eyes were shining. "There's me," she said.

Mr. Hedges peered over his spectacles at her for the longest time.

She banged her fist on the counter. "Oh, don't look at me that way. I'm an old maid. I live alone and it's not because I want to. But I'm not an old enough old maid that they don't gossip about me. I'm almost afraid to bring you an icecream cone unless I know there's nobody in the store." She stopped. Then she said almost in a whisper, "I hate them."

Mr. Hedges almost acted like he hadn't heard her because he took up where he'd left off. "Sassoon isn't any different in that way from anywhere else in the world. People are always curious and gossipy about alluring single ladies."

Miss Wilson almost jumped at him. "What do you know about the world? What ..." she trailed off. "Alluring?" She said the word as if she'd never used it before.

He touched her hand again. "I can cash in for almost seventy thousand dollars, store and all," he said in a careful tone. "You didn't know I had that much, did you?"

"No," she said. She sounded excited, kind of startled and dreamy. Mrs. Jack Knudsen came in then and started to take her list from her purse. Mr. Hedges shook his head and said, "I'm sorry. We're closed up."

Mrs. Knudsen jerked. "Huh?" she said.

"Closed up," Mr. Hedges repeated. "Go over to Burton's."

Mrs. Knudsen looked at Miss Wilson, a hard, mean look, then back at Mr. Hedges and bustled out of the store.

Charlie Hedges laughed. "I can close with Owens in twenty minutes," he said, walking over and locking the door. "They'll flag the Limited if we take a drawing room."

Miss Wilson tried to say it twice before she said it: "Today?"

He didn't answer. He just looked at her.

"I'm frightened, Charlie."

"Of course, you're frightened," he said. "I'm frightened too. Who wouldn't be?"

She grabbed his hand like it was a pup and held onto it. "All right," she said; "but once — one time — before we *really* get going, I want to come back here."

"I aim to humor you," he said; and then he pulled his hand away. "But nobody has spoken about love." He paused, sadly. "I found out while I was thinking about old Samuel last night, Louise, that I got an awful lot of that for you."

Miss Wilson practiced the word. "Love," she said. "Love." Just then she looked over toward the stove and saw me. Her mouth flew open, and Mr. Hedges looked back, too.

He frowned for a second and started to say something. Then he thought better of it and said, "Hello, Ed. You been here long?"

"I don't know," I said. I got up, looking at the floor, and thought maybe this would be a good time to run out of there as fast as I could. A long minute passed. I looked out of the front window because I couldn't look at them, and I saw Doctor Ramsey go by in his buggy.

Finally Mr. Hedges laughed. "Ed, listen," he said. "If you don't understand what just went on, don't worry about it. We won't, either."

"I didn't hear anything," I lied. "I was half asleep. Honest!"

Miss Wilson saw me staring at her — I couldn't help it, she was so different; I didn't mean anything by it — and she gritted her teeth, mad. "Yes," she said. "Like everybody else in this whole town is half asleep! You're going to be here 'til you die," she said, "and you'll say, just like the rest of them, isn't it a shame that the poor Wilson girl never got married!" She stopped and took a breath. "Well, let me tell you this —" I backed away. "I'm alluring. Do you hear that? And if I want to go away with Charlie Hedges here, and do some of the things I've dreamed of doing, then I'll go — and I won't have any silly little boy telling me not to!"

Mr. Hedges said, "Now, now, you're just upset, Louise. Ed's all right." He winked at me. "Don't you think she's alluring, Ed?"

I nodded my head fast. "Uh-*huh!*" I said.

HE TOOK a piece of paper from his pocket, and his hand shook a little. He adjusted his spectacles and wrote something on the paper. Then he folded it and handed it to me and went over to the cash drawer and got out two silver dollars. "Have Harry send this message," he said, "and you keep the change."

I could hear Miss Wilson's breath go in between her teeth and it made a sort of sighing sound. "Charlie," she said, "you're going to be good to me?"

"That telegram'll stop the Limited," Mr. Hedges said to me, "if it goes right away." He turned to Miss Wilson. "I aim to humor you," he said.

I told him that the Limited would be here in two hours.

Mr. Hedges popped his watch open. "Yep, two hours and two minutes," he said, "and if it wasn't for the fact I got a little business to attend to, I figure it'd be a pretty boring two hours."

"Boring?" She sounded shocked.

He looked at her. "Louise," he said, "I've been bored for forty years."

He let me out of the store then, and I went in and gave Harry Mott, the telegraph operator, the piece of paper and paid him. He keyed it out.

I saw people trying to get into the store, which was locked, and they were all puzzled. I didn't let on what had happened. They'd find out soon enough is what I thought.

Finally I went back into the office and told Harry Mott I'd be back in a little while, and then I went out and got my bike and rode down to the station. In a while I heard the Limited whistle down past the Post Oak grade, two longs, and I ran and looked in the waiting room but no one was there. I came on out of the station and sat down on a baggage truck.

The train whistled again, coming up the levee grade, and I knew that in just a minute now it would start gaining speed downgrade through Sassoon.

I looked all around once more as the watchman came out to let down the black-and-white arms on either side of the tracks where they crossed Main Street, and the ticket agent came out with his hoop that the engineer would lean down and catch on his arm.

The engine came around the elevator, and all at once somebody behind me said, "Goodbye, Ed," and I like to've jumped out of my skin. It was Mr. Hedges, with a silver dollar in his hand. "Here's something for you," he said. "I want you to play as if you weren't in the store at all this morning. Okay?"

Miss Wilson looked pale, but Mr. Hedges looked just like he always did, only he had taken off the alpaca coat he wore in the store and put on the gray coat that matched his pants. They didn't have any suitcases or anything.

"Okay," I said and took the dollar.

The train ground to a stop. When it was still, Mr. Hedges ruffled up my hair and walked two cars down to the sleeper section, solemn and slow, with Miss Wilson on his arm. He helped her up the steps, and went up himself.

Sassoon never was much of a stop, so the Limited built steam right away and began to move. Then it was gone.

It didn't take long for Sassoon to find out. I remember my dad and mother talking about it that very night. Dad, he looked kind of sly and kept saying, "Who'd of thought the old goat had it in him?" But my mother said it was *perfectly all right*; that they'd simply been seeing each other all their lives but hadn't ever really *seen* each other, and that Charlie Hedges had probably never thought that Louise would look at him twice but that Louise had dropped a hint and he'd taken her off in an *elopement* before she had a chance to change her mind. And what's more, Mom said, doing something romantic doesn't make a person an old goat.

TIME PASSED right along, one day like the next. School was almost ready to start, and it was my last day at the telegraph office, which puts it about one month after the day the old goat jumped the fence (as my dad called it; Mom called it the day of the romantic elopement). I was sitting out in front of the office on a bench we had there on the sidewalk, watching Mr. Williams over in his drugstore window taking down some strips of flypaper.

He was just pulling down the last strip when I heard the explosion. An automobile came around the corner by the People's Bank then and pulled up in front of the drugstore — a great big long thing, not like any I'd ever seen before. It had a man sitting up in front with goggles on and two people in the back. At first I didn't recognize them at all.

Then the woman got out of the automobile and took off her veil and shook it, and I saw that it was Miss Wilson and Charlie Hedges with her. People started to gather around and say hello and gawk, but it didn't bother Mr. Hedges any. He acted, even in the fancy clothes he had on, just like he always had — friendly and congenial. But Miss Wilson — she was *pretty!* She had paint, only somehow it didn't look cheap on her.

They went into the drugstore. Two or three people went in with them, and I kind of walked in too and hung around the candy counter, waiting to see what would happen. I wanted to go out and look at the car, but I was afraid I'd miss something.

They ordered sodas, and then Miss Wilson took a cigarette out of her bag and Mr. Hedges leaned over and lighted it for her.

Mrs. Knudsen, who had been trying to talk, stopped trying, and her eyes got like beads. "That's a cigarette," she said, sharp and cold.

Miss WIlson picked the cigarette out of her mouth and looked at it and then took a puff. "You're right," she said.

Mrs. Knudsen snorted and snatched up her purse and left. Then Mr. Williams came back and said something to Mr. Hedges, and Mr. Hedges started to answer him but then I saw Miss Wilson kick him good under the table and he grinned at her.

"We'd be mighty glad to accept your congratulations, Henry," he said to Mr. Williams, "but to tell you the honest truth, we're not married. Miss Wilson, here, just won't say yes."

And then Miss Wilson leaned over and took Mr. Hedges by the ears and kissed him. Right in the drugstore!

The folks watching just looked. Then Mr. Hedges and Miss Wilson got up and went out, and I went out, too.

He saw me and said, "Hello, Ed. What's new?"

I told him nothing much, and he winked at Miss Wilson. When we got to the car, there were a lot of people standing around. The man with the goggles up in front looked put-out, but he sat straight. When he saw Mr. Hedges he hopped out, ran around in front of the car, took the crank out of a leather sling, and fixed it in. One turn and the engine fired, sweet as anything. It had a wonderful roar.

Miss Wilson and Mr. Hedges got in the back seat. The driver adjusted his goggles, and then Mr. Hedges whispered something to Miss Wilson and she nodded. He leaned out of the car. "Where's your bike, Ed?"

I pointed across the street.

He got out of the car and went over to it. "If I tie this on behind," he said, "so you can ride back on it, would you like to take a little spin?"

I looked back at the ring of people staring at us, and gulped.

"Come on — I want you to see how she runs. We'll go out the graded road through Post Oak Bottom."

We got the bike tied on and I climbed in beside the driver. He backed out, and we drove away from town.

When we got to where the road gets level and smooth through the Bottom, Mr. Hedges had the driver stop, and he got up in front himself. There was a kind of clattering, and I could hear the driver in back with Miss Wilson muttering something about stripping the gears. Then we were off.

Mr. Hedges pointed to the thing that looked like a clock on the board. "Watch the needle!" he yelled. I watched it. It crept around to 20, then to 30. The wind was whipping at my face, and my shirt collar hit my neck and I had tears in my eyes. I looked at Mr. Hedges, and he was different from what he'd always been before.

The little needle said 50, then 55, and finally, in a roar that shook the green trees by the side of the road, and blurred them, with Miss Wilson squealing in the back above the noise, the speedometer said 60!

Then we started slowing down. When we slid to a stop I tried to swallow, but nothing went down except some dust. Mr. Hedges got out of the car and handed the driver back his goggles. "When you get to Sassoon, Ed," Mr. Hedges said, "tell 'em that you rode a mile a minute." He started untying my bicycle.

Miss Wilson looked down at me, just as I started to get on the wheel. She beckoned me to one over to her. "I'll tell you a secret," she said, "if you won't tell anyone, ever."

I promised.

"We're married, all right," she said. "We got married the day we left. And we're very happy. But you mustn't tell."

"Why not?" I asked. It seemed like a funny thing not to want to get told.

Mr. Hedges laughed. "Because," he said, "she doesn't want to spoil everybody's fun. This way, Sassoon'll have something to talk about for years."

I said sure, but I didn't understand.

They drove off and left me standing there. Mr. Hedges yelled, "She don't smoke cigarettes, either!"

He was right in one way, though; people did talk. They didn't have any other subject of conversation for a long time. My dad allowed that it was the best thing that ever happened to Sassoon; that other countries had their kings and queens to do the things people dreamed about doing, but that Sassoon had Charlie Hedges and the Wilson girl. My mother said she *could* hardly *approve*, of course, but she did hope they had a gay time.

I never told anybody about them; even when I heard Mrs. Knudsen and the other women talk, I never let on.

Fourteen is different from eleven. I'd quit my job at the telegraph office because I figured I was too old to be running around the town with little pieces of paper in my hand. And now sometimes I would wonder whether Mr. Hedges and his wife would ever come back, and think how pleased they'd be that I hadn't told their secret.

I WAS the first to see them, this time. They came in on the morning local and got down out of the coach and then the porter set their bags down. It was wonderful luggage, and a lot of it, all over stickers — Cairo, Naples, Shanghai, all the cities in the geography, almost. In spite of the fact that Mr. Hedges was kind of dirty he looked fine. So did Miss Wilson — I mean Mrs. Hedges. Jake Wells, who met the trains in his new Reo, helped them put the suitcases in his car and drove them off toward the old Wilson place.

I ran home and told my folks, and then at noon I was going down by Mr. Hedges' old store that Mr. Owens had painted white, and there was Mr. Hedges behind the counter.

He called to me and asked how I was, like always before. I went in and told him I was all right. "You buy the store back?" I couldn't help but ask.

He shook his head. "Nope. Owens needed a clerk and he hired me."

"How come you came back?"

"Ran out of money."

I thought of how you'd go about running out of seventy thousand dollars in three years. Then the door behind me opened and a voice said, "Charlie!" It was his wife. "Sure is a mess up there, but —" Then she saw me and stopped. She smiled. "Ed! Why, it's just like it was when we left."

Mr. Hedges smiled. "Yes," he said.

There was a silence and then I said, "I saw you come in on the train, and I saw your suitcases. Have you —?"

Mrs. Hedges looked at me. "Yes," she said, "we've been all those places," and her voice was a contented whisper.

"But is that why you came back, really?" I asked, "because you spent all the money?"

"No," Mrs. Hedges said. "Sassoon's a good town, and I wanted our baby to be born …." She quit.

Mr. Hedges laughed good and loud.

But Miss Wilson — Mrs. Hedges — went on dead serious, "You go away from where you live," she said, "full of hate for people, and then you get to remembering them and you remember the good about them, and you want to come back, to have a place to come back to where ... where people are interested enough in you to talk about you."

"Which only happens," Mr. Hedges said, and he was serious too, "at home."

———————————————

Novelettes

The rustlers shoved the quiet Easterner around until his sure eye and wounded pride exploded into lightening action.

THE TIMID ANGEL

EDGAR TUTWILER was a blond young man from the civilized city of Philadelphia, where the hall of records was a building with records in it, written in precise language and script and properly filed. In 1859 in Los Angeles, California, the records that had not been lost or stolen from its hall of records were mostly written in spidery, illegible Spanish.

In Los Angeles, the sun hung in the air like God's branding iron, and twenty per cent of the male population were gamblers or pimps. It was hot and dusty. Indian laborers on benders from nearby farms got into drunken brawls and white men strode in the streets, stooping under the weight of a pocketful of octagonal fifty-dollar gold pieces. In the beef-hungry mining camps to the north, they spoke of Los Angeles in awed tones as a "tough town." It had a permanent population of only four thousand or so, but it gave refuge to all sorts of thieves, murderers, and cutthroats.

The town was surrounded by ranges where the Spanish grant-holders ran enormous herds of cattle for themselves and various rustlers. It was the kind of land where a man could lose forty thousand head of cattle and never get them back.

Edgar Tutwiler, after six weeks of searching records, knew that, and he wanted to go home. But he wanted his land and his cattle — and he wanted Candace Forest. Candace lived with her father, Major Forest, outside the town; and she was high-breasted, high-spirited, demure, daring, and slim. Edgar's heart thumped at the thought of her and pounded when he saw her. It sank, though, when he thought of Jonathan Gault.

He was thinking of Jonathan Gault as he slumped into a chair in Pete Bigg's barber-shop. Pete Bigg's was a black, portly, bilingual gossip, diplomat, and social arbiter. He could also trim whiskers and cut hair.

"Pete," Edgar said, "who have you seen going in next door — the record place — well, kind of frequent during the last few months?"

"Nobody much," said Pete. "Nobody much 'ceptin Mr. Jonathan. But he got the run of the place most anywhere."

Jonathan Gault was a lean, handsome man who was making a fortune selling cattle bought from the Spanish grandees to the northern gold-mining camps. He wore silver spurs as big as saucers and tight-fitting pants. It was said that he was engaged to Candace Forest.

"Somebody's stolen a paper out of there," Edgar said. "It's an important paper. Got a name on it ..." his voice trailed off as Pete swathed his face with a wet towel. Back in Philadelphia, it had sounded fine from the exuberant letters that Elisha Farrow had written. A gold strike traded for forty thousand acres of land and eight thousand head of cattle! And when the news of Elisha's death had come, with a will bequeathing all his land and cattle to Edgar, it had seemed like an easy thing to come out West and take title to them. That's what you did with an estate in the East, where things were civilized. Pete removed the towel. "Man named Elisha Farrow," Edgar finished. "He was my uncle."

Pete Biggs, unheeding, stiffened. There was a good deal of noise outside, and both Pete and Edgar hurried to the door to see what was going on. Out into the dusty street, men were pouring from Gresham Greeley's Oroport Saloon. A slim man, all in black, was backing daintily away from the door of the saloon, his hands at his sides; and a big, bearded, dirty man was moving after him. The big man held a gun, and the crowd fanned out, giving the two figures plenty of room in the hot sun. Finally, the black-clad figure paused in the middle of the street. The dust rose and puddled in the air and settled, and the crowd grew still. The soft voice of the man in black carried in the white, hot air, as he spoke. "Do you have silver bullets in your gun, Mr. Streeter?"

"Draw!" the big man growled. "I'm gonna kill you whether you do or don't." He aimed carefully and, a moment later, fired.

The black figure staggered back, and black cloth was torn above his heart. The powder smoke was black and acrid, and it mixed with the dust.

Slowly, with nerve-snapping deliberation, the black-clad figure let his hand go to his belt; when it emerged, it held a long slim knife. You could hear him whisper. He was icily amused. "No silver bullets, Mr. Streeter?"

The man called Streeter fired again, steadying his gun hand with the other. Again the black figure was driven staggering back; again there was the horrible wait for him to fall. Again he spoke. "I'm going to cut your heart out, and give it to the dogs." He walked forward.

Streeter fell to his knees. Then, with a cry, he leaped up and threw his gun at the man, stumbled, and fled wildly through the crowd.

The black-clad man shrugged, replaced his knife in its hidden sheath, and walked to a big grey stallion tethered at the rail. He mounted the horse and said loudly, "No mortal man can kill Mort D'Angel!" He sat slim and straight, the gaping holes in his black coat mute evidence of the truth of his statement. He looked over the heads of the still crowd and repeated what he had just said, in Spanish. Then he headed for the mountains and was, at last, out of sight.

Edgar moved back into the barbershop and sat down in the chair, weakly. The heat, the sun, the filth, the violence were bad; but this strange fight that hadn't been a fight at all made him sick.

Jonathan Gault elbowed his way through the crowd, his huge spurs jingling in the dust, and picked up Streeter's gun. He looked at the gun carefully; then, carefully, he fired at the sign that swung above the Oroport. The sign swung wildly, a large new hole in its tattered planking.

Gresham Greeley came out of his saloon, looked at the sign, and spoke briefly to Jonathan. Gault handed him the gun and came across the street into the barbershop. "What really happened, Pete?" he asked. "You always see everything."

Pete Biggs said, his voice strained, "What they tell you happened?"

"Said an argument broke out in the Oroport between the little man in black and a fellow been around a few days they called Streeter. Said they went out in the street, and the big man shot the little one twice from ten feet, in the chest."

"That's right," Pete said. "They told you true."

"Nobody ever saw the little man before. Said the bullets either went in him or missed him or through him or something."

"They tear his clothes," Pete said, "heart-high."

"And didn't hurt him?"

"You see him layin' out in the road?" Pete asked.

Jonathan Gault turned his contemptuous eyes to Edgar. "And you saw that, too?" he said.

Edgar said slowly, "Yes, I saw it, too."

Gault shrugged. "No one hurt, I guess. Nothing for the Committee." He grinned and added, "Found your land yet?"

"No," Edgar said. He started to add something else, but Gault walked from the shop.

"Funny thing," Pete Bigg's said, musingly. "Lose a patch of ground the size of Philadelphia." He picked up the shears again. "You be goin' back there?"

Edgar said grimly, "I don't know."

Pete grinned with a sudden remembrance. "Seem a shame for a shot like you be goin' back to Philadelphia."

Edgar laughed without humor; that was the only amusing thing he had found in the West. He had expected every man to carry two guns and to be able to shoot the spots out of the deuce of hearts at fifty paces. What he'd found was that the men out here had all they could do to handle one gun, and any marksmanship beyond point-blank range was largely luck. There were exceptions, of course. But it seemed to be the custom in personal combat to come upon your antagonist from the rear, or to let him have it from six feet or so.

Edgar Tutwiler had belonged to the Rod and Gun Club at home. And one day, not long ago, he had hit a whiskey bottle thrown into the air while testing a dueling pistol that Pete had picked up as a curio. As a result of Pete's gossiping, he had achieved a fabulous reputation overnight. Diverted by the picture that Pete had created of him, he had never had the heart to spoil it by mentioning that, on the only occasion he had ever gone hunting, the appearance of a living thing in his sights had given him a case of buck fever so bad that he had been unable to pull the trigger.

The sun was throwing long shadows down Commercial Street and the town was coming to violent life as Edgar left Pete's shop. He was vastly refreshed by Pete's ministrations, and, stepping into the street, he felt the beginning of the coolness that would be complete after the sun had set. Tonight, Candace Forest was having a party, and he reflected with pleasure on the good things there would be to eat.

That thought increased Edgar's good humor to the point where he could actually nod pleasantly to the barkeep in the Bella Union as he passed down the open courtyard to what the management called his room. The horses in the corral behind the hotel went into their usual simulated panic and kicked up the usual cloud of choking dust when he opened his door. He took off his heavy gun and belt with relief and hung them on the wall. He had bought and carried the gun as a concession to local custom — Pete Biggs said it would discourage footpads. But he wouldn't wear it to a party.

It took him an hour to get ready and half an hour to walk the mile to Major Forest's house. Candace said at the door, "Mr. Tutwiler! I was beginning to think you'd forgotten us."

He quelled his shyness and began a carefully rehearsed speech. "Hardly," he said. "As well expect the desert wayfarer to forget the oasis he has —"

Jonathan Gault appeared at Candace's side. Edgar stammered to a halt, Gault's short jacket was stiff with beadwork and silver embroidery, and his wide-bottomed charro pants were plain black except for a thin line of silver down the side. He was wearing a big, white-handled gun. Edgar's well-cut eastern clothes looked drab in comparison.

"Excuse me," Jonathan said. "May I speak to you a moment, Candy?"

Edgar moved away, spoke to one or two of the other guests, and then to Candace's father, Major Forest, who was a prosperous vintner. Major Forest kept him pinned against the wall for five minutes, while Candace, wandering about among her guests, threw him an occasional teasing smile.

Finally he broke away and took her by the arm. He didn't look back, forward, to right or left; he guided her into the big patio and out into the cool grey moonlight. He said, "Candace, are you engaged to Jonathan Gault?" He said it fast while he had his courage up.

"No," she said, gravely. "We —"

She may have been going to say something else, but Edgar Tutwiler took her in his arms, quickly and roughly, and kissed her. Far off, a dog barked, but Edgar didn't hear. He heard his own heart. He heard the heart of Candace Forest. He felt her breasts against his chest, and her hair smelled like silk and lilacs.

The girl said, "You are very, very bold, Mr. Tutwiler."

Edgar clenched his teeth, and his voice came muffled. "I can't help myself with you. Will you go back with me? Will you marry me?"

"No," the girl said.

Three dogs barked closer, and Edgar heard them then, with a tiny, numbed portion of his mind. A dog had barked at a galloping rider, and now the rider came a little closer and the first dog was joined by two others. And when the first dog had grown bored with his senseless baying, three fresh dogs, nearer, took up the cry with the two that had joined the first.

"No, I won't go away with you." She paused maddeningly. "And I won't be hurried into any decision. But I'll forgive you."

The dogs were in full cry now, and above their sound came the sound of hoofs. Then a horse, hard-ridden in the dust, came running up to Major Forest's house and stopped. The music in the house stopped too.

Jonathan Gault came out onto the patio, and said in a voice that was like a rock thrown through glass, "Candy."

Candace called to him. "Yes?"

Jonathan Gault walked toward them, and finally he was close to them, his eyes two leaden spheres of hate. "They've raided Don Juan Rivera's lower range," he said flatly. "The Vigilance Committee's going out." He paused and looked at Edgar. "Now," he added. "We'll need you, Tutwiler." A smile showed on his lips.

Edgar smiled back, but his stomach was heavy and cold. "Oh, I hardly think so. I have no horse. No gun. And after all I'm only an Easterner."

"You're the best shot in town according to Pete Biggs," Gault said. "And we'll get you a horse and a gun."

Edgar heard Candace's voice, warm in the night. "They need *bold* men, Mr. Tutwiler, wherever they call home."

"I'll take care of you," Gault said, still smiling.

"That will hardly be necessary," Edgar said stiffly. He turned to Candace. "May I borrow a horse from your father? I'm sure he'll lend me a gun."

Sanchez, Don Juan's foreman, told of the raid. The rustlers had run off two hundred head. They'd been led by a slim man on a big grey horse.

The Vigilance Committee rode out into the night. They rode for an hour and then stopped. The men nearest Edgar made signs for silence. He listened, but, except for the sound of horses breathing and the clink of bit metal, there was nothing. Then, finally, he heard it. Thunder muted close to the realm of silence. The distant drum of hoofs on adobe.

Gault rode away and the others waited. After a time, two spaced shots came from far ahead. Then two more shots close together. Then a ragged volley — and silence. The men around Edgar spurred their horses and rode forward into the bright gloom of the moonlit night, but Edgar stayed where he was and waited, alone.

Three horsemen came through the chaparral. One of them was Gault. He was holding his gun on the two men who rode ahead of him, and Edgar realized with a strange shock that one of them was Streeter—the man who had shot at the person who called himself Mort D'Angel that afternoon.

Gault said, "I thought I'd find you back here. Take care of these two. They won't give you any trouble." He turned to the two men. "Get down."

The two men dismounted silently. Gault got down too.

"I'll tie them to be sure," he said. He cut the reins from the horses the rustlers rode, put the men back-to-back against a small tree, and busied himself with the leather reins.

"I'm afraid," he said, straightening up, "these are the only ones we're going to get for our trouble." He looked at them speculatively. "Don't shoot them unless you have to," he said. "We'll hang them in town, in the daylight. They'll make a pair of good object lessons, kicking in the sun with their faces going black."

He climbed on his horse and rode away.

Edgar stood back from the men, holding Major Forest's big gun pointed toward them. Nobody spoke. Edgar felt he ought to say something — but what was there to say? His heart pounded, not so much from fright as from a nightmarish sense that this wasn't real.

Streeter said abruptly, "How do you feel, Ab? Wrists hurt?"

"Yeah," said the other man.

"He sure tied us." A short silence. Then, "It'll be a lot tighter around our necks, come sun-up."

"Yeah, that's right," said Ab.

There was another silence. Edgar felt the moisture coming through the pores of his hands.

Streeter said, "Son, roll me a smoke, will you?"

"I — can't," Edgar said finally.

"Sure you can. There's a paper and dust in my pocket. I'll tell you how." Edgar didn't move. "It ain't like I could do anything to you, tied up like this," the man said.

That was true. Edgar had always heard about the last requests of condemned men. He moved forward and took the papers and sack out of the pocket of the man's grimy shirt.

"Fold the paper about a quarter way up the edge," Streeter said. "Look, son. You can't roll it with one hand. You gotta lay that gun down."

Edgar hesitated. "Hell," said the rustler, "lay the gun down, son. We're tied up tighter'n the collar on a suck-egg hound."

Edgar put the gun down carefully on the ground and bent his head to the unfamiliar task.

There was an enormous splashy explosion of blackness and he bit his tongue, where he'd had it between his lips in concentration, so that it bled. But he didn't know that. He didn't even remember hitting the ground....

GAULT LOOKED DOWN at Edgar in the grey dawn. Beside him was a fat rancher named Sam Smith. "So you turned them loose?" Gault said.

Edgar felt his sore tongue quiver. "No. Of course not." He told them what happened.

"I tied those men tight," Gault said.

Smith said, "And he had a gun."

More men rode up. Gault's pale eyes were cold. "We've never known anything about you," he said, "except what you've told us yourself. Until now. Now we know you turned two rustlers loose."

"I didn't help them." Edgar said, panic mounting in his voice. "I told you what happened."

Gault didn't answer him. "Put him up on Sam's horse," he said. Edgar rode back to town on

Smith's horse, sitting behind the fat rancher, holding onto him.

When they rode down Main Street, there was a knot of men in front of the Bella Union Bar. Three dazed Mission Indians were huddled together on the lower gallery.

As he got down from the horse, Edgar heard a name he'd heard before. Mort D'Angel. The Indians had confessed that a man of that name, a man invulnerable to lead bullets, had recruited some of their number during the past weeks. But they were innocent; they had nothing to do with him.

There was an angry murmur from the crowd at this. Smith got off his horse, his attention momentarily diverted from Edgar. Edgar took two instinctive steps backward, and then suddenly realized that he was unnoticed. He turned and ran.

He ran down the side of the hotel and into his room. There were no shots, no pursuit. Apparently they were preparing to hang the Indians. He grabbed the gun from the holster on the wall and stuck it in his belt. Then he lifted the edge of the mattress to get the money he kept under it.

"Hell," Sam Smith said from the door. "I let you go a' purpose. I figured you'd hide the money them outlaws give you."

"They didn't give me any money."

Smith grinned. "Give me the money and let's get back," he said.

He stepped forward. The adobe-walled room was only six feet wide, and he wasn't more than a yard away. Edgar reached for the gun in his belt. He had to tug to get it free, and Smith laughed as his hand flashed for his own gun.

There was a deafening roar, and the force of the bullet from the gun in Edgar's hand knocked Smith backward and almost completely around. He hit the side of the door facing outward, and slowly slid to an untidy heap on the dirt floor.

Edgar was at his side in two short steps. He leaned down, and, as he did so, Smith coughed once and a thick stream of bright red blood gushed out of his mouth. Edgar turned away and leaned against the door. The nausea that seemed to be lurking in his throat shook him and he retched painfully.

Finally, he stepped backward and out. He walked backward until he came to the end of the corral, then climbed through the rails.

There were shouts behind him now. He crossed the street, turned a corner, found himself on Main Street. It was empty except for a saddled horse tethered to a rail in front of a shuttered store.

He got the reins loose and jumped into the saddle. A shot sounded and he heard, for the first time in his life, the angry hum of a bullet cleaving the air near him. He grabbed the pommel with his left hand and hit the horse with the gun he still clutched in his hand. The horse bounded forward. There was another distant shot, another more distant whine.

Edgar slashed his horse again with the gun. Once he could gain the open, he could lose his pursuers and would be safe. The scent of dust and gunpowder was in his nose. The scent of blood and fear. Faintly, he smelled silk and lilacs. He hit the horse again.

He rode on for a mile or so until the terrain roughened and there was vegetation to hide him. Then he struck off at an angle into the chaparral, twisting and doubling among the yucca and greasewood and manzanita, and headed south. San Pedro, he remembered, was a day's ride away. He rode on in the bright dawn, and before long the sun burned through the fog and began to get hot. His broadcloth suit wasn't meant for riding, and he shucked his coat and rolled it up on the saddle in front of him.

Soon his head began to hurt, and he remembered he wasn't wearing a hat. He was going to have to find one. Before he did anything about getting food or finding a place where he could sleep for a while, he'd have to find a hat. He tried knotting the corners of his handkerchief and wearing it like a nightcap, but that was effective for only a couple of minutes. He understood, for the first time, why the high crowns of Mexican sombreros were more than just decorative: they provided an air space between the top of a man's head and the surface hit by the broiling sun.

Finally he saw a few live oaks near enough together to make shade that wouldn't keep moving with the sun, and he headed for them. In their shade, he dismounted, tied the horse to a tree, and sat down on a rock. He put his elbows on his knees, rested his chin on the heels of both hands, and dropped off to sleep immediately. He wasn't sure how long he slept before his chin slipped off his hands and he was jerked back to wakefulness.

This happened several times, for, though he needed sleep badly, he didn't dare to succumb to his fatigue to the extent of lying down.

When, at last, he made himself get up and saddle the horse again, he still felt weary. But he knew he had to keep going.

He saw the square roof of a house while he was still a half mile away from it. When he got close enough, he dismounted and tied the horse and crept toward the house, taking care to keep himself screened from view. There were two horses standing by the door, and near them were three men. One of the men was Jonathan Gault; the second was someone Edgar recognized as having been of the posse the night before; and the third — a squat Mexican with a scattergun in his hand — was apparently the owner of the house.

Edgar could hear them faintly, but he couldn't make out what they were saying because they spoke in Spanish. He could follow it out well enough, though. In a few moments, Gault and his man mounted and loped off toward the south. The Mexican watched them go, then stood looking carefully around him. Finally, he went back in, closing the door behind him.

Edgar took stock of his situation. Gault was ahead of him on the road to San Pedro. It wouldn't be safe to head in that direction now — he'd be picked up at the first house he passed, and there was a good chance of encountering Gault himself. That meant he would have to avoid all traveled roads. At any other time such a prospect would have terrified him; now he didn't have time to be scared. Or maybe it was the sun. He was puzzled by the effect the sun was having on him. Then, too, he'd not eaten for twenty hours. The two most urgent things were food — and a hat.

His mind made up, he pulled the gun from his belt, moved swiftly to the door of the house, and pounded on it. There was silence inside and he pounded again. There was still no answer, so he pushed at the door — and it fell open. His heart was pounding in his throat and his body was tense with the effort to keep from showing the panic that now shook him, but the Mexican, more frightened than he, dropped his own gun and raised his hands.

Edgar, his mouth drawn in panic, but outwardly a tight-lipped killer, glanced swiftly around the place and saw what he was looking for. It was a large sombrero hanging by its chin cord to a wooden peg set in the adobe wall. Edgar moved toward it and took it down. An involuntary cry of protest came from the Mexican's lips. Real pain showed in his eyes. It was the only bright thing in the poor, puncheon-floored room. And Edgar had a moment's compassion. He jerked his tie open and off. Then he unfastened the gold studs that held his long shirt with its stiff front, and undid the collar. Silently, he handed these to the Mexican.

The Mexican looked at them wonderingly, then suddenly grinned. Edgar could speak no Spanish, and so he asked for food in English and French. Finally, the Mexican understood. He got together a pile of tortillas and handed Edgar a gourd filled with water.

When Edgar was out on his horse once more, he looked back and saw the Mexican standing, wearing the shirt and waving genially. He felt the beginnings of laughter in his throat and, doffing the big gay sombrero, he waved it.

As he rode, more comfortable now, he worked out a plan of action. Gault had figured that he would head for San Pedro and the harbor, and so Edgar gave up that idea. The only other possibility was San Francisco. It was a lot farther, but there were compensations. For one thing, after he got a couple of days' ride from the City of the Angels, there would be no further pursuit. There were towns to the north. There would be food along the way, and water. He would write to Candace from there, from San Francisco.

He rode eastward until mid-afternoon and then, when he was satisfied that the new direction wouldn't take him through any of the outlying settlements of Los Angeles, turned northward.

The sun went down and the air chilled. He unrolled his coat from the pommel and put it on, but he was still cold. Finally he came to a dry wash that would hide a fire from anybody who might come too close.

He made two fires and cleared the rocks away between them. He lay down on the bare sand, scooping a hole for his hips, and in less than five seconds he was asleep.

He woke up feeling very cold and lay there staring at the sky, thinking that it was funny the fires had died down so much that there wasn't even a glow from them. Then, as he turned his head a little, the skin prickled across the back of his shoulders. Not a yard away from his eyes was a pair of boots — heavy boots made of thick creased leather. New soles had been recently nailed inexpertly over the old ones. Whoever was wearing the boots was sitting down. Without moving his head, Edgar slid his eyes up the stained pants until he saw a pair of thick hands clasped around a pair of knees. In one of the hands was a gun — held idly, but pointed straight at his head.

A familiar voice said, "He's awake, Ab."

Edgar didn't move. His mind was fighting the terror that had settled over him again, trying to decide what to do, knowing there was nothing he could do.

A foot prodded him in the back. It belonged to the man called Ab. "Get up," he said in his flat voice. He kicked again — this time with jolting force.

Edgar got up. Fury, washed over him in a tidal wave, moved his hand to the man's shirt. His other hand, fisted, swung to the stubbled chin. He held the man for a moment, then dropped him like a sack of wet wash on the rocks.

The man called Streeter laughed. "Ab," he said, "I told you before never to judge a man by his pretty clothes. And, besides, this hombre saved our lives."

The man called Ab said, "Gault never ... "

"Shut up!"

Edgar's hand went to his belt, but the gun wasn't there. He looked at Streeter, saw it at his side. Streeter tossed the gun to him. "We only took it to play safe," he said. "You kinda got you a reputation this mornin' as bein' a little hasty, and we didn't want you to shoot us before you got full awake."

Edgar picked up the gun and stuck it in his belt. "What are you doing here?" he asked.

"Same thing you are," the big man told him. "Headin' for more congenial company. We been hidin' since you co-operated us outta a necktie party, waitin' for a chance to travel. This here is Ab Heath." He nodded toward the other man. "My name's Joe Streeter. Which way you pointin'?"

"North," Edgar said. Then he added, "I saw you shoot at Mort D'Angel."

"Shoot *at* him?" Streeter said. "Hell, I took him heart-high both times."

Edgar didn't say anything and he heard Heath chuckle. "Joe oughta be a stage actor."

"Which way you say you're headin'?" Streeter asked, ignoring Heath.

"North."

Streeter was silent a moment. "Well," he said finally, "we're goin' that way too. We might as well travel together."

"I'll stay by myself," Edgar said.

Streeter rubbed his hand over his bristly cheek. He got up slowly. "Be more sensible to stick together," he said. "We're goin' right up the Big Tujunga."

Edgar thought for a moment, while the two men waited in silence. He needed help to get straight on the way to Frisco. Better do it with an appearance of friendliness. "Maybe you're right," he said at last. "Wait'll I find my horse."

"We got your horse," Heath said in a flat voice.

"We saddled him up for you," Streeter said. He chuckled. "You know you're about the best *quick* horse thief I seen. You stole Don Juan's top cuttin' cayuse."

Somehow this geniality worried Edgar more than open hostility would have. When they were mounted and on their way, Streeter rode a little behind him. It was plain that he was, in a way, a prisoner.

There was a certain relief, though. These men, even if he was their prisoner, seemed to know where they were going. Edgar's flight had been thus far so amateurish and panic-stricken and he had been so overwhelmingly alone, that now moving *someplace* with someone else gave him a sense, almost, of security. This time last night he'd been at a party — maybe in the garden with Candace. The memory of Candace, her vision now close before him, made him smile.

Four hours of riding brought another dawn, red and clear. The country was vast and magnificent, the valleys spotted here and there with cattle. They saw deer, tame and incurious; and once a grizzly bear stood up behind a rock and looked at them. They threaded their way up a little stream and crossed and recrossed it many times, winding up and down the precipitous ledges which the horses of Streeter and Heath seemed to find familiar.

The sun grew as it climbed the sky, but the high crown of the sombrero shielded Edgar's head and the wide brim shaded his eyes. He found himself whistling.

They had just rounded a promontory when they suddenly found themselves in a camp. Suddenly and immediately. Well-fed horses grazed at the sweetly grassed end of the cul-de-sac and a woven willow corral held other mounts. Indians cooked over small, strangely smokeless fires, and two white men were playing cards on a rock. Aside from the absence of women and children, it presented a strangely tranquil and domestic scene.

At one edge of the clearing was a thatched lean-to, and in its protective shade sat a man clothed incongruously in black. He sat on a satin-wood box and studied a map.

He looked up at Edgar and smiled an animal-toothed smile. "Welcome!"

The man's eyes were opaque grey. He was the man that Streeter had shot. Edgar stepped down from his horse. "Thank you," he said.

An Indian took the horse, looked at it for a moment in admiration, and led it to a little brook, where he removed the saddle and rubbed it with dry grass. Edgar watched him, questions racing through his mind. He'd seen Streeter flee from this man in terror — and yet Streeter had led him here.

"Hungry?" said the man in black.

"I am," Edgar said. "I don't want to impose, but...."

The grey-eyed man barked an order; and Heath retreated sulkily to one of the groups of Indians by a fire, gathered food from their pot into a wooden bowl, and brought it back to Edgar.

Edgar thanked him and dipped in with his hands, as the Indians seemed to be doing; he plucked forth a chunk of hot and seasoned venison. It was delicious.

The man watched him. "I know a great deal about you," he said. "It is a fetish of mine to be informed about people. But there is one small foolish thing. I don't know your first name. I like to address my *compadres* by their given names. I want them to feel at ease with me."

Edgar realized, almost with dismay, that he *did* feel somewhat at ease, anyway, but he said around the second bite of venison: "'Gar."

"Gar Tutwiler," the black-clad one mused. "A purposeful name. Gar. It fits you."

Well, Edgar thought, he never had liked Edgar; it was too — well, not enough like Gar. He rolled the new name over in his mind as he swallowed the meat. He had a new and purposeful name. He would be purposeful. "I'm on my way to San Francisco, but I'd appreciate staying here until tomorrow morning."

The man nodded. "I can understand your motives, Gar, but your judgment is clouded. They'd pick you in a day and hang you."

Edgar said nothing, waiting.

"You see," he went on, "I told you I knew a lot about you. You went out with the posse the night before last when we ran off our little rehearsal, and then you let Streeter and Heath here get away. Or so Johnny Gault can prove. For which he'd have you strung up before Miss Forest could say 'Please.' Sam Smith would have testified against you." He paused. "If you hadn't murdered him. And Don Juan would kill you on sight for stealing his top horse."

"You are going to San Francisco?" Edgar asked.

"Indeed! And you are going to help me."

"I am?" Edgar said.

"Let me tell you a little story," Mort D'Angel said. "You are a confederate of rustlers, you are a murderer and a horse thief. Furthermore, you are a thorn in the romantic side of Jonathan Gault, heretofore self-assayed as the greatest catch west of the great divide. You haven't a chance — alone." He paused and licked the cigarette he was rolling.

Edgar was silent.

"I have, scattered strategically about these hills, a hundred and fifty Indians. They are good Indians, of stern and wonderful stuff, having resisted the white man's religion, whiskey, and diseases. And I am their leader. I am," he said, getting up, "almost their god."

"And your name is Angel de Mort," Edgar said.

"I call myself Mort D'Angel," the other corrected gently. "It signifies death to Los Angelenos — the angels, as some of them humorously call themselves."

Edgar looked at him. Mort D'Angel returned the look blandly.

"The raid that you so gallantly rode to prevent was a rehearsal," he said. "Part of a stage setting — like my invulnerability to lead bullets."

"Yes," Edgar said. "I saw you shot. With my own eyes."

"You understand the necessity of such chicanery in dealing with impressionable savages. You are a man of culture like myself," Mort D'Angel said, dismissing the episode with Streeter without further explanation. "My next move on the City of the Angels will net me twenty thousand head of fat beeves. And fortune — my fortune, which has never failed me yet — has delivered you to me. You will be useful."

Mort D'Angel made a gesture of dismissal and turned away.

They gave Gar Tutwiler blankets to sleep in that night. They weren't very clean, but they were warm; everybody treated him with an offhandedness which you couldn't call friendliness, but it had no hostility to it.

It was only after the whole camp was asleep that a chill of terror crept slowly over him. He was wide awake, looking at the stars, and he thought about everything that had happened in two days. He had killed a man; he was a fugitive from the law — or, rather, Johnathan Gault's law. He was Gar Tutwiler — Wanted. That was Edgar Tutwiler, the well-brought-up young man from Philadelphia, who had journeyed to the Great West to claim an inheritance.

Mort D'Angel regarded him as a kindred spirit. Joe Streeter regarded him as a good horse thief. Ab Heath knew him as a man who would slug another man senseless who kicked him.

Slowly, carefully, he stood up. The sleeping forms near him didn't stir. The friendliness of D'Angel hadn't extended to letting him keep his gun. His horse was in the corral, too far to try to reach. A coyote howled far away and sent a chill through him, but wild animals didn't attack men. Only men attacked men.

He walked a few steps, casually, framing an excuse if he were challenged. He walked like that, slowly and casually, beyond the edge of the little encampment to where the ground began to slope toward the north ridge. It was so simple that he thought for a moment of going back for his horse — he was considering Don Juan's prize mount his own now, he reflected wryly. But even that great steed could not walk on tiptoe.

In a half-hour he was on the ridge. He knew that. The ground began to slope away before him, but the brush was too thick to see what was below. Then he stopped, his skin prickling at a tiny sound behind him. He turned, but there was nothing. He resisted a panicked urge to run. Finally he moved.

The brush crackled behind him, but he never got turned around. Something hit him and he was down in a tangle of brush. Grotesquely, the enormous sombrero slipped half off, and he felt the chin cord cutting into his neck.

He struggled in the brush, trying to get up, trying to see what he was fighting. Something landed solidly on the back of his head. He lay still.

A VOICE cut through the vast, throbbing emptiness that was Gar Tutwiler's head. "That's better," the voice said. "He's all right, now."

His face and head were wet; water had trickled coldly down the back of his neck under his coat. He opened his eyes and saw daylight made dim by the roof of a thatched lean-to. He moved his head a little — painfully — and saw a man bending over him, a man with opaque grey eyes that even now held no expression except one of detached interest.

"You left quite a trail," Mort D'Angel said. "The Indians were amused, following it." He stopped. "Heath really did you a kindness. You wouldn't have got five miles through these hills alone. And he hit you very scientifically."

Edgar got the world steadied a little. He put one hand tenderly to the spot on the back of his head that seemed to be the center of the trouble. It was just an aching head, now. He felt a damp mass of moss. "What time is it?" he asked.

"The next morning," Mort said.

"All right," said Edgar. He considered a moment. "I won't try to get away again." He hesitated, then added, "I guess maybe I'd better decide to come in with you after all."

D'Angel gave him a long, amused look, and Edgar was glad that the pain in his head gave him an excuse not to meet it.

"That's fine," the rustler chief said, finally. "We can use a man that handles a gun like you do."

But he didn't offer to give Edgar a gun. The day passed slowly. By midafternoon Edgar was sure it was the longest day he had ever lived through. The white men in the camp played cards endlessly. The Indians cooked their meals, ate them, slept, cooked again. D'Angel rode out for a short time just before sundown, but he was back before dark. After dark, the cardplaying went on by the light of fires. Nobody asked Edgar to play and he wouldn't have known what to do it they had. He rolled up in his blankets finally, but he didn't sleep for a long time. The pain in his head was miraculously almost gone now, with only an intermittent ache to remind him of his foolish attempt to escape.

When he woke in the morning, it was as if he had passed from one dream to another — and opened his eyes to still a third. Nothing was different the second day. The cardplaying went on almost without talk; the Indians moved about silently or sat talking in undertones. And a little while before sunset, D'Angel rode away again, and this time he was gone deep into the night. But he spoke no word when he returned of where he'd been, and no one questioned him.

The third morning, it was as if the early sun were an insult. The same sun in the same cloudless blue sky; the same filthy figures rolling out of their blankets, coughing and spitting, moving stiffly on sleep-numbed legs, cursing over their breakfast, cursing the sun. Edgar washed his face and shaved with D'Angel's razor, but the others never thought of it. He found himself seized with an almost uncontrollable fury at the tedium of all this.

He wasn't the only one who felt it. Before noon, a fight broke out among two of the gamblers. Out of the usual silence came a spate of curses, the crack of fist against flesh. They rolled on the ground, flailing with fists and feet. The other players drew away a little and watched. There was no shouting now — only the harsh breathing of the fighters.

D'Angel came out of the lean-to and watched for a few moments. He walked over and stood above the fighters until they had almost spent themselves. Then he reached down, put a hand on the collar of each, and pulled them to their feet as if they had been two empty sacks. He said nothing to them, but, as he turned away, he called "Gar!"

Edgar went over to the lean-to. He found the rustler chief sitting on his satinwood box.

"You see," he said, "what waiting does to animals. Every day it becomes harder to hold them in check. We are not yet ready to move, and so these stupid men grow impatient. I must give them something to keep them busy — and in that I shall need your help."

Edgar said nothing.

"Tomorrow," D'Angel said, "there is a stage due from San Bernardino. There won't be a great deal of money on it, I suppose, but there will be passengers — perhaps a few bottles of something to drink. It will entertain them to hold it up. You shall lead them."

"No," Edgar said.

D'Angel looked at him. He said, "I have had great difficulty keeping my white men from killing you. I alone appreciate the kind of man you are. They resent you. They think you consider yourself better than they are." His thin lips moved imperceptibly toward a smile. "The fact that you wash your face in the morning, that you shave. If you led them on a raid, I think they would feel more kindly toward you."

"I can't help it," Edgar said. "I won't do it. If you feel the way you do, why don't you let me go? I don't care how many head of cattle you steal — nor what you do to Los Angeles. Give me my horse, a blanket. I won't even ask for my gun."

D'Angel shook his head. "No," he said. "It is too easy for me to put myself in your place. You would get out of sight of this camp, and you'd start thinking about our plan. You'd get word to them, warn them. You might even be so quixotic as to go back yourself. No matter what you promised, I am sure your better nature would be too much for you to resist."

Edgar wondered briefly if that were true. He hadn't thought of it.

"Besides," D'Angel said, "*I* want you to lead the raid on the stage. I have my reason. There must be no bloodshed, no one harmed. If they went without you, they might get too excited. They're not men who can think far ahead, and I let them do this only to keep them happy until the time comes."

"Well," said Edgar. "I don't give a damn why

you're doing it. That's up to you. But count me out."

"Just as you say." D'Angel shrugged. "But I am going now and tell them what I've decided. If you want it otherwise, you can tell them." He walked a little way and paused. In a mildly curious voice, he asked, "Did you ever see a man staked down in this country, spread-eagled and staked down? Ants, you know."

Edgar saw the change in the men when they heard what D'Angel told them — they were like grotesque caricatures of children being promised a party. The cardplaying stopped immediately. The two men who had fought went over and squatted together and in a moment were in deep, amicable conversation. Streeter took out his gun and sighted at an imaginary stage moving swiftly along an imaginary road. Edgar looked down at the ground. Large red ants were scouting about. He saw one of them pick up a grain twice its size and start away with it. When D'Angel came back to the lean-to, Edgar said nothing.

The next day they rode out of the camp, up over the south rim and down. D'Angel had given Edgar back his gun — Major Forest's gun — and he hoped to be able to use it to make his getaway. But he was surrounded by D'Angel's men, each watching his every move. There was nothing he could do but ride along with them.

They stopped on a hump of land that rose a bit above the evenness of the slope. They didn't have long to wait. Far to the east, a thin plume of dust formed and moved slowly along the faint scar on the scorched land that was the road to Los Angeles. Soon the four horses and the lunging vehicle behind them were in clear sight.

Streeter's voice barked, "Here we go!" Somebody gave Edgar's horse a cut on the rump, and he had to grab the saddle to keep from being flipped out.

The stage came up over a small rise and the horses came to a roaring stop at the sight of the motionless figures in front of them.

Streeter called to the driver, "Which way to San Gabriel, friend?"

The stage driver looked around quickly. Heath knew what he was looking for and his hand went to his gun, but Edgar grabbed it without thinking and tore it out of Heath's hand. The driver reached for his carbine, and Edgar fired then; the rifle twisted away, like a live thing, out of the driver's hand.

There was a stunned silence. Then Edgar said, "There will be no shooting, please." He said it in a low voice, because if he had said it any louder, he couldn't have controlled the shaking of his throat.

Streeter said to the driver, his gun unobtrusively on Edgar, "You better come down off of there," and the driver, his hands above his head, jumped to the ground.

"Tell 'em to come out," Streeter said.

The driver spoke over his shoulder and the door of the stage opened. Three men, a woman, and a little girl got out and lined up — all of them, except the little girl, obviously terrified. Edgar's mind was working with all its power to keep panic from his face as he felt their eyes on him. To them he was the personification of everything they had ever heard about bad men. The neat, well-cut broadcloth suit, the bright scarf at the neck. The incongruous but somehow becoming sombrero. It all fitted perfectly into the picture. And his polite reminder about not shooting would have completed it.

Streeter and one of the other men searched the stage, then the passengers. They showed an unexpected rudimentary politeness to the lady, although it didn't prevent them from emptying her reticule. Edgar saw her distress. "Leave the lady's things intact," he said sharply.

Streeter looked up at him, but Streeter's hands were full and Edgar held a gun. Streeter gave the woman back her things.

The haul included several hundred dollars in gold, a few trinkets, and eight bottles of whiskey. The passengers got back in the stage and the driver climbed up on his box.

Streeter said, "Tell 'em in Los Angeles that you met Gar Tutwiler."

Edgar tuned indignantly. But Streeter was mounted now and his hand held a gun. Edgar called to the woman. "If you see Miss Candace Forest, please tell her that I will explain everything." The triteness of the remark made him color and he added, "Tell her that she will hear from me."

Streeter said, "We'll be gettin' back now, son. You lead the way." The stage swung into motion.

The last thing Edgar heard was the little girl's exclamation: "Gee, Maw, ain't Miss Candace Forest lucky?"

That night the white men got very drunk. The Indians watched and said nothing. D'Angel thanked Edgar for his part in the raid. "I knew if I put you in command, I could depend upon there being no bloodshed. The love of man is a powerful weapon." The thin lips twitched in an ironic smile. "I understand that your forcefulness in enforcing orders impressed the others, too."

Edgar said, "Why are you holding me? I know your reasons aren't what you say they are."

"You're very valuable to me," D'Angel said, amiably. "After the stage holdup, your reputation in Los Angeles will be such that it will serve my purpose well to have you stay here."

Edgar looked at him sharply. He opened his mouth to speak, then closed it again.

"You will go with us on the raid," D'Angel said, "but we shall leave you there when we leave. As I said," — his voice became bland —"I have complete faith in the loving heart of man to prevent pursuit, but I feel that having you in their hands will make the law-abiding element feel they haven't completely failed in exacting justice."

Edgar thought about this for a grim moment. Finally, he asked, "And you think a commonplace fellow who unsuccessfully sought a title for inherited land will satisfy them?"

"I don't leave a commonplace fellow," Mort D'Angel said. "I leave a mysterious, dapper stranger, the best shot in town, a road agent who has recently held up a stage, a man who *said* he sought title for land owned by a fictitious person with the unlikely name of Elisha Farrow."

"Uncle Elisha traded a claim for the land," Edgar said doggedly. "Perhaps he *was* never in Los Angeles."

"But *you* were, amigo," Mort D'Angel told him. "You spent six weeks in town — the six weeks or so before the raid — in some mysterious preparations that you tried to cloak by saying you were looking for a deed."

Edgar began to understand. It was strange how poorly the prosaic life of an honest city dweller fitted you to understand the minds of men like Mort D'Angel. But it came into focus gradually. Chance had given him a man wanted for killing another man. He had planned it so that the killer looked like a bad man of a stature sufficient to satisfy most of the Los Angelenos that they were holding the rustler chief — if they caught him.

Mort D'Angel smiled. "Jonathan Gault will be grateful to have someone in his hands with whom to silence the public reaction to our raid," he said, drawing the toe of his boot through the dust. "Especially if that someone has been seen kissing his girl in the moonlight."

"You seem to know a lot," Edgar said.

"I've been in love," Mort D'Angel said. "That's why I trust it as a dependable factor in an operation. But I like you, Gar. And that is bad. You can depend on love, but friendship is unreliable. It troubles me to like you."

"I think you're crazy," Edgar said at last.

Mort D'Angel smiled again. "I guess I am. Because I like you, I am tempted to tell you things that you are too naïve to guess. But I will tell you one thing. Mark it well."

"I'm listening," Edgar said; and he made no attempt to keep the sarcasm from his voice.

"It is this," D'Angel said, serious now — and Edgar could see a troubled man behind the opaque eyes. "When it comes at last and you pull the trigger, *do not stop. Keep on pulling the trigger.*"

ONE LARGE DROP of rain fell in the dusty street of Los Angeles. It made a puff of dust, a small depression, and then around it fell other drops, little explosions in the dust. People came out of the cantinas and stores and stood a moment, sighing luxuriously, letting the first big drops hit their unprotected faces.

The big drops stopped and became tiny drops, incredibly fine, incredibly close together, and where the big drops had dappled the dust on the pale green leaves of the trees, the little drops washed them clean; the whole country changed color from grey and brown to light green, and the sullen tan of the ground turned brown.

But no water ran upon the ground. The ground drank up the water, absorbed the water, blotting it up; and when a column of men moved down the big arroyo far to the east they moved silently, and no dust arose from the walking feet of their horses.

Other bands of mounted men were moving into the big coastal plain, through the grey rain. They moved carefully and slowly, combing the coulees where the cattle bunched, moving the cattle down, forming the herd, moving slowly. They were bunching the cattle subtly into a herd by guile and gentle persuasion.

Every fall the rains came, and every fall it was a fresh surprise. The streets that teemed the clock around were deserted, and the Angelenos watched the miracle of the rain in pleased astonishment, all activity suspended.

A hundred and fifty Californians moved on their horses. They were true Californians—stoic, brown. Their gods had brought the rains to this plain for a thousand generations and they were not surprised that their gods had not failed them. These one hundred and fifty Californians had taken the language of the Spaniard, but that was all. They stood by their own gods who always brought the rain. They rode now for a black-clad man who knew their gods well and had them for protection even unto lead bullets full in the chest. They bunched the cattle slowly and with skill — the Spaniards' cattle and the white men's cattle — and pushed them north.

Up in the mountains in Mort D'Angel's camp, there was much attention to firearms, to keep them dry. There were more people in the camp, now that it was breaking up. Other white men had ridden in — four or five of them — and each one brought a few Indians. But these Indians were armed and their faces carried anticipation like the white men's. They saddled the big grey stallion for Mort D'Angel — saddled him with his black saddle that was heavy with silver. They put Gar Tutwiler on his horse and crossed his hands and lashed them to the pommel with lengths of rawhide.

Mort D'Angel climbed laboriously up on his big horse and looked at his watch. The satinwood box lay empty in the rain. "It's been raining five hours now," he said slowly. "Now we move. It's all going off according to plan. In town we gut the gun shop, then break open the main cantinas and leave the liquor around. We want 'em to have free liquor. Rob the stores that sell lamp oil and candles, and run off any horses that you see. Tear down the poles of the Bella Union corral. Every man knows what to do. Be sure he does it."

Streeter said, "What about Gar, here?"

"No change in what I told you." He looked at Edgar speculatively and smiled a tiny smile. "No change at all."

And down in the town, things were in suspension. "Nobody does nothin' in California when it rains except set around and marvel."

They had something to marvel at. After nine months of choking dust, Commercial Street now ran three inches deep in water, and still the rain fell relentlessly. Six hours after it had started raining, it seemed that it had been raining forever.

Far out on the edge of town, the big grey stallion picked his way in the gathering twilight daintily, slowly, and then his rider gave a high cry and he broke into a lope. Behind him fifty horsemen followed, standing in their stirrups. They came with a purpose. Each man moved to where he had been assigned.

Two white men with two armed Indians behind them hit the Oroport. They came in, eight guns leveled, and one went behind the bar and put his shoulder to it and turned it over. It made a mighty crash and Greshem Greeley let a sudden cry of pain as liquid profits ran in rivulets upon the floor. The other white man, from behind him, opened his scalp with his gun barrel and turned and shot down the big hanging lamp. It fell, still burning, and the flames started licking up one wall before anyone knew what had happened.

Shots sounded up and down the streets as D'Angel's men moved through them, shooting for fun and for effect. Occasionally, somebody drunk or brave would try to rally a resistance and then they dealt swiftly with him, and the pocket of resistance would melt. There was no sense to it and there was no defense because the Angelenos had no clear idea of what they were defending, or why, and that created an element of stultifying shock.

And then the rain. People didn't operate in the rain — not in California. The rules had been broken, and it left everything out of focus.

At last, the gunmen rode out of town, and at the edge they met again. They dispersed the horses they had captured into the darkness and Mort D'Angel took a roll call. Every man was there that had ridden into Los Angeles, save one. Edgar Tutwiler was missing.

They had left Edgar Tutwiler at his hotel. Right at the door. They had cut the thongs that bound his wrists and set him down in the mud. Heath looked down at Edgar standing shivering in the rain. He rubbed his jaw. "Mort said to give you this," he said at last, and tossed down a package wrapped in oiled cloth. He turned his horse and moved away.

Edgar stood quite still a moment, his hands automatically searching the outlines of the package. It was a gun.

And suddenly Philadelphia seemed very close. He ran to the cubicle that had been his room in the hotel. Smith's blood still stained the floor where, in the wet darkness, he burrowed in the bed. The money belt was still there, still reassuringly heavy. He buckled it on. He stuck the gun, still wrapped, in the waistband of his pants. He stepped out and looked about. The ship that would take him to Philadelphia would be lying even now in San Pedro harbor. He had a gun. He had his money. But no horse whinnied in the broken corral of the Bella Union, and up the street a fresh volley of yelps marked the progress of two riders. He eased the gun under his waistband and stepped into the deeply embrasured doorway of the room next to his own.

The horses hard-ridden, pulled up in a long, splashing skid, and he heard the voice of Jonathan Gault. "Tutwiler's still here! He's armed but afoot. We've got to get him! He's the leader."

Major Forest's voice came to him then, tight and frightened. "But Candace …"

"She'll be all right. We've *got* to get Tutwiler!" Four booted feet moved to his door. "We've got to get Tutwiler while we have the chance."

Major Forest said again, "But my daughter …" and then his voice was drowned by the sound of a heavy shoulder against wood.

Edgar Tutwiler walked quietly to the horses, started to mount the one he recognized as Major Forest's, then stopped and moved to Gault's horse and, taking out his penknife, cut the cinch. He wouldn't have done it a week ago. It made him feel good.

There was a light in his room now and enormous shadows played vaguely from the door. He stepped up to Major Forest's horse, cut him once with the end of the reins, and headed out of town at a hard run. Rittenhouse Square seemed just around the corner. He heard Gualt yell. He heard Gault run to his horse. He heard Gualt step into the saddle — and he heard the saddle fall upon him in the mud. It was a sound that he would cherish.

The ship that would lie in San Pedro harbor would take him home. Home to an ordered life in a civilized town. It was as if he were awakening at last from a distorted dream that was peopled with men who thought they were gods. With Vigilantes who would hang a man for sport.

With Candace Forest. With the scent of silk and lilacs. With warm lips and teasing eyes.

With Candace Forest.

Gault knew that I was in town and afoot and armed. Is Gault clairvoyant? How did he know that?

Edgar pulled his horse to a walk, and Rittenhouse Square seemed vague now. For suddenly he knew where Candace Forest was tonight. He knew what Mort D'Angel had meant with his phrase about the loving heart of man that would prevent pursuit. The loving heart of a man who would not see his daughter harmed — even if it meant rustlers going undisturbed!

Edgar pulled his horse to a stop.

He knew a lot of things, now. And he sat quite still, relishing the impact of his knowledge, the sure impact of his emotions. You can count on love. Mort knew that.

Edgar thought for a moment without nostalgia, of Philadelphia and of the dull people there who would never have a chance to fall in love completely and at once upon a moon-drenched night. And learn of it completely and at once upon a rainy night. He knew he'd never see Rittenhouse Square again as he stepped down from his horse.

He unstrapped the heavy money belt, moving to the side of the road, and hid it under a rock that he marked by a lonely oak. Money wouldn't buy the things that he must have now, and the belt was heavy. He felt the dry gun in his waistband as he moved back to his horse. Suddenly he stumbled, felt the ground come up, felt his head hit a rock. He stood up shakily and touched the cut above his eye. It was bleeding freely, but he wiped the blood away abstractedly and climbed up on his horse. He started towards Los Angeles in the rain.

Jonathan Gault would find him, all right. The blood caked in his eyebrow and gave him a rakish appearance. The blood dyed his gay scarf. The horse loped easily, heading home.

They would be organizing now. He stepped down from the horse and tied him lightly in the shelter of an abandoned shack at the edge of town. The honest citizens would be organizing now, planning what to do. Jonathan Gault would be there. Edgar came around a corner and saw light pouring from the Oroport Saloon.

Greshem Greeley had his head bandaged, and the rain had put out the fire and he'd swung new lamps. He'd got the bar upright and had swept up the broken glass. He'd tapped a fresh keg of whiskey so that no brave Vigilante need ride out unfortified.

Edgar walked toward the Oroport, keeping close to the wall. Fifty feet from the entrance of the saloon, he stopped and flattened himself in a door. A group of riders were stopping in front of the Oroport, tethering lead horses. The Vigilantes were organizing now; they were bringing in fresh horses to replace the ones the riders had driven off.

Edgar moved between buildings to the back of the saloon, and, finding an empty whiskey barrel, he stood it by the wall. There was a charred hole in the low roof of the building at that point. He pulled off his shoes and set them aside and climbed onto the barrel and then to the roof.

Keeping his face from the light that shone through, he looked down through the hole. Jonathan Gault stood drying his muddy clothes by the crude fireplace at the end of the room where they had kindled a small fire. His coat was off, hung over a chair, and his big six-gun swung on his right leg.

Edgar heard him speak. "Tutwiler is the head of this scheme and he's the one we've got to hang. That'll break the back of the raiders and we can go out and get our cattle then."

"But, Johnny," Major Forest said, pacing paley from wall to bar. "They've got Candace! We've got to get *her* back!"

"We can't get her back," Gault said patiently. "If we go out after the cattle, they'll kill her."

Major Forest sat down and buried his face in his hands. "If you only hadn't come by and led me away on the wild-goose chase after Tutwiler, I'd have been home."

Pete Biggs appeared in Edgar's line of vision. He said, explaining apparently to late-comers, "Mr. Tutwiler steal the Major's hoss and leave Mr. Jonathan floppin' in the mud. Wonder how come Mr. Tutwiler was afoot?"

Jonathan Gault said angrily, "Shut up! If I find Edgar Tutwiler, he'll —"

Edgar Tutwiler's long legs swung down out of the hole and he held himself by one hand an instant while he freed his gun and brought it up. Then he was standing on the floor, gun in hand. In his bare feet, his face covered with blood, he stood, half crouched, his gun on Jonathan Gault. There was a long silence. Then the sigh of twenty escaping breaths.

"You found him," Edgar said.

Jonathan Gault stood still a long moment, and then slowly his hand moved toward his gun.

Edgar pulled the trigger. There was a click. He snapped the trigger twice more as Gault brought his gun up, and then he dived.

The roar of Gault's gun filled the room and there was suddenly great scrambling. Edgar pulled the trigger, lying on the floor, not aiming, and there was a roar. *"Keep on pulling the trigger." That's what Mort had said.*

Edgar scrambled to his feet. The room was clear and Gault was standing under the hole in the roof now, their positions almost reversed from Edgar's long, sliding leap.

An errant rivulet ran down the hole, fell toward the floor. Gault brought his gun down carefully and squeezed. The hammer clicked.

Edgar fired and the lead tore at Gault's hat. "Don't move. Drop your gun and raise your hands."

Gault obeyed.

"So you lured Major Forest away so they could steal his daughter. And you are strong against pursuit. *Your* plan is to hang me, Jonathan Gault."

"Do you believe him?" Gault asked the crowd at large.

Edgar whirled halfway around and fired at a point slightly above Don Juan Rivera's head. Don Juan took his empty hand quickly from his side. "Don't do those things," Edgar said softly.

Major Forest said, "The man's mad."

"He's in it," Edgar said, and his voice was a little weary because he saw that he would never be believed. Suddenly, though, he smiled. "Pete," he said. "Go take the gun from Major Forest's holster and put it in Gault's."

Pete Biggs moved rabbit-like, obeying, then scuttled to the wall.

Edgar shoved his own gun into his waistband, and no man moved in that long room. Slowly he raised his hands, and his voice was almost a whisper. "You knew my gun was empty before, but Mort D'Angel gave me a tiny chance. He left three bullets in the last three cylinders. I've got just one more." He raised his hands and stood facing Gault, both his hands above his head as he watched the other.

"Draw, Jonathan!"

Gault swept his hand down, and his gun was out and up when Edgar fired. The bullet tore Gault's shoulder above his heart and spun him around. He dropped the gun and cried out.

Edgar swept his eyes around the room, watching for movement. There was none. Gault cried out again, then, and Edgar moved, barefooted and silent, backward toward the door. He turned at the door and plunged through it, and they heard his bare feet pattering in the mud for a moment; then there was silence.

Pete Biggs went to the door and looked out. When he came back, they had Gault on the bar and were bandaging his wound. Major Forest was looking down at him speculatively. "Johnny," he said at last, "you'd better answer a few questions. I think you'd better ...."

IT WAS dawn and the rain had stopped for a little while when Edgar Tutwiler walked the Major's horse out of a clump of trees. The girl saw him first; her eyes flew open and she gave a little exclamation. Then Mort D'Angel was reaching for his gun.

"Don't do it, Mort!"

Mort D'Angel's hand stopped. He turned and saw the gun in Edgar's hand and pulled his horse to a stop. Far behind them they heard the slow and muffled beat of thousands of hoofs. "It was a hell of an idea, Mort," said Edgar, "but it didn't work out."

Mort D'Angel said nothing. He sat measuring his chances and Edgar grinned, his gun leveled at Mort's head. "It's full of silver bullets, Mort. I'll shoot you in the head."

"I left you three bullets," Mort D'Angel said. "I was told by Gault to leave you an empty gun. But I was a sentimental fool. You see what I said about friendship." He paused and smiled a little smile. "Do you have one left?"

"It's easy to find out, Mort. Go for your gun."

Mort looked at the girl. "I told you," he said, "he was much man." He turned to Edgar. "We were talking about you," he explained.

"And Jonathan Gault talked about *you!*" Edgar lied. "It's all finished. And you are finished too."

Mort looked at the gun, at Edgar. "I wonder ..."

"Turn the herd, Mort. Send back word to turn the cattle. Take his gun, Candy. Ride beside him and take his gun."

The girl, her eyes shining, brought her horse alongside the black-coated figure, reached under his long coat, and pulled the gun from its holster. She gave it to Edgar, her eyes wide with wonder.

"Fire three times," Mort said finally. "They'll turn 'em."

"If it brings armed men to help you," Edgar said, "You'll have silver in your brain. Or lead. Lead will do as well if I miss the chain mail waistcoat, won't it, Mort?"

"You know about that?"

"Chain mail or something like it. How else can you take a bullet in the chest?"

Mort laughed for the first time since Edgar had encountered him. "You make bigger magic than I do, Gar," he said finally. "The shirt was an ingenious idea, I thought. Evolved by a white man I met in Haiti. The natives worshipped him almost as a god."

Edgar threw away his own empty gun.

"Your gun was empty?" the girl said, and her voice broke with the realization.

Mort said, softly, "He was clothed in valor, my

dear, and, as I have told him, love is a powerful weapon."

Behind them the top of the moving column had come to a halt. Some of the Indian drivers were riding up.

"There may be difficulties," D'Angel said. "Superstition was enough to keep my Indians in order before the raid. But now they have something else. The smell of gold in their nostrils. It may not be easy to make them give up the cattle."

"You can persuade them," Edgar said.

D'Angel talked to the Indians. Edgar listened, knowing Candace's eyes never left him, but not daring to take his from D'Angel. The black-coated man spoke rapidly in Spanish and the Indians listened without expression. The words formed themselves into long, lilting cadences like some savage song, and Edgar thought he understood how simple people might believe in silver bullets and the superhuman might of one man.

Even so, the deciding argument was not the man's who called himself Mort D'Angel. It was the sight of a line of men, ant-size in the distance, riding over a hill far to the south. One of the Indians pointed and D'Angel spoke quickly. The Indian turned and kicked his horse to a run on the slippery floor of the valley. In a moment another followed. After that, they broke like frightened deer.

D'Angel looked thoughtfully at the line of men riding hard far to the south. Then he turned to Edgar, and the curtain of opaqueness was down from his grey eyes. "My life may not seem valuable to you, but it is to me and I will give you something in return for it. Eight thousand of these." He jerked his head at the cattle.

"Thank you," Edgar told him. "But you only stole them a few hours ago. We would say in Philadelphia that your title is a little cloudy."

"They're yours," said D'Angel, "and the land we are on now." He pulled the big stallion around, facing north. "Look through Gault's papers for Elisha Farrow's title." He spurred his horse, but Edgar shouted at him and he stopped.

"You left me three bullets," he said. "Three empty chambers and then three bullets. You gave me my life then, or a chance for it. Why did you do that?"

Mort D'Angel thought about it a moment. "Gault lured you out on the futile pursuit of our men the night of the party. By mistake, he caught Streeter and Heath. He'd seen you and Miss Forest, there in the garden. So he brought Streeter and Heath back and left you to guard them. He purposely didn't tie them, and of course they got away. It gave him a perfect excuse to hang you."

"I figured that," Edgar said. "But why did you leave me three bullets?"

Mort D'Angel let his eyes fall and the truth came hard from him. "I hoped you would kill Gault," he said. "And then it would save a split with him in San Francisco."

He held up his hand as Edgar started to speak. "That is a little of it, but not all." He looked at Edgar and Candace. "You were a coward, a timid man, and then you fell in love and you became a brave man — braver far than I, for I seldom feel fear. You may not have known those things, but I knew them, and I wanted you to have the woman that made you what you are now."

Edgar looked at him a long time. And he looked into himself. Then he looked at Candace. "You are," he said at last, "the only honest man I've ever known."

He threw the outlaw the loaded gun that Candace had taken from him. "Goodbye and good luck, amigo," he said softly.

Mort D'Angel blinked twice. He stuck the gun in his holster, tried once more to speak, and failed. He raised his hand in a salute and dug his big horse with his spurs.

Edgar looked up and saw Major Forest galloping toward them at the head of the column. "Gault isn't dead," he said quietly. "At the final instant I couldn't kill him."

The girl was beside Edgar and her arms were up and she was leaning perilously in her saddle. "As if I cared," she said.

Two Indians rode by, heading for their hills, abandoning the herd. They stopped and stared at Edgar, and then bowed and made a sign. Edgar released Candace, blushingly, and said wrathfully in English, "Now what?"

One of the Indians pointed and said gravely to the other, "It is as Mort D'Angel said just now. The new god prevails with an empty gun and rides barefoot when it rains."

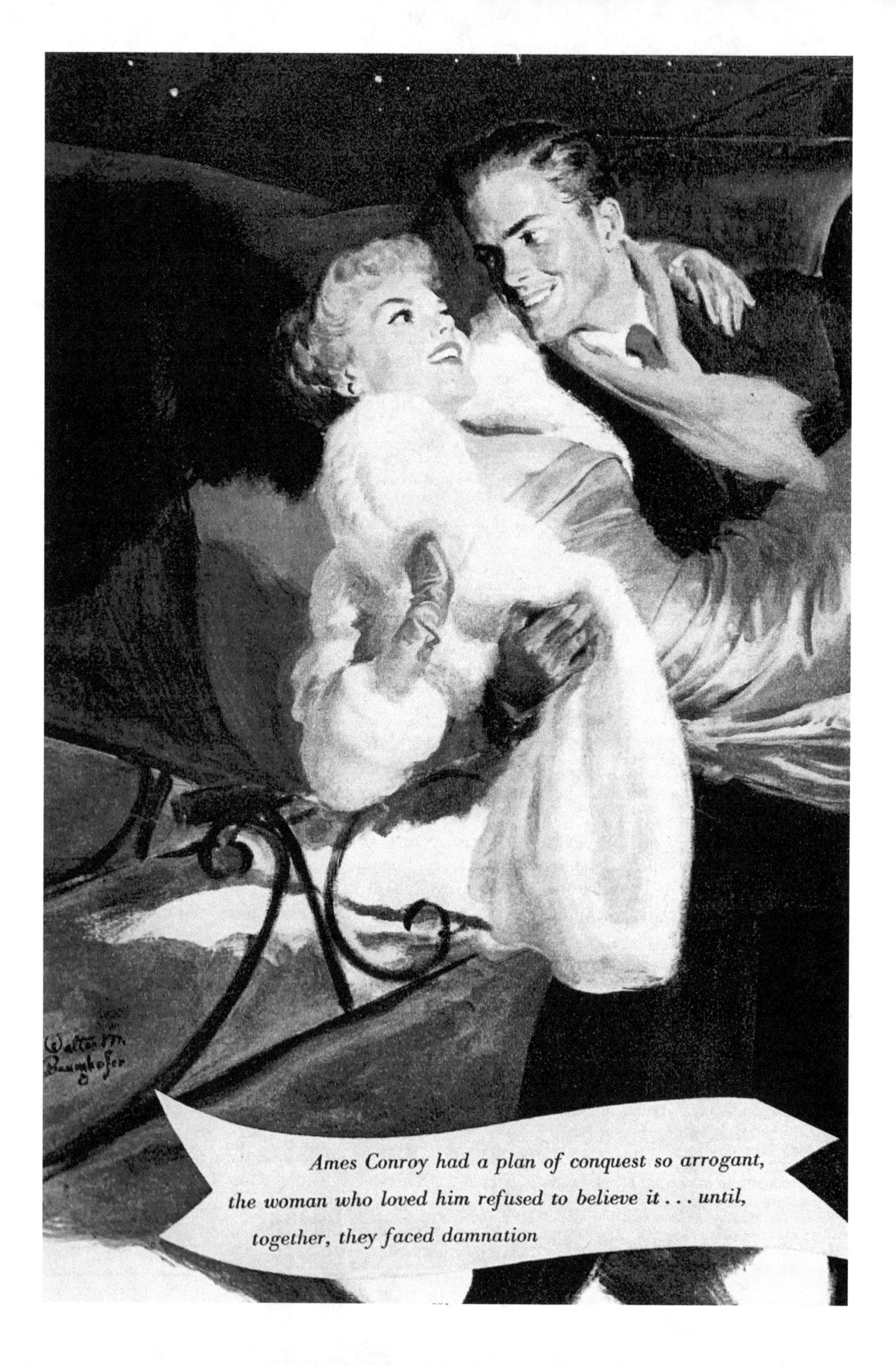

Ames Conroy had a plan of conquest so arrogant, the woman who loved him refused to believe it... until, together, they faced damnation

THE POWER DEVIL

IT WAS HOT in the little room. Hot and still, even with the window open.

Ames Conroy sat in a cone of yellow light in the center of the room, with a book before him on the table. Under heavy brows his slate-colored eyes moved across a line, back and down, across the line again. He was tired and his eyes moved slowly, methodically, taking hold upon each line, each word, and jamming it back into the recesses of his memory.

When the phone rang, it made him jump.

He picked up the receiver. "Ames Conroy?" the voice came up the wire.

"Yeah."

"Listen, Conroy; come down to the bar a minute. I got somethin' you might like to know."

"Who is this speaking?" Ames asked.

"My name's Rolly Henderson," the voice said, "but that don't matter. I knew your old man back in the old days. He done me a favor once, and I never got around to evenin' off with him. Maybe I can give you a break."

"If you'd hang up and let me go to bed," Ames said, "you'd be giving me a break." The mention of his father edged his voice.

"Listen, mate," the voice said. "You been sittin' up there studyin', ain't you? Sure, you have. You wasn't asleep. Well matey, you come down here a minute, and maybe you won't have to study so hard and lose so much sleep."

Ames Conroy's eyes narrowed. "I'll be down in a minute," he said, and hung up the receiver. It was ten minutes of two.

Rolly Henderson was a round little man with round little eyes behind thick glasses. He sat hunched over a corner table, his two hands circling a big glass of beer. When Ames came in, he motioned to the seat opposite him.

"Somethin' to drink?" he asked amiably.

Ames Conroy looked over, caught the bartender's eye. "Double brandy and plain water on the side," he said. He turned to Rolly Henderson. "Thanks," he said, grinning bleakly.

"That's all right, kid," Rolly Henderson said. "I'll even go for a glass of the bubbly if you want it." He stopped and sipped his beer. "You look kind of like your old man," he said, "and your old man bought me plenty of drinks in his day."

Ames said, "Yeah — get to talking. I'm tired."

"No foolin' around, eh?" Rolly said. "Well, matey, that's a symptom suits me perfect." He took another sip of beer. "What'll you pay for the questions to the examination that starts next Monday?"

Ames Conroy sat perfectly still, not answering. Then he reached out and took the brandy the waiter had put on the table, drained it off, and drank half the glass of water. "The bar examination?" he said.

"You takin' any other examination startin' next Monday?"

"No," Ames said, still expressionless.

"Listen, matey," Rolly Henderson said. "You been to law school two years. You're gonna try the examination without gettin' that third year — you're gettin' old. I don't blame you. But not goin' back for the third year — that leaves you a little drafty in a couple of regions. But say you got the questions — you knock 'em over standin' on your head. It's a cinch."

"How do you know all that?" Ames said.

"Listen," Rolly said. "A guy with a proposition like mine would know where he was goin', wouldn't he? Sure he would. I knew your old man when he was the hottest mouthpiece in River City, and I knew him after he was disbarred. I —"

"You can skip that," Ames said. "How much?"

Rolly Henderson leaned back and grinned. "Now," he said, "here is a guy I can deal with. Matey, I ain't gonna keep you up long. Not long at all." He finished his beer, and leaned forward. "Two hundred clams and eighty cents," he said.

Ames Conroy looked across at him and grinned. "What's the eighty cents for?" he asked.

"My beer's a dime," Rolly said. "The brandy's thirty-five cents a slug. I thought I'd let you buy the drinks because you was so tough with me over the phone."

"We haven't closed yet," Ames said. "How do I know the questions are the McCoy?"

"You don't," Rolly said. "You gotta go along with me."

"Keep talking," Ames said.

"Well," Rolly Henderson said, patting his pocket, "there is eighteen questions — no, twenty-one. They give you seven a day and you take your pick of 'em for six. You answer eighteen questions. They're pretty long. I got 'em here in my pocket."

"And you want two hundred dollars for them," Ames Conroy said slowly. The brandy, warm in his veins, gave him a feeling of exultation. To eliminate any chance of failing the examination, of having to wait and take it over again, that was worth every cent of Rolly Henderson's price.

He reached into his pocket and counted out two hundred. "Let's have the questions. But you buy the drinks."

Rolly Henderson looked over; the bartender was out of sight. There was no one else in the place. He took the money, drew a long envelope out of his pocket, and handed it to Ames.

Ames opened the envelope, took out the thin pages. He looked at the first question, drinking it in. Then he laughed. "Okay, pal," he said. "This round's on me."

THE OLD MAN was quite handsome, with silver hair, straight back.

"Gentlemen," he began, "you are about to embark upon an examination that most of you won't pass. You who are about to fail, I salute — and wish you better luck next time. To those of you who will pass, my congratulations. The Common Law is a ponderous accumulation, but it stands as the distillation of man's wisdom in dealing —"

Ames Conroy grinned sardonically to himself as the sonorous phrases rolled forth, then straightened to attention when the speech ended and they began passing out the examination papers. The page handed Ames his pamphlet with this session's questions, and passed on.

Ames took out his pen, checked the ink, loosened his tie. His mind was alert and clear.

He opened the pamphlet and looked at the first question. And with a remaining shred of his cool alertness, he knew that the question was entirely different from any that Rolly Henderson had sold him.

He felt the sweat start on his forehead, glanced instinctively about, almost expecting everyone to be looking at him, jeering at him.

"I've got to get back on base," he thought. "I've got to get going. I can't sit here in a daze forever. I've got to forget about Rolly Henderson and everything else and read the question again and try to answer it."

Finally, haltingly, he started writing.

THE NEXT THREE DAYS passed like one long day, broken by naps, with food, with study. When he had finished the answer to the last question, he felt his mind unwinding like a tight spring, gradually relieved of tension. He got up from his chair, felt his knees shake a little, and realized with surprise that there hadn't been a single question that he hadn't felt he had answered in a well-reasoned and competent manner.

He walked out across the grounds of the Capitol. The buildings were lovely, tempered with age, set up on a hill above the river and the town. He wondered why he had never noticed them before. Walking slowly, almost drunkenly, he became aware of the man who had made the speech three mornings before. That would be old Colonel Anderson, Chairman of the Bar Examining Committee.

Ames drew abreast of him. "How do you do, sir?" he said.

The old man peered at Ames. His eyes lighted with interest. "Why, you must be Daniel Conroy's boy. Though I must say you're a sight less handsome." He laughed.

Ames smiled at him. "Yes, sir," he said.

"Were you down taking the examination, my boy?"

"Yes, sir," Ames said again. "Pretty tough, too, isn't it, sir?"

"It's as hard, lad, as we can conscientiously make it," Colonel Anderson said. "There are too many bad lawyers in the world." He coughed in embarrassment and looked away. "No reflection on your father, my boy. As a matter of fact, I saw him try a case once, and I believe his was the most brilliant performance I ever witnessed."

"Maybe that was his trouble," Ames said evenly. "Maybe he was too brilliant." He lit a cigarette. "I'm pretty sure," he added, "that won't bother me. I base that on my performance on those exam questions."

"And the worst of it is," Colonel Anderson said, relieved to change the subject, "that you won't know how you came out for a couple of months."

"Well," Ames said, "I hope I get a fair shake."

"Oh, you needn't worry about that, my boy. You take the examination as a number. That number is substituted for another one before any of the graders are permitted to see the paper. You are doubly anonymous. There is no possible chance of anyone's knowing whose paper he is grading. However," Colonel Anderson added, "among those who fail there will be lamentations and accusations."

"I guess so," Ames said. "Well, I hope I make it."

They walked a few moments in silence. Finally Colonel Anderson said softly, "How is your father, son?"

Ames Conroy took five steps. "He's dead," he said.

"Oh, I'm sorry —"

"Don't be," Ames said. "He's lucky to be dead."

"I saw him quote verbatim and at apparent random from a volume on psychiatry once," the old man said. "He told me later he had committed large portions of the book to memory the night before." He paused. "A mind like that, I suppose, is a very dangerous thing without its proper balances."

"Yes, sir," Ames said, turning off. "Good day, sir."

"We'll not discuss my old man," he thought. "My old man was a drunken bum most of the time I knew him, and I will remember him that way. I'll let that thorn stick into my memory just deep enough to prick me every time I want to make the mistakes my old man made. I'll remember my father my own way."

At the hotel, he went through the bar and up to his room. "I passed," he said aloud. "I know I did. I've got two months now to look over the field and pick my spot."

IT WAS NINE WEEKS later, and Ames looked up from the steamy water, saw the cook standing there holding a letter against the light from the bare electric bulb that hung over the long stove.

"Here's a letter for you, Suds." he said.

Ames straightened up from the big dish vat, wiped his hands, and then grabbed for the letter. He unfolded its single page. The type swam, then crystallized: *We are honored to inform you that you have successfully fulfilled* —

Ames said, "I'm a lawyer, Cookie."

The cook grinned. "A man who works two shifts a day trollin' for china deserves better."

Ames was taking off his apron. "I've only got half a day's pay coming. If you can get it you can have it."

"So long, Suds," the cook called.

Ames went out the back way, around to the front. Walking toward his hotel, he ran into Colonel Anderson. He stopped, grinned.

"I just heard," he told the old man. "I made it."

"I'm glad to hear that," Colonel Anderson said.

"I don't suppose," Ames said, "you ever know how you did, whether you just squeezed through or —"

"There were four or five top papers that the entire Committee examined," Colonel Anderson said, his face perfectly bland. "Those showing exceptional reasoning, lucidity of expression, originality. Some name among them began with a C. Carney — Conrey — Conroy — something of the sort. Could have been you, son." The Colonel took his stick from his arm, raised his hat. "Good day," he said. "Congratulations."

THE CLUB CAR was full except for one table, and Ames sat down there and ordered a whisky and soda from the waiter. It hadn't come yet when he saw the girl come into the car.

She stopped at the end and looked the place over. For a fraction of a second she looked squarely at Ames; neither of them changed expression, but he knew she was going to come and sit at his table. He stood up as she came near, exactly as if they were meeting by prearrangement. He hadn't meant to stand up, and he felt his face redden as he did it. They sat down, and the girl opened her purse and took out a cigarette. Ames held a match for her.

"Thank you," she said.

He sat staring at her. She wasn't tall and she wasn't small. Her eyes were green and they slanted up a little at the corners. Her beauty was by no means perfect, nor was the manner that she wore a thing of practice.

She looked at him and smiled. "We might play gin rummy."

"Okay," he said. The waiter came with his drink then and he ordered some cards. The girl ordered a lime squash, a drink he couldn't remember ever having seen. He thought it had a vaguely church-social sound; but he decided not to say it.

"Of course," the girl said, "you shouldn't play cards with strangers on trains."

Now was the time for him to tell her his name, to get hers. But this wasn't a pick-up. He knew that, and it kept him from speaking.

"Shall we play for something?" she asked.

"Don't gamble with strangers," Ames said.

"I see," the girl said gravely. "Deal."

Ames dealt. He picked up his hand, but he didn't look at it. He was looking at the girl again. She smiled at him, sorting her cards.

"Going through to the coast?" she asked.

"No," he said. "I'm only going a hundred miles or so. I just got on at the capital. I'm going to a little town called Ozarkanna. I'm going to open a law office there."

The girl looked up from her cards. "Why Ozarkanna?"

Ames took a deep breath. "Well," he said, "it's like this —" He stopped. "You don't want to hear all that."

"On the contrary," the girl said, "I'm sure I do. It sounds interesting."

Ames Conroy looked out the window; his eyes, unfocused, were soft, reflecting the green and tan of the countryside that slid by the train.

"My old man was a lawyer," he began abruptly.

"He was the most brilliant lawyer that ever hung his shingle in River City, I guess. He could do anything; he was terrific. And when he started practicing, River City was run by a machine. Old Tom Gates's machine.... I suppose you don't remember the government sending Tom Gates to the penitentiary?"

"Yes, I do. I remember reading about it."

"Well, when my father started to practice in River City, Tom Gates was just starting to run the town. My father liked money; he liked clothes; he liked horses and dice. My mother died when I was four, and my old man liked women, too. He figured the fastest way to get all of them was to tie in with the organization."

AMES STOPPED and looked at the girl. "I don't want to bore you," he said. But, suddenly and desperately, he wanted to tell this girl the whole thing. He wanted someone in the world to know what he had done and what he was going to do. It couldn't hurt anything; she would be out of his life in an hour and gone, no telling where.

"If I didn't want to hear it," she said, "I could get up and walk away."

Ames grinned. "My old man was a success — he grew up with prohibition and the organization. Maybe it got too easy, or maybe when they put Tom Gates away, it broke his nerve. He got on the bottle, and then it got tough and he tried to bribe a juror, and he got disbarred. Then he died. I decided not to be his kind of chump."

"What did you decide to be?"

"A lawyer — only different."

The girl didn't answer.

Ames went on: "My old man was brilliant, see, but actually he was a chump. I didn't have the time nor the money to finish law school, so I crammed and took the bar exam after two years. I made it."

"Oh."

"I decided to be a success, too. To be powerful. I figured if I got some power, the money would take care of itself."

"How did you happen to choose Ozarkanna," the girl asked, "to begin this rags-to-riches saga?"

Ames said, as if he hadn't heard, "Did you ever see a broke ex-governor or ex-senator? Did you ever see a broke ex-congressman?"

The girl answered dutifully, "No."

"Neither did I. And here's the way I figure: The way to get power, the quickest, simplest way in this state, is through politics. The way to get ahead in politics is to get elected to office — make a record, run for something better. That's a lot easier than it sounds. And so we come to Ozarkanna. Let me sum up the advantages, the perfection, almost, of Ozarkanna."

"Sum, by all means," the girl said.

"Ozarkanna," said Ames, "is safely one-party. So you have only the primary to worry about if you are running for office. Election is a formality. Two, it's the center of a Congressional district that is just Ozarkanna and Hill County — of which Ozarkanna, by the way, is the county seat — on a larger scale. There is no city in the district with a city's problems — labor problems, racial problems, and so on. In other words, if you run for Congress in Ozarkanna, the campaign you make is the same campaign you are making for a county office, only a little bigger."

"You seem to know a lot about Ozarkanna and its environs."

"I DIDN'T pick it out on the map with a hatpin," Ames said. "I did it after weeks of research and calculation. Of course, I was washing dishes two shifts a day, but still I gave it a careful look. There are other features."

"Such as?"

"The incumbent congressman from that district is old," Ames said. "He's going to die some day. I would prefer him to die four years from now. Four years or five, maybe. I'll come to why I want that in a minute. But about Ozarkanna again. It's a small town — seven thousand, with a static population. Its successful people are the ones that had enough get-up-and-go to get out of town. Thus, the people left, especially the lawyers, are a bunch of mediocrities. People who were afraid to try it elsewhere."

"*All* of them?" the girl asked.

"There are a couple of semi-exceptions," Ames

conceded. "An old boy named Milburn. Judge Marshall Milburn. He's in his sixties, has probably got such practice as makes any money — retainer from the power company, the big bank, the railroad, that sort of thing. He was prosecuting attorney way back, then circuit judge a couple of terms. To me, he's no threat. As far as I'm concerned, he's just sitting around waiting to die."

"Which isn't really necessary," the girl supplied, "as it is for the congressman."

"You make me sound pretty cold-blooded," Ames said.

"Aren't you?"

"Well, yes. I suppose I am."

"You mentioned a couple of these semi-exceptions."

"One other. A guy named Weldon."

"From the tone of your voice, I would guess him to be young and healthy."

'He's the prosecuting attorney now."

"I see."

"But about the congressman. I want to run for prosecuting attorney next election. Then I want to make a record. And I'll make a record. I'll get my name in the metropolitan papers; and if the congresman'll die, I'll be in there running for Congress. Well, that's it." Ames stopped abruptly.

THE GIRL mashed her cigarette into the tray. "I have a suspicion you'll get where you're going," she said softly. "You may have to revise your values a little. Maybe everybody in a small town doesn't think he's a failure. But I expect you'll get where you're heading for…. Now, one more question and the State will rest."

"Yes, ma'am."

"Why is it you bought a Pullman on an extra-fare train to ride a hundred miles? That somehow seems a grievous waste for you, the way you figure things."

"It fits," Ames said. "You see, I ride into Ozarkanna on a crack train — they flag it and let me off. I get off, and that makes me a person. That makes an impression. I'm immediately of more than average interest. Not broke. I mean, it makes me *look* as if I'm not broke."

"I see. And what about the dishes?"

"What dishes?"

"The ones you were washing. Remember? Before you ran for Congress."

"Oh. Money. A guy let me work two shifts: seven in the morning until midnight, two hours off in the afternoon. He gave me sixteen dollars a day and meals. It was the best quick deal in town. While I was waiting to hear on the exam, I saved my train fare for Ozarkanna."

The train whistled, hurled itself around a curve.

"I think we're coming to your station," the girl said.

Ames looked at the girl. "Funny thing," he said. "You're about the prettiest girl I ever saw."

"Thank you."

He hadn't meant it for a compliment; he hardly paused. "And, for a minute, I felt you were more important to me than the things I've been telling you. I felt like riding right past Ozarkanna to find out your name and where you lived."

"There's nothing secret about any of that." She smiled.

"No," he said, stopping her. "I don't want to know." He stood up. "Thanks," he said. "Good-by."

Without waiting for her to answer, he walked to the end of the car. He stopped, fighting an almost irresistible impulse to turn; then he forced himself into the passageway leading to the vestibule.

The train was losing speed rapidly now, and he bent down to look out of the window. They were coming into the edge to the town. Across a trestle laid through dry swamp, over a river with an island in its center where odd clumps of nondescript shanty-boats were moored, then onto a bluff, and past a few scattered cabins where ragged, dirty children stopped in their play to watch the silver train go by. Then came the first streets, quiet and elm-lined, with old-fashioned houses behind their wide front yards.

The train hammered into a cut, under a wooden bridge, and the brakes went on again for the last time now. Ames saw a big mule barn fronting on a dirt street along the right of way. Beyond, he could see a dome, partially visible through a clump of trees. The courthouse. And suddenly Ames Conroy felt the weight of fear. Fear born of loneliness. He didn't know anybody in Ozarkanna, and nobody knew him. No one knew he was coming, and even after they knew he was there, they wouldn't care.

THE TRAIN STOPPED. Ames went on to the vestibule and down the steps, to find himself in the middle of Ozarkanna's main street. He tipped the porter, picked up his bags, and hurried toward the depot.

Even before he reached the little red-brick building, the train started to move again. Ames cursed himself. What harm could it have done to learn the girl's name, where she lived?

The station agent was coming back to the depot. Ames stopped him: "Could you send a wire to the conductor at the next stop?"

The station agent guessed he could.

"There was a young lady on the club car," Ames said. "I borrowed her fountain pen —"

The station agent said to somebody beyond Ames, "How do, Judge? Miss Gay?"

Ames turned. The man was tall and straight and tanned. The girl was the girl on the train.

He held his face grave, immobile. He bowed. He followed the station agent inside. "Who was that?" he asked.

"Judge Milburn. He's about the biggest lawyer in town."

"Yeah?" Ame's voice had an edged sound.

"Daughter Gabrielle was with him," the station agent said. "Pretty girl."

Ames had hold of himself now. He put a smile on his face. "Yes, sir," he said heartily. "Pretty as a poke in the nose." He turned, walked a couple of steps. "Never mind the wire," he said.

The knock on the door was gentle but insistent, pushing through the walls of his slumber. "Yes?" he said.

"It's seven-thirty, Ames."

"All right," he said mechanically. "Thank you."

"Don't go back to sleep now. Breakfast will be ready by the time you come down."

It was the sixth morning he had awakened in Ozarkanna, and on the first Mrs. Doughty had invented the myth that he would go back to sleep if she didn't warn him against it. He lay a moment watching the September breeze stir the white organdy curtains. Then he got up.

He wondered if he'd ever get used to this room. It kept reminding him of something way back in his childhood, although he had actually never known anything like it. Its high ceiling made it look larger than it was, and the furniture made him think of antique shops. But no decorator could arrange stuff from one of those places like this. These things had always been this way.

AFTER HE HAD DRESSED and was on his way downstairs, he decided once more that he couldn't let Mrs. Doughty go on giving him breakfast like this. And once more his resolution evaporated before the comforting fumes of coffee and fresh toast.

"You shouldn't do this," he began weakly.

"You just sit down," she told him. She was a tiny widow with a mouth of unalterable gentleness and a turn-of-the-century pompadour whose gray was still brown-streaked.

"It's awfully good of you." He felt foolish and inadequate, but he had to say it.

"It's little enough," she said, "to do for Marhsall Milburn's daughter's young man."

"Mrs. Doughty," he said, "I think I ought to make one thing plain: I'm *not* Gabrielle Milburn's young man."

"Don't worry," she said. "I've not told anybody, and I'm not going to."

"But I can't let you think —"

"Besides," she said, "I've never thought Harry Weldon was good enough for her."

Mrs. Doughty poured coffee into Ames's cup. "I knew how the wind blew," she said, "when she called me up and asked me to find you at the hotel and give you a room." There was more than a hint of archness in her manner.

"It was a thoughtful thing to do —"

"Of course it was. Just what I've been saying. I've known Gabrielle Milburn since she was a baby, and if you think for one minute she'd pick up with just any young man on a public train—"

"It wasn't like that."

"I should say it wasn't. Now, don't you worry," Mrs. Doughty said reassuringly. "Your secret's safe with me. Just eat your breakfast."

He ate his breakfast.

At nine o'clock he turned in at the door beside Greer's Hardware Store on the east side of the courthouse square, caught himself on the verge of a salute to his bright shingle —"Ames Conroy,

Attorney at Law" — by the entrance, and went up the dark, narrow stairs to the second floor, where his office was.

In the upper hall by his door was a packing box, long and narrow but solidly heavy. With his key already in the lock, Ames hesitated, looking at the box. He took his key out again and went back downstairs.

Old Man Greer, which is what Ames had heard people call the hardware merchant, was pouring nails into a scoop that sat on the scales. He answered Ames's good morning and continued about his business. He was lightly built, with heavy white hair which he was vain of. He didn't wear a coat in the store; he had a long apron with the strings passed around him and tied in front, and a pair of woven straw cuffs that came halfway to his elbows.

Ames said, "Who is the freight agent, Mr. Greer?"

"Whit Sales. Rassled you a heavy box upstairs, hour or two back."

"Yes, I see he did. I owe him some charges."

"Guess you do."

Whit Sales was behind the counter in the freight office.

Ames went in and said, "I'm Ames Conroy. I see you brought me my new books."

Sales, tall and spare, with rimless glasses, slid a bill of lading toward him along the counter. "Dollar eighty charges," he said.

Ames took a five-dollar bill from his pocket and handed it over. By the time the other man gave him the change, he would have to make a decision. It would be important. He took the change and held it in his hand a moment. "You don't have to deliver freight," he said.

"You ain't got a car."

"You didn't have to carry it upstairs."

"That's right," Sales agreed.

Ames made his decision and put the money in his pocket. "It was a thoughtful thing to do," he said. "I want you to know I won't forget it." He held out his hand and smiled.

Whit Sales took his hand and smiled a spare smile. "That's okay," he said.

WALKING BACK up Holden Street, Ames thought, "I guessed right. He wouldn't have liked me to offer to pay extra. He's a voter. He's done me a favor now, and I've got a hold on him — more than if I'd done him one."

He was pretty well furnished now. Stationery, freshly printed by the *Hill County Courier's* job printing department, was stacked neatly on his desk. A client or two now, and he would be set.

The window was open, and the hills beyond the town were gunmetal blue, splotched with orange and scarlet, the work of an early frost. He walked over and looked out toward Market Street. He could see a small stretch of it if he stood well over to the side of the window. He looked at his watch.

He went out and hurried down Holden Street to Colton, and then east to McGuire. It was exactly twenty minutes later when he turned back into Market Street and headed toward the courthouse.

He passed the Milburn house just as Gabrielle came out of the front door. "Hello," he said, stopping.

"Hello," she said. Her face was grave except for a crinkling at the corners of her green eyes. She said, "Aren't you a bit late getting to work?"

He was grave, too. "I've been to my office."

"I'm on my way to shop."

THEY WALKED along the sidewalk together.

"I expected you would be," he said. "I've watched you from my office window. You're very punctual, every day."

She didn't answer that.

He said, "I wanted to talk to you. I didn't feel that I should call."

"It would have been all right. I told Father we'd met — nothing more. He doesn't know he's just waiting around to die."

"Aren't we all? But I wanted to thank you for getting me the room with Mrs. Doughty."

"You're welcome."

"I can't help wondering why."

"I guess it was the picture of you in the Martin Hotel. Just you and your plan of conquest. It made me lonely just to think of it."

He smiled down at her. "I wasn't thinking of my plan of conquest, then. I was thinking of you."

"The money you pay Mrs. Doughty," the girl said, with no change in her voice, "will be a vital help to her."

Ames put his hand over his heart, ignoring the interruption. "And you're the only person I ever thought of whom I didn't want to think of."

"Is that all?" she asked.

"Oh, no. I want to marry you. I just wanted you to understand how things were before things started."

They were at Main Street now. He took off his hat with a faintly awkward shyness that the brashness of his words couldn't quite conceal. "I've got to run over to the jail," he said. "A possible client."

The girl looked at him thoughtfully, trying to see behind his words.

Ames grinned. Then he turned and fled. "Grin to keep your heart out of your mouth," he thought. "Grin so she won't know how young and in love you are." He ducked his head and plunged across the square toward the jail, fighting not to run.

The man was named Joiner. He had been in jail for several weeks, awaiting trial for "stealing chickens in the nighttime," as the legal phraseology quaintly put it. Ames had found out about him his second day in Ozarkanna and had offered his services as defending attorney free of charge.

Joiner pulled himself up from the bare bunk and shuffled toward the door of the cell. He was thirty and looked fifty.

Ames said cheerfully, "How are you today?"

Joiner said that he was all right.

"Well," Ames said, "we'll have you out of here soon. Court convenes day after tomorrow. You're on top of the docket."

"Uh-huh."

"The whole case against you swings on what's-his-name —"

"Fellow's name's Harris."

"— Harris identifying his chickens. Well, I sent a boy out there, and he bought four from Mrs. Harris. I took them up to Sassoon, to the poultry yard, and bought four to match. We'll see how well Mr. Harris can tell his four from my four in court."

"Yeah?" Joiner smiled. "Four enough. I taken seven. Sack wouldn't hold —"

"Hush!" Ames broke in. "I don't want to hear that. Just keep your mouth shut. Let me do the talking." He paused. "Remember. Don't say anything to anybody."

"Okay."

Ames stood up. In the gloom of the next cell another man stood up, too. He was a big man with a short red beard. "What's your name, mister?"

Ames said, "Ames Conroy. I didn't see you."

"I saw you," the big man said.

"You heard what I said?"

"I forgot what you said."

"Thanks," Ames said.

"Come see me."

"All right," Ames said automatically.

HE LEFT THE JAIL, and saw Gay across the square. He took the long way around and managed to come up to her while she still stood talking to a man in front of the store. He was about thirty, handsome as men are who have never had to worry about anything in their lives, and poised from a record of success. Ames sensed who he was before Gabrielle introduced them. The self-assured young man was Harry Weldon.

"The Prosecuting Attorney," Ames said. "I'm particularly glad to meet you before we face each other in court."

"Are we facing each other in court?" Harry Weldon said.

"The day after tomorrow. You hadn't heard about it?"

"It slipped my mind," Weldon said.

"Well, I hope I won't give you too boring a time," said Ames.

Weldon looked at him thoughtfully.

Ames smiled blandly.

"The Joiner case, isn't it?" Weldon said.

"Yes," Ames answered, still smiling.

"Well, I hope it won't put you out. I'm dismissing the case for lack of evidence."

There was a long silence. Ames's face showed nothing of what he felt. "When did you decide that?" he asked.

"Just now." Weldon's smile was bland, too. "I just realized you were about to tell me that the State's case was shaky. He's guilty, all right, but we couldn't prove it, probably, if he was intelligently defended. Besides, he's done thirty days awaiting trial. I think he's paid his debt to society. Also Mr. Harris got his chickens back."

"Well," Ames said cheerfully, "that's fine. I hope I don't win all my cases that easily, though. An unbroken string of successes, and I'll starve to death."

He went on to his office. About his only emotion at the moment was a desire to punch Harry Weldon in the nose. He picked up his phone.

"Mrs. Doughty?" He said. "Those chickens in that box in the garden. Let's eat one for dinner."

HE SPENT most of the next day at his desk trying to find something to occupy his mind. But there was little room in it for anything else but the question: How does a lawyer get his first client? He thought regretfully of the chicken-stealing Joiner, and then suddenly he remembered the big man in the next cell. He stood up abruptly and walked out of his office.

The sheriff's residence was built onto the front of the jail, of the same aged pink brick, and the sheriff was sitting on his little porch, picking his teeth. He didn't get up. "Joiner's left."

"I know," Ames said. "Who's the big guy, red-head, in the cell-block?"

"Why," the sheriff said, "that there is Stepper Keith."

"What's he do?"

The sheriff looked at Ames and the he looked at the floor. "Well, now, the Stepper can do a collection of things. He's a gambler and a fighter, and a stone mason and a carpenter, and a fisherman, and a whole collection of things." The sheriff paused. "But I guess you'd say mostly the Stepper was a pirate."

"He looks the part, anyway," Ames said, and waited.

"He's a shanty-boater," the sheriff said, as if that explained everything.

"Those boats I saw from the train, coming into town?" Ames said.

The sheriff nodded. "Down on the river, where McGuire hits the bluff. That island out there in the middle's where the river cut through the horseshoe in the wet year of oughty-ought. The shanty-boaters tie up there. They fish and trap acrost the river, in the swampland yonder. The Stepper, he steals from their traps and runs their trotlines for 'em, or sometimes he waits and takes their money from 'em gamblin'. He comes in, sometimes, and works. He's a real good man, can lay stone, carpenter, but mostly he's a pirate, like." The sheriff, an old and stringy man, said all this with a slightly wistful air. "I always kinda liked the Stepper, myself. I've had him here off and on quite a bit. I'll miss him."

"What do you mean you'll miss him?" Ames asked. "What's he done this time?"

"Kilt his wife. Harry filed first degree against him. Murder."

"Oh. Can I talk to him?"

"Sure. I'll let you in. Holler when you want out."

AN HOUR later he was back in his office. He had a client now. He'd told Stepper he wasn't sure yet that he'd take the case. But he'd made up his mind.

First case, first-degree murder. Not stealing chickens in the nighttime, but taking a life. And for that the people demanded a life in return. The State v. Stepper Keith. All organized society against Stepper Keith. Against Stepper Keith and Ames Conroy.

He sat there a long time. It was the first time he'd known what the law was. They had told him, but he hadn't known. It all turned on him. The whole thing, all liberties that people had, all freedoms, turned on him, counsel for the defense. He was starting his career with a fight for the highest stakes there are: life itself.

He walked to the window and looked out at the patch of Market Street near Gabrielle's house. "I've got to free him," he said aloud, "or I'm through before I start."

The telephone on his desk rang. It was Mrs. Doughty.

"Ames," she announced, "you'll be contributing to the Community Chest this year."

"If you say so, Mrs. Doughty," Ames said. "How much can I afford?"

"Pledge twenty-five dollars, and spread it out. I'm on the committee this year —"

"I'll fill out a form tonight," Ames said, a little puzzled.

"I put you on Gabrielle's list," said Mrs. Doughty coyly. "She's on her way to your office now."

He had barely time to cradle the phone, when Gabrielle knocked.

"Come in, Gay," he called.

Gabrielle came in.

"Hello," he said casually.

"How did you know it was me?" she said.

"Contrary to popular belief," he said, "love is not completely blind. The eyes of love can see right through a door."

She looked at the window. "You certainly didn't see me come along Market Street. I came down Holden from the other direction."

"I know," Ames said seriously. "It's just that I can already recognize the sound of your step."

Gay looked incredulous, then confused. She said, "I don't believe you."

"Of course you don't," he said. "Won't you sit down?"

"I wanted to talk to you about the Community Chest," she began.

"I got another client," Ames said irrelevantly. "Stepper Keith."

"Oh-h. Oh, Ames! He's guilty, you know."

Ames kept his voice smooth: "I suppose he has a long record of killing wives."

"He has a long record!"

"So you think Stepper should hang?"

"I didn't say that."

"But you've already tried him and found him guilty?"

"Well, I think it's pretty obvious."

"And the whole town, I suppose, thinks just like you?" Ames tried to sound ironic to keep the despair out of his voice.

"I don't see how they can help it."

"Do you think he's entitled to counsel, or do you think lynching would be best?"

The girl colored. "I was just trying to help you," she said. "If you had been appointed by the court, it would have been different. But accepting the case — I don't want to be disagreeable," she went on. "I was just trying to give you some advice. Harry has talked about the case a little bit."

"I see. I know nothing of the case. I just feel that the boys had something when they wrote the due process amendment into the Bill of Rights."

"And so, if you free him by some miracle, you will contribute to a miscarriage of justice; and if he hangs, you've started with a black mark against you."

Ames had a hot retort on his lips, when the door opened and Harry Weldon came in.

Gabrielle said, "Hello, Harry."

Ames didn't say anything.

Weldon said, "I saw you turn in here, Gay. I was on my way out of the courthouse. I thought I'd see if I could sell you on a little golf."

Gabrielle stood up. "Yes, I'd like to," she said, and turned toward the door.

Ames said, "I've got another one for you to dismiss, Mr. Weldon. I'm defending Stepper Keith."

Weldon, on his way to the door, stopped, turned. But when he spoke, it was to Gabrielle: "We can have lunch and get in eighteen holes."

He went out, closing the door behind them.

THE SELECTION of the jury went swiftly, and Harry Weldon addressed them briefly:

"The State will prove that on the night of August fifteenth, Mary Keith was throttled to death by the defendant, Stepper Keith. That witnesses, whom we will put on the stand, heard the sounds of a fight on the Keith shanty-boat, and that in the morning, when other shanty-boaters, alarmed at the now ominous quiet, called the sheriff, he rowed out and found Mary Keith dead. And that while he was there Stepper arrived in the dinghy with rope and a large rock" — Harry Weldon became amused and sarcastic —"which he *said* he had been using as a substitute anchor, having lost his while out fishing that night. He was going to use it as an anchor, all right, gentlemen. He was going to anchor to the bottom of the river the body of his wife — the wife he had killed in cold blood."

There was more of this, a good deal more, and at noon the court recessed what promised to be the shortest murder trial in Hill County history.

Ames saw Gay and Judge Milburn in the corridor. Judge Milburn said, "That's the worst jury I ever saw, Conroy."

"They look all right to me," Ames said. "Better than Gay, here. She has already convicted Stepper."

Harry Weldon came up, and Mrs. Doughty appeared in the circle. She said, "I want you young people to come home with me to lunch. Ames, I fried the last of those chickens. It was one of the ones you said that Joiner person stole, and I must say it's tenderer than the ones you bought."

Ames took Gabrielle's arm. "I'm sure we'll accept, won't we Gay?" He moved after Mrs. Doughty, and the girl went with him, apparently shocked into silence.

Judge Milburn was laughing, and Weldon was trying to.

Harry Weldon said pointedly, "Aren't you going to invite me, too?"

Mrs. Doughty said, "No; I never have approved of lawyers opposing each other in court and hobnobbing outside."

The trial ground on through the afternoon. Ames put Stepper on the stand.

"Did you kill Mary Keith?" The State asked Stepper.

"No. We had a fight. I kind of knocked her around, and maybe I choked her a little, but she was all right when I left."

"And when you came back, after fishing all night, she was dead and the sheriff was there?"

"That's right."

"And the shanty-boat was down-stream, anchored out from the shore, and you had the dinghy?"

"Yes."

NEXT MORNING Harry Weldon began summing up the state's case. He made use of Stepper's record, his wrongdoing. And there had been a fight.

Ames finally stood before the jury. He looked out and saw Gabrielle. He said, "Stepper Keith was in love with his wife. People in love do funny things. Sometimes they fight. Sometimes they hurt each other."

He paused. "Mary Keith was a city girl. I want you to remember that. Mr. Weldon has sought to prove that Stepper Keith killed the defenseless girl in cold blood. He has brought out, very skillfully, the fact that Stepper Keith has a bad record. I didn't bother to object to these entirely irrelevant innuendoes. It wasn't necessary. You told me under oath that you would not convict an innocent man. I trust Stepper Keith. I trust the emotion that we call love, and I trust you.

"Now, Mary Keith showed no marks upon her of wounds that would cause death, so the assumption was that she was throttled. Such a death might possibly have occurred without marks indicating a fatal application of force upon her windpipe. So she was choked to death. Or so the prosecution, to make it murder, contends.

"But I know Stepper wouldn't choke her to death, and we all know that there were no external marks of violence upon her that would cause death, and that nobody else was on the boat."

Ames looked at the floor. "So it has to follow that she died from an *internal* cause. Well, she was healthy, so it now has to be a poison. But she wouldn't commit suicide; she wasn't that kind of person. So it has to be a poison that she didn't know she was taking. So it has to be a food.

"Witnesses heard a fight; later, Mary Keith was dead. The prosecuting attorney put two and two together. And Stepper Keith is on trial for his life.

"I put two and two together — because I know you don't kill the person you love if you are sane, and Stepper Keith is sane — and I get an entirely different answer. She was poisoned by food, and she didn't know it was poison. She was a city girl. If she was sick she couldn't get off the boat. She loved mushrooms."

Ames turned and looked at Stepper Keith, and then he whirled around to the foreman of the jury. "How would she die?" he asked.

The foreman said almost automatically, "Toadstools."

"Thank you, sir." Ames turned to the bench: "The unprecedented speed with which this case was brought to trial now becomes the factor that saves Stepper Keith's life, for the type of poison that occurs in toadstools does not remain constant in the body for very long and subject to analysis. In other words, if the prosecutor had not been so anxious to hang an innocent man he probably would have been successful."

Ames said quietly, "Will the court permit the exhumation — immediately, for time is vital — of the body of Mary Keith? I have caused to come here Dr. Morton, a famous toxicologist from River City, who will be able, at the conclusion of his examination, to assure the court, the jury, and the prosecuting attorney that the continuation of this case is unnecessary."

The word was on the street by nightfall: Ames Conroy had been right. The soft haze of Indian summer became crystal-blue and gold and scarlet with the sharpening of fall, and Gabrielle Milburn and her father went away to spend Thanksgiving with friends in River City. Ames tried not to recognize the emptiness he felt at not being able to see her start on her morning shopping tours. When he finally did see her, he hurried downstairs and met her, just as she turned into Main Street.

"Well, well." he said. "Fancy meeting you here. When did you get back?"

"Yesterday," she said. "How have things been going, Ames?"

"Pretty good." He smiled at her. "Better now."

"Dad would like you to drop by Christmas afternoon. Quaff an eggnog. There'll be loads of people there you haven't met. The wax-museum segment of Ozarkanna society."

"Thank you very much."

Gabrielle dropped her eyes. She said evenly, "The Christmas party is partly to announce my engagement to Harry Weldon."

THE DAY before Christmas it started to snow. In his office, Ames stoked the pot-bellied stove, and tried not to think about the season. He still wasn't the busiest lawyer in town, but he had clients enough to keep him occupied and, at the moment, work that would keep his mind off Christmas Eve.

He had supper in a lunchroom called Joe's, near the depot. He was the only diner, and Joe said "Merry Christmas" when Ames paid and went out.

Mrs. Doughty had gone to her daughter's for Christmas, but she had left the porch light on for him, a beacon of warmth and hospitality in the storm. He shook the snow from his coat and stamped it from his shoes before he went in the house.

He stood there a moment. On a night like this, he thought, anything could happen — the sound of tiny hoofs on the roof — anything. His eyes suddenly smarted with tears and, setting his teeth hard, he hurried to his room.

Ames wasn't to go to the Milburn's until midafternoon on Christmas Day. He had breakfast at Joe's and was in his office by eight-thirty. Just one more stretch now, and the holidays would be over. The dread of days like Christmas was nothing new to him; as a child it had meant a period of horrible nightmare: More toys and bigger toys than you knew what to do with, grown-ups drinking — your father drinking more than any of them — and nothing under your feet, nothing solid and safe in the whole world to stand on.

He was looking out of the window when footsteps brought him back to the present.

Gabrielle walked in, a gaily wrapped package in her hand. "I brought you a present. I knitted it myself. I'll have the other one finished by next Christmas — It's a sock."

"Oh. I thought we were still on the books-and-flowers basis," he teased.

"There are really two socks. The last one is almost perfect."

Ames said, "I thank you." Then suddenly he added, "You know the old Crouch place out on Miller Street?"

Gabrielle nodded.

"They're trying to sell it."

"I know. It's a good house — but it's the Crouch place."

"I'll buy it," Ames said, "and it'll be the Conroy place."

Gabrielle shook her head. "People will say, 'Mr. Conroy? Oh, yes, he lives out at the old Crouch place.' It will *always* be the Crouch place."

Ames sat down, thinking about that.

"Now, there's a darling pie-shaped lot out on the dead end of Water Street," Gabrielle said. "They laid out the town kind of catty-cornered out there to leave a big tree standing in Colonel Brigg's side yard. I think it's all tied up in taxes and litigation, but I'm sure it could be straightened out."

Ames frowned. "I don't think I remember the tree."

"It was struck by lightning long before I was born, but Grandfather remembered it. The place is just short of an acre, and wedge-shaped."

"I'm caught up in it now," Ames thought. "The tiny strands of Ozarkanna. I'm going to have a house on a pie-shaped short acre. It's lucky that's the way I want it."

THERE WERE TWENTY people at Judge Milburn's house when Ames got there that afternoon. Presumably, they would hear of Gabrielle's engagement to Harry Weldon.

He stayed an hour, watching Gay, waiting. Finally, he left. He went to Joe's place, and questioned Joe for ten minutes. Then he departed on an errand that took him the rest of the afternoon.

About eight o'clock that evening he drove up to the Judge's house in the result of his search — an old-fashioned cutter drawn by a mettlesome bay gelding. They drew to a stop with a jingle of sleigh bells.

Ames was told that Gay was dressing. Presently, she appeared, looking deceptively demure in an off-the-shoulder beige satin evening dress.

"I didn't know you were going out," Ames lied, and added, "You look lovely," which was the truth.

"I'm sorry you didn't know," Gay said. "It's the dance at the Club. We have it every Christmas night."

"That's all right," Ames said. "I just wanted to show you something."

She followed him to the window and looked out. "A sleigh!" she exclaimed. "Where in the world —?"

"Oh, I tool about in my sleigh every Christmas night," Ames said. "It's an old Conroy tradition. I take people for rides who like to ride in sleighs."

"I haven't seen one since I was a little girl," Gay said. Then, "Harry's calling for me."

As if on cue, Harry Weldon's car came slowly through the snow and stopped behind the sleigh.

"Look," Ames said suddenly. "If you'd like a ride, why don't I take you to the Club? I am, by coincidence, equipped with a genuine buffalo robe, mint condition."

"I don't think it would be quite the thing to do," Gay said, but her voice lacked conviction.

She met Harry at the door. "Would you mind," she asked, "if I rode with Ames to the Club?"

Harry looked ruefully out of the window at the cutter. "No," he said. "I mean, yes, but what's the use? I wish I had thought of it myself."

THE HORSE trotted with spirit, and the runners sang on the crisp, dry snow. A warm, yellow, waning moon crawled over a tree-dappled hill and cooled to silver, climbing the sky.

Finally, nearing the Club, Ames pulled the horse to a walk. "How'd it go?" he said.

"Go? What?"

"The announcement."

"Oh. The announcement," Gay said slowly. "Oh that."

Ames didn't answer nor turn his head to look at her. He took her hand from under the robe, held it against his cheek a moment, then put it back under the robe.

"You've been trying very hard to be nice to me, haven't you?" she asked.

"Well, yes," he admitted, "I've been trying. Not pressing, I hope, but trying pretty hard."

"It's turned out very well, Ames. You've been nice to me."

"It's for myself," he said. "It's for me, if I have. It unshrivels my soul."

"Well, thanks a lot," Gay said, "In fact — a million."

They were near the clubhouse now. They could see the shiny cars parked in the frosty night; they could hear the music, the trumpet, fine and wonderful. He sighed, "Well, here you are."

He stopped the cutter, jumped down, and walked around the sleigh. He picked her up from the seat and swung her around and carried her to the cleared drive. "Have a time, baby," he said. He winked at her as Harry Weldon came down from the veranda, and he jumped back in the sleigh. "Okay, Prancer."

She called after him, "Thanks again, Ames."

He clucked the horse into a trot. "I got her worried," he said exultantly to himself. "She didn't announce her engagement."

He let the horse trot a hundred yards.

"What am I laughing about?" he said to the horse. "*She's* got *me* worried sick."

BY THE MIDDLE of March, winter was over. There would be a late frost or two, maybe a snowfall, but it wouldn't stay on the ground overnight. In the three months since Christmas, Ames had defended two men accused of robbery, one of assault, and one of manslaughter. He'd won them all but the last, which he didn't try, but settled for a minimum sentence, because the man was obviously guilty.

One day Ames sauntered down Main Street toward Bailey's Garage, near the railroad. Everyone he passed nodded to him now, or spoke.

He found Jim Bailey under a car in the back of his shop.

Ames said, "They tell me you've got some used cars for sale."

Bailey slid into the open and sat up. "That's right, Mr. Conroy. Are you in the market?"

"I've been in Ozarkanna six months. How long do I have to be here for a guy my own age, who fought in the same war, to call me by my first name?"

Bailey grinned, embarrassed. He didn't answer.

Ames shrugged. "Well, it was a good try, Mr. Bailey. Leave us see some chariots."

Bailey laughed outright. "Okay, Ames. Hasn't anybody in this town called me 'Mister' since I was born. Come on and I'll show you what I've got." They went out back. "They're all too high," Bailey said, "but I figure they'll stay up a while…. Nope — quit lookin' at that one. I wouldn't sell a comrade-in-arms that car. Not 'til I've worked on it."

Ames finally found one that Bailey would sell him.

"I know this car," Bailey said. "Rebored it myself." It was eight years old and not a great deal to look at. But Jim Bailey guaranteed it.

Ames took it without further questioning. "And now I wonder if you'd throw in a little advice for nothing."

"Sure," said Bailey.

"Ever since that Stepper Keith case," Ames said, "I've been wondering what would happen if I ran for prosecuting attorney."

Bailey thought about it for a while. "I think you'd lose," he said finally.

Ames said, "I know, they always elect a man two terms in this county, and that gives Weldon one more time around. But I thought if I sort of went out and made a few calls, it might get people to know who I am. Then I could run again next time."

"Seems like a good idea," Bailey said.

"You don't think it would make anybody sore? Make 'em think I was too pushy?"

"I don't see why it should. If a man don't push in politics, he's not going to get very far. Why don't you just tell 'em what you're doing — the way you told me?"

Ames grinned. "I guess you know what I'm doing without being told. A lawyer can advertise, but he can't get along any more than a guy like you if nobody knows him. I'd really be campaigning two years ahead. Your advice is to go ahead?"

Bailey nodded. "I think I would," he said.

Ames thanked him, got in his new car, and drove way. "He's advised me to campaign," he thought. "He'd just about have to vote for me. Can I go from man to man through a whole county like that? Can I think up different ways to get them on my side?"

HE TURNED into Market Street and stopped thinking about anything else but Gay Milburn. He parked in front of her house, went up the walk, and rang the bell. She came to the door in a house dress and apron.

"I wanted to show you what I have bought," he said. He nodded toward the car at the curb. "I would have consulted you before I decided — you know, color, upholstery, all the things dear to the homemaker's heart — but my buying range is limited."

She looked at him, levelly, and he returned her gaze blandly. At last she laughed. "Really!" she said.

"How about coming for a ride?" he asked.

"I'm busy."

"Or perhaps you don't want to run the chance of being seen with me."

"Why not?"

"Well, being engaged to Harry Weldon and all —"

"Oh, for heaven's sake!" she exclaimed. "Wait a minute."

She went in for her coat, and Ames grinned to himself. In a moment she reappeared, and they went to the car.

As they started, Ames said, "They smoke a lot of

ham in this county, I understand. Who's the best at it?"

She considered briefly. "Abel Grant."

"Where does he live?"

She told him, and he turned the car. She looked at him questioningly, but he didn't let on that he noticed.

"When will you marry me?" he said.

She kept looking at him, but he didn't take his eyes from the road.

"Are you really that sure of yourself?" she said finally.

He said slowly, "No — I guess maybe I'm not. But I'm mighty determined."

"You don't believe in — well, I guess the word is courting — before asking such questions?"

"I believe in whatever is necessary to get what you're after," he said. "I could tell you I'm mad about you. I could get you out under a moon some night and repeat the prescribed formulas for such occasions. They wouldn't be any truer — or less true — than they always are."

"I'm afraid you're a dreadful cynic, Mr. Conroy." she mocked.

"Oh, no," he said cheerfully. "I believe in love, all right. I just don't believe it happens quite as fast as it's supposed to. I don't think more than maybe one out of a thousand couples do love each other before they marry. It isn't possible."

She didn't answer that.

"Do you love Harry Weldon?" Ames asked casually.

"That," she replied, "is a question that could be asked only by an unscrupulous lawyer."

He chuckled, and dropped the subject. "Tell me about this Abel Grant," he said.

BY THE TIME Gay had given him an account of why Grant's hams were the best in Hill County, they had arrived at the farm. Ames found Grant, lean and middle-aged, in the barn, mending harness.

Ames told him who he was, explained that he was thinking of running for prosecuting attorney.

"I'm for Harry Weldon," Abel Grant told him, without even thinking about it, "strong as horse radish."

"That's honest," Ames said. "You vote for him. It's not going to matter to me really, one way or the other, because, as I told you, I have no idea of winning. What I mostly want is a chance to get acquainted around the county." He paused, smiled. "Miss Milburn tells me," he added, "that you smoke the best hams in the county."

"Gay Milburn?" Abel Grant said in surprise.

Ames nodded. "She's out in the car."

"Why didn't she get out?"

"I guess she thought she wasn't dressed for calling."

Abel Grant strode indignantly around the house, and was somewhat mollified to find that Gay had gone inside to talk to his wife.

"Well!" he said signifying that that put a different light on the matter. "I didn't think Gay Milburn would have to dress up to call on her old friends."

The visit lasted about a half-hour. When it was over, and the farmer and his wife were walking back to the car with them, Ames said to Grant, "Come next fall, will you give me a chance to buy one of your hams?"

"I'll give you one," Grant said. He shook hands heartily. "And I'm glad you came by."

"By the way," Ames said as he got into the car, "who lives on the next farm?"

"Some of the Joiners."

"Party people?"

"Yeah." Grant's voice was uninterested. "But a shiftless lot."

After a round of goodbyes Ames drove away. In about a half-mile they could see the Joiner house. The senior and limpest of the clan half reclined on the front porch in a broken rocker. From there he could survey the road, a weedy garden, and serial pieces of discarded and broken farm machinery that littered the front yard.

Ames stopped the car so that a tree hid it from the front porch.

"I'll only be a minute," he told Gay. He got out and walked across the unkempt front yard. He introduced himself, explained his mission. His name was known, of course, because he had almost defended one of the family.

"I was anxious to see you," Ames said. "Fellow next door's for Weldon, he tells me. Man gets kind of discouraged, even if he isn't figuring on winning."

"So he's strong for Weldon, is he?" Mr. Joiner spat over the rail. "Well, they ain't but him and his old lady, and they's a passel of us Joiners."

It became all very comradely.

When Ames came back to the car, Gay said, "One would almost get the impression that you were running for office."

"Would one?" He grinned.

"It doesn't particularly amuse me," she said. "I don't like being used."

"I wish I could say I'm sorry," he said.

"The Grants are old friends. You deliberately let them think there was something between us. It seems a bit crude."

"It would be," he answered amiably, "if there were any real chance of your marrying anybody but me."

She declined to answer. But, though Ames kept his eyes on the road, he knew she stole a puzzled glance at him from time to time. "She can't hate me," he thought. "She can't even be angry very long — you can't hold anger against anybody who loves you."

Half a mile ahead he could see the grouped buildings of another farm. A perverse impulse made him ease his foot off the accelerator.

"I wonder who lives up there?" he said. "Know their names?"

He turned, to find her eyes on him, wide with incredulous anger. He grinned.

"I know their names," she said. Her voice was startlingly quiet. "Galway."

"I might as well stop in," Ames said.

AS HE BROUGHT the car to a stop, Gay turned and looked at him. Her eyes were grave. She said, "Are you going to let them think — about us —?"

"I can't deny you're here," Ames said. "I'll tell Mr. Galway we aren't formally engaged if that'll make you feel better."

She said, "Ames —" She stopped. He went on.

John Galway, a man of about forty, was taking a bale of straw into his cow barn from a tarp-covered stack in the yard. He stopped when he saw Ames.

"My name's Conroy," Ames said when he was close enough.

Galway nodded. His hand, which he didn't offer, was enormous, with fingers perpetually curved.

Ames said, "I've been sort of driving around the county, getting acquainted."

He stopped and smiled, but Galway didn't say anything.

"To tell the truth," he said frankly, "I've got political ambitions, and so long as I was just driving by —"

"My eyes are all right," John Galway said in a flat voice. "I seen you from a quarter-mile down the road. You and that Milburn she-devil."

It was one of those things that simply can't happen. But Galway was still speaking:

"I can't do nothin' about the high road. But you can get offa my property right now. And I'd just as lief you wouldn't leave your car out front with her in it. Spoils the look of my place."

Ames heard all this with only half his brain, but he acted, instinctively. Remembering to set Galway up with a left, he clubbed him in the belly with his right. He felt as if he'd hit a washboard, then something fell on him, taking him under the eye, and he went down.

He scrambled to his feet, just as Galway moved toward him again, and this time Ames fought with his head, too. He raked the man's face with a long left and moved back, to the side, and tried downstairs again. The washboard bent a little, and he brought his right up and felt it connect with the point of Galway's chin. Galway went down.

Ames turned and walked toward the car. He felt the big mouse rising on his cheek, closing his eye. He got in the car and started it without a word.

"I was going to tell you," Gay said a little shakily, after a hundred silent yards, "that Dad sent Mr. Galway to the penitentiary once when *he* was prosecuting attorney. He's hated the Milburn's ever since."

Ames said, "Oh."

"Did he say anything about the Milburns?"

"Nope."

"Did he say anything at all?"

Ames turned to her, and the big welt under his eye pulled his face off center and made his grin crooked. "He said he didn't believe he'd vote for me."

Gay's eyes were wide; she looked scared and

miserable, strangely childlike. She tried to speak, but the tears welled out and down her cheeks.

"Okay," he said gruffly, turning back to the road. "Skip it."

ALL THAT SPRING he made his way through the county. He never made a speech, and he made no effort to line up the so-called leaders. But he saw everybody. He even hit the shanty-boats — sixty registered voters of the opposition party. They hung together, a solid front. But Ames knew he'd cracked it for one vote: Stepper Keith's. It wasn't much, but Ames wasn't overlooking anything.

On the first Tuesday following the first Monday in August, the sun walked up the sky like a round brass ingot pulled slowly from a fire with invisible tongs.

The asphalt bubbled in the gutters of Main Street, the consistency of chewing gum, and it looked to Ames, hauling voters to the polls since six o'clock, that there wasn't a Conroy supporter who could get to the voting booths under his or her own power.

But he got them out, with hired cars and workers. He got out all his vote, knowing it wouldn't be enough.

When the polls closed, he went wearily to the crowded courthouse. Harry Weldon was there. So was Judge Milburn.

Ames told Harry Weldon, "I suppose I ought to wait until the returns are all in before I congratulate you."

"It will be close," Weldon said without malice. "Surprising."

"Nothing," Judge Milburn said, "responds to work like a political race. Ames, you made a remarkable campaign."

"Thorough," Ames corrected wearily.

The returns started coming in. Almost to a vote, Ames could have called them. Bristle Ridge: Weldon 67, Conroy 92. Post Oak: Conroy 36, Weldon 50. They came on in.

"I'd have to come to town with a five hundred majority," Ames said, "to win."

"Would you?" Harry Weldon said.

"Yeah. You must have gone to school a long time. Ozarkanna seems to be composed entirely of your old school-mates."

"A man makes friends, I guess," Harry Weldon said.

Ozarkanna came in. First ward: Weldon 421, Conroy 26.

"It looks like you carried the out-county by three hundred," Judge Milburn said, making his way back through the crowd. "Really remarkable."

"That won't be enough," Ames said.

Second Ward: Weldon 309, Conroy 231.

"I do better with the not-so-near neighbors," Ames said. "I forgot for a minute that you lived in the first."

Third Ward: Weldon 245, Conroy 222.

Ames walked over to the big board. The returns were all in except the Fourth Ward.

Ames slid his arm out and looked at his watch. It was ten minutes of nine. Mentally, he added the figures on the board.

"In the stretch," he said, "it's Weldon 2,208, Conroy 2,191."

THE PHONE RANG. "Here comes the Fourth at last," Judge Milburn said. "I wonder why they are so slow."

The clerk was talking into the phone. "Give me that again."

There was a long wait. "They did?" the clerk said. Finally, he put down the phone and paused, dramatically. "I'll read the returns on the Prosecutor's race first," he said.

"Well, go ahead," Judge Milburn said impatiently.

"Conroy 290, Weldon 244," the clerk said slowly. Then he added, "Sixty shanty-boaters appeared at the polls at sundown, swore to affidavits that they would support the party ticket in the fall, and voted."

There was a long vacuum of shock. Then Weldon said, "It looks like every one of them that switched over, voted for you, Ames."

The corners of Ames's mouth turned down in a wry grin and he said, "Yeah — I suppose so. A man makes friends." There lay the lot; a short acre, pie-shaped. It had been cheap in money, but expensive in time and work, as it was deeply enmeshed with overlapping tax liens. It was a bare brown hill. But it was his, the first piece of ground he'd ever owned.

And so, the day after primary election, Ames Conroy, Prosecuting Attorney-elect, drove out to inpsect his property.

He parked the car near where he figured the driveway would curve in from the road to the house. He got out and walked slowly up the rise to where the ground leveled off.

Ozarkanna lay below him, no longer a strange, unfriendly town. The courthouse dome, rising above its surrounding elms, was an important landmark to him now.

It was funny the feeling that owning land gave you. Not merely pride, nor the sense of accomplishment. "Interest" was the word, he guessed. He felt interested and important. The ground itself was important to him now.

He scuffed the ground with his shoe. It was dry from the long summer heat, and the grass was dead. But if you dug a little it would be black and damp. Good ground. He looked around, seeing visions of rows of vegetables, neatly laid out. He grinned to himself. Better let that wait a bit. No use planning a vegetable plot in what might turn out to be the living-room floor.

He went back to the road. In the back of the car was a hedge post Mr. Greer had got for him. He'd lent Ames a post-hole digger. Ames walked along the front of his land, figured out the best place to put the post, and started to dig.

A car came up the hill and stopped where he was working. Gay Milburn was at the wheel.

"Hello," she said. "You're starting work on your house sort of early, aren't you?"

"I'm just putting in this post," Ames told her. "Quite a job." He picked up the digger again.

When the time came to set the post, Gay got out of the car and held it for him. He pulled in dirt, tamping it around the post with the handles of the digger.

"Should have been set in concrete, I suppose," he said. "But I know even less about concrete than I do about tamping dirt — and I didn't want anybody else to do it."

Gay nodded.

Ames looked at her a moment, undecided. Then he shrugged. She'd know some time, anyway — everybody would. It was nothing to be ashamed of.

He went over to his car and took out a large, tunnel-shaped mailbox of aluminum-painted metal. Inscribed on it in bold black lacquer was his name. He stole a glance at Gay, but he could see no sign that she was tempted to laugh.

"I thought I'd get this up," he said, fitting it on the post. "I'll be coming out here pretty much every day, so I might as well get my mail here, too."

Gay nodded and said, "It looks like a good box. I hate those little dinky ones."

Ames felt good. When he had finished with the box, he took her on a tour of the short acre.

"It's wonderful, Ames," she said. "Nobody can ever build near enough to block you off in any direction. I've always thought this was one of the best lots in town."

"Really?" Ames said, pleased.

Gay looked back toward the road. "Here comes the mailman," she said.

As if they understood it to be a natural thing to do, they went back to the mailbox. The car stopped behind Gay's and the mailman got out. His name was Chauncy Barriss; he was from over near Post Oak, and he'd been an RFD carrier for twenty years. Ames had met him on his electioneering trips around the county.

He said, "Hello, Chauncy."

The mailman nodded, more interested in the box than in Ames. "Nice box," he said. He put a letter in it and slammed the door shut.

"Vote for me yesterday?" Ames asked.

Chauncy Barris looked at him, and a grin crept over his weathered face. "I'll sure vote for you in November," he said. He held out his hand, and Ames took it. "Good luck," Chauncy said.

Ames watched the car until it dipped below the rise. Then he turned to the box, took out the letter.

"'Supreme Court' —" He read the return address on the envelope aloud. "You don't suppose they're offering me a place on the bench already, do you?"

He tore open the envelope, unfolded the single sheet. He read silently: "It has come to the attention of this Court through the testimony of one Rolly Henderson —" Ames's eyes leaped to the end of the letter: " — to appear before this Court and show cause why you should not be disbarred."

Ames did not move. He stood there, his eyes on that one word, "disbarred."

"Ames!" Gay was at his side. "What is it? Tell me."

"Nothing —"

She took the letter out of his hand. There was a silence, a long silence. "Is it true?" she asked.

"No." The detached half of himself said, "That isn't a lie. I didn't pass the examinations on stolen questions. I bought stolen questions, but they didn't do me any good. I'm not lying, technically. A man on trial for his life has a right to any technicalities he can use — and this is my life."

"Then what is there to worry about?" Gay asked.

"The truth won't make much difference," he said.

"It will to you," she said. "And to me."

AMES DIDN'T LOOK at her. He fought a sudden impulse to smash at the new mailbox with his fist.

Gay took him by the arms. "Ames," she said. "Look at me."

He looked at her. Her eyes seemed to be searching for something behind his own. Words raced through his mind. He let them all go and said the ones that came last. "I couldn't drag you through all that," he said.

Gay said, her eyes still on his, "Do you think if I loved a guy, it would make any difference to me what I was dragged through?"

A moment of torturing self-consciousness almost made him turn and run. So often he had resisted an impulse to take her in his arms. Then, without his knowing how it happened, she was there and he was holding her hard, desperately hard. With the evening, it had become cooler, and Gabrielle had thrown a jacket of Ames's across her shoulders. Wrapped in it, she felt wrapped in his love. It was a married thing to do.

She glanced up at him, and his eyes crept from the road and met hers. She laughed a little shyly.

"Say it, baby," Ames said.

"What?"

"You wonder what you've got, don't you?"

"I got my guy," Gabrielle said. "I got Mr. Conroy, my true love." She looked at her watch. "We've been married two hours. You wear wonderfully as a husband."

Ames grinned.

They had been married at the Milburns' home in the afternoon. Ames remembered the pounding in his throat as Gabrielle came down the stairs on her father's arm. It was a moment when he had been completely unaware of himself, and he remembered it with a kind of pride. But now he was thinking, whether he wanted to or not, of Rolly Henderson, and the charge that he would have to answer before the State Supreme Court that he had bought questions to the bar examination from Rolly.

That was why Gabrielle and he were honeymooning in the capital. The night clerk at the hotel grinned at him knowingly, and walking behind the bellboy to the elevator, Ames said to Gabrielle, "Marriage brands you, doesn't it?"

She held his arm and said, "Yeah, man!" and then they were in the elevator.

They followed the boy down the hall, and he opened their door and put the bags down, opened the window.

Ames said, not tipping the boy, not looking in the bathroom, "Go get me some big towels, a couple of bars of soap, and tell room service I want a bottle of champagne, Pol Roget '29" — he'd prepared on that one —"and leave the transom closed and don't monkey with the radiator. And bring some more coat hangers when you bring the towels."

The boy grinned and left.

Gay watched her husband snap open his luggage, start unpacking. "How practiced you are," she said.

He stopped and looked at her, and then said slowly, "I'm home, baby."

She just looked at him.

"I lived off and on in hotels for twenty years. They're pretty much all alike." He smiled a little crookedly.

"Oh, darling." Gay's eyes were soft and she came over and put her hands on his shoulders and kissed him. "Oh, darling, darling —"

Now that he was facing his accusers, Ames' nervousness vanished.

AMES PICKED her up and carried her to a chair. He knelt down beside her and said, "I'm the luckiest guy in the whole world." He paused, feeling her hand in his hair. He went on, "I told you I was going to marry you, but I didn't believe it. I couldn't believe it. I said it aloud to you, and I wrote it on little bits of paper to try and make it so."

"You made it so."

"*You* made it so —"

The boy knocked, brought in the towels, the soap, the hangers. He let in the man from the bar with the bucket of champagne and the glasses. Ames tipped them both too much.

When they left, Ames poured two glasses of champagne. "Stay the same, Gay," he said.

She was gone after a little while, and he sat, the thoughts churning through his head. The wedding service came back to him, word for freighted word, like a record in his mind.

And Gay came back in negligee and stood before him, her eyes frightened and melting, and he stood up and moved toward her. He said, "My lovely wife."

"I'm glad you said that word."

They were having breakfast in their room, and it was the third day of their stay in the capital. Gay was looking at him, her eyes reflective. "And," she said, "I thought I loved you when I married you."

"Didn't you?"

"So much more now."

Ames looked at her, and a sudden wave almost of resentment swept over him. This was the day he was to appear before the Supreme Court — and she cared only about keeping intact the mood of the honeymoon.

He stood up abruptly. He said, "I'm due in court at ten."

Her eyes didn't leave him. What else could a woman offer a man at a time like this except her love? "And I don't want anything else," Ames thought, suddenly contrite.

"I wish I could be there," she said.

"You will be — in my heart." He leaned down and kissed her.

ROLLY HENDERSON stood below the bench, and the seven black-robed figures watched him, listening. Ames fidgeted, wanting a cigarette.

Rolly told his story, omitting only that the questions had been the wrong ones. He finished, looked at Ames, and then looked away.

Ames sat still. Finally the presiding judge said, "Mr. Conroy."

Ames stood up and walked to the bench.

"The Bar Examining Committee," the judge

said, "found a number of papers of such startling similarity and such patent and unimaginative correctness that an investigation seemed warranted. As a result of their investigation, Rolly Henderson was arrested. He confessed to selling the questions, which he had stolen. You are named as one of the purchasers."

Now that it was happening, now that he was standing up in court, Ames's nervousness vanished. He felt good, in command of the situation.

Ames said, "Your Honors, I have been summoned before you to show cause why I should not be disbarred —"

Like a lawyer, half his mind said, "Not too fast. See that the proper foundation is laid for everything." Then he nearly chuckled aloud, because, suddenly, he saw exactly what he was going to do.

He went on, "I am summoned here on the strength of a statement by one Rolly Henderson that I bought from him a copy of the questions for the bar examinations. Now, as I understand it, Your Honor" — he faced the judge who had last spoken — "Henderson was arrested as the result of an investigation, which, in turn, was made because the Bar Examining Committee found a 'number of papers of such startling similarity and such patent and unimaginative correctness that an investigation seemed warranted.'"

The judge, smiling almost imperceptibly at this verbatim quotation, nodded.

"Did you find in my papers," Ames asked, "a 'startling similarity' to any other papers?"

"No," the judge said.

"Colonel Anderson, the Chairman of the Committee," said Ames, "told me after the examination that I had turned in a pretty good set of answers. Would you, Your Honor, describe them as having 'patent and unimaginative correctness'?"

The judge glanced at one of his colleagues, then said, "No."

Ames looked at Rolly Henderson.

"Next," he said, "I should like to cite the case of the Commonwealth v. Rolly Henderson some years ago. I have purposely not looked up the date of the trial. It happens to be a date which, for a purely personal and, I am afraid, rather cowardly reason I don't want to remember."

AMES STOPPED and looked at the floor, knowing he had the judges' full attention.

"It was a few days after one of my father's wedding anniversaries," Ames said. "That is a date I've never known exactly, a date I've never wanted to know. Perhaps you can understand that," he went on, his voice lower. "My mother died when I was four, and my father never quite got over it. He used to get drunk on his wedding anniversary, and stay drunk for several days. It was after coming out of one of those bouts that he appeared in court to defend Mr. Henderson on a felony charge. He was suffering from a hangover, and he pleaded Mr. Henderson guilty."

Ames looked at Rolly Henderson. The little man's face was red, contorted in a grimace of hate.

"Rolly Henderson placed some rather forceful curses on my father as the result of the incident — on my father and all his posterity. Rolly Henderson did offer to sell me the questions, of course, but even if I had been inclined to buy them, I should have hesitated to take my trade to this man."

Ames looked at Rolly Henderson, and this time he smiled. He could feel the judges on his side now.

"Two years before his death," Ames said, "my father was disbarred. I suppose it might be assumed that disbarment runs in the Conroy family, like a disease. Or perhaps disbarment was only the end symptom of a deeper weakness, and perhaps I inherited that. A tendency, let us say, toward disbarment."

Ames stood up a little straighter.

"My father," he said, "was disbarred for bribing a juror. The action was proper and deserved, and he knew it. My father's action showed a lack of faith in himself, a lack of faith, we may say for the purposes of my argument, that I have inherited. But my father's action showed no lack of faith in the validity of the law and the dignity of the courts. He believed in those things, and if I could not biologically have inherited that belief, I assure you my father never ceased trying to teach it to me. For me to have bought those questions from Rolly Henderson, I would have had to descend to a level of self-distrust that was reached, in my father's case, only after years of drinking."

He stopped for a moment, timing the silence instinctively.

"But I would also have needed," Ames went on,

simply now, "a contempt for the law as an institution, and of the courts as the instrument of the law, that my father never reached. It would have been a contempt so deep that it must have shown in my every action since I have become a member of the bar. Your Honors — I rest my case."

THERE WAS A SHORT silence, and then one of the other judges said, "We're sure that there was never any real feeling on the part of the Examining Committee that you were guilty, Mr. Conroy."

The first judge said, "The wording of the letter sent you was a matter of formality. You have stated your case ably. I think" — he glanced at his colleagues and smiled slightly —"I think we can say that your case is dismissed."

"Thank you," Ames said.

A third judge said, "There will be an action for perjury against this man Henderson."

"They talk about him as if he weren't here," Ames thought. "Well, he isn't — not really. The Hendersons of the world don't matter — even to themselves."

"I hope you won't be too hard on him," he said.

No one answered that. Henderson was taken away and the Court recessed.

Ames said goodbye to the judges. It was saying goodbye to friends now.

He went slowly out the big doors of the courtroom; he came into the sunlight and looked across at the Governor's mansion. Then he turned and looked down at the gray block of the prison by the river. The Governor's term was four years. The maximum for perjury was seven. He tried to feel an amused pity of Rolly Henderson. Instead, he thought of Gay, and suddenly he was troubled. He looked at himself, and what he saw, for the first time, was not good.

The somber mood deepened by the time he got back to the hotel.

Gay was sitting before a mirror in their room, when he came in, trying on a hat he had never seen. She looked up no said, "Hello, darling." Her level eyes searched his for a moment, and then she added, "Did they apologize?"

"Yes," he said, "they apologized."

She rose and kissed him.

He said, "I love you, Gay."

That evening, Ames got slightly but firmly drunk.

AMES STOPPED by his property the day after their return to Ozarkanna. Some time before the wedding he had got an architect down from River City, and he and Gay had seen sketches of their house. Meanwhile, they were living in a furnished apartment.

He pulled off the road and stopped where the flagstone walk would lead to the front door. A half-dozen men were busy on the foundation and the wall of stone masonry that was beginning to take form around its edges. Ames knew them all by their first names.

They called him Ames. They didn't ask him what he thought of the work so far; they knew he liked it. This house was going to be built right; it was an Ozarkanna house for an Ozarkanna man who was one of them.

That was the thing. A house was important, but a man's roots had to go deeper than that; they had to go down among the people he lived with.

As he went to the office he got thinking about his timetable. Now that he had a place in the world, now that he belonged somewhere, he could move along faster. He would take office as prosecuting attorney in January, but a man could die, politically, in that job. Unless he was smart enough to create his own opportunity.

It wasn't until March that his chance came. The man was about fifty. He wore a jacket made in England, bright heather, a nice match for a complexion bonded in Kentucky. He groped with his right hand for a bottle on the seat beside him, took a swig, and laid it down again.

There were a hundred and sixty horses under the long hood of the big sedan he drove, and he goaded them gently with his right toe on the accelerator. The man looked at the clock on the dash. The sign wavering insecurely in the breeze at the right side of the road said STOP.

The boy rode out of a side road on his bicycle.

The big wheels of the sedan screamed and the car slowed. The man got out of the door away from the wheel and picked up the whisky bottle and tossed it in the weeds and ran back to the boy.

The boy was sitting in the ditch, screwing his face to cry, his left leg folded grotesquely at his side. A woman was running from a cabin on the right.

Suddenly there were several people.

The man looked at his watch. He reached for his wallet and gave the woman some money. He turned to a man beside her who had climbed out of his car, and arranged to have the boy taken to a hospital.

When they had all gone, the man walked down the shoulder on the right side of his car, stooped for the whisky bottle in the weeds. He dropped it into his side pocket and got in his big car and started it up. He drove off slowly.

THE NEXT DAY the paper carried a couple of obscure paragraphs about the incident. Ames called the editor of the *Courier* and asked who the driver of the car was. His name was George Holcome, a man of some wealth and prominence in River City. Ames asked his friend the editor, jokingly, if the *Courier's* story was brief because of Holcome's position — and the next day there was a slightly larger story.

It grew. With judicious handling, it grew.

Then came the day in court.

Ames said quietly to the judge, "I have a statement to make."

Harry Weldon sat with his client, George Holcome, who was a little pale and quite sober.

Ames said, "A city slicker, a big shot, drunk, hurtles his big car through a small town and crushes the leg of a poor widow's son. He contemptuously gives the poor widow a few dollars and goes on. Then he writes back to his lawyer.

"The poor but honest prosecuting attorney files charges of drunken driving against this big shot. The underdog is not ground down in Hill County without a fight."

Ames paused, waiting for Harry Weldon to say something. Harry Weldon remained quiet. Ames looked out of the window. He saw people walking around the courthouse square, people he knew by name now. He thought, errantly of Rolly Henderson. Well — if Rolly didn't do time for perjury, he'd do it for something else. Rolly Henderson was born for trouble.

Ames wheeled, said almost fiercely. "I made a mistake. I went out to that corner and took a picture, and the picture showed I had made a mistake."

George Holcome *wasn't* drunk. There is no evidence that he'd been drinking. And Tom Allgood did run *his* STOP sign on his bicycle. George Holcome arranged for Tom to be taken care of, gave Mrs. Allgood money.

He took a picture from the table and handed it up to the judge.

"Mr. Holcome couldn't see the STOP sign that he was supposed to obey. It was gone, so he couldn't see it. The picture proves it."

He was silent, and all the eyes in the courtroom were upon him. "They can't see inside my mind, though," he thought.

"The picture proves the STOP sign was gone, all right. It's gone, because I went out at night and knocked it off before the picture was taken. It was loose, anyway — all I had to do was give it a shove."

He straightened and faced the judge. "I will not prosecute a man," he said, "for not obeying a sign that wasn't there. I won't prosecute a man for drunken driving when he wasn't drunk." He stopped, then added harshly, "I am dismissing this action for lack of evidence."

When it was over, of course, the reporters wanted a statement.

"Look, boys," Ames said; "you've got to go easy on me. I'm in a rough spot here. This case has had a lot of publicity, and no matter what I did the chances are that it would have been wrong. If I prosecute, I'm out for cheap notoriety for knocking over a prominent citizen. If I don't, I'm toadying to the interests. Do me a favor and just forget it."

But he had an idea they wouldn't forget it, and of course they didn't.

The story made front pages all over the state. One River City paper even had a short editorial. The Governor was planning to appoint a Crime Commission. The Chairmanship would have political significance. Why not, the editorial suggested, go outside the ranks of the party regulars for the man to fill it? Why not a man who was interested in seeing justice done first — and in his career second? In any case, Ames Conroy was a man worth watching.

AMES LEFT GAY doing her hair, stepped out into the hall, and closed the door softly behind him. The first guests for their housewarming wouldn't show up for an hour at least. He hadn't had a chance to walk around the house by himself yet, and he wanted to do that. Never in his life had there been anything like this, solid and enduring — and his.

From downstairs he could hear the dim party-preparation sounds. He didn't want to walk around the downstairs, though. The first floor of anybody's home was pretty much public property. The upstairs was the family part of a house, where people lived and loved and were born, got sick and well, and at last died. All his life he'd never been able to go to the upper floor of a house without feeling like an intruder, but now this upper floor was his.

The room Gay and he shared was on the southeast corner. There were two more bedrooms along the front of the house, all furnished, as the entire house, from that miraculously inexhaustible supply of fine old furniture that Judge Milburn had stored away.

The room at the southwest corner was Ames's study. From its window he could see the bunched elms and the dome of the courthouse in the midst of them.

Then he remembered the appointment to the Crime Commission and he knew that he wasn't really going to spend much time in the Ozarkanna courthouse or in his study.

But this was an important room, the most important part of the Conroy place. The realization came to him; he just hadn't seen it until now.

He wanted a son. This was a boy's room, a place where a kid could live and grow up. It wouldn't have much character until this boy put it there, with the pictures and posters and books, or whatever it was that boys decorated their rooms with. He'd never had a room of his own, so he didn't have a real idea. But this kid would have it; and he'd be able to look up from his desk when he was studying and see the dome of the courthouse, and he'd think, "That's where my old man got his start. My father, Ames Conroy."

A son. That was the next thing.

Ames went quietly out of the room, the way you'd walk out of a room if there was a baby asleep in it. He went back through the hall, and into his and Gay's room. Gay was still at her dressing table. She had finished her hair; she was just sitting there, looking in the mirror.

He walked over to one of the windows. "It's a wonderful house, Gay," he said. "I never knew how a house should be until you made this one."

Gay said, "Thank you," in a low voice.

He turned and walked over to her. "My beautiful wife," he said.

SHE LOOKED UP at him, smiled almost imperceptibly, then looked away again.

He took her hand. "I got to thinking about something," he said.

She looked at him again, her eyes calm.

"That room," Ames said. "My study. It isn't really my room."

"No?" She didn't seem surprised.

"No. It's a kid's room, Gay."

She looked at him with a cool and level regard. "Is this the first time you've thought of that?" she asked.

"I guess it is," he said.

Gay said, "You'll want a son?"

"I'd be glad if it were a son," he said.

Gay looked down; she was silent and thoughtful for a long time. "I'd hope my child was a son, if that's the way you wanted it," she said finally. "I'm afraid, though, that I'm a little bit old-fashioned. I've never been able to look on children as simply matters of biology," she said. "Loving the father would be the most important part — to me."

"Don't you love me?" He said it before he thought, then grinned.

She didn't smile, but there was a flicker of expression in her eyes that might almost be called longing before she looked away. "Ames," she said, "why did you dismiss the Holcome case?"

"Would you want me to try to convict an innocent man?"

"Why do you think he's innocent?"

"That may be too strong a way of putting it. Let me say it this way: It's my sworn duty to prosecute cases against people accused of crime. If it seems to me that they are guilty beyond a reasonable doubt, I try to persuade a jury to convict them."

"You think there's a doubt about George Holcome's guilt?"

"Yes, I do."

The short silence was broken by the sound of a car on the gravel drive.

"We'd better go," she said rising.

He followed her to the door and out.

"I feel left hanging in the air," he said in the hall. "There's something on your mind, Gay. What is it?"

"Nothing," she said. "Only that —"

"Only what?" he prompted.

"You didn't ask me what the connection was between our having a baby and your dismissing the Holcome case," she said. "I wish you had. I wish you had known without having to ask."

He followed her downstairs.

The first guests were Jim and Harriet Bailey, and for a few minutes there was no chance to talk about anything but the house. Then Whit Sales, the freight agent, and his wife came, and after that it was as if a human log jam had broken.

Everybody in town was there.

After the gigantic shuffle attending the buffet supper, Ames found himself in a group that included Harry Weldon. And, as he had expected and hoped, it was Harry who mentioned the editorial in the River City paper.

Ames grinned. "It was just delayed retribution, Harry. I was getting back at you for dismissing that case against my first client in Ozarkanna."

"You saved me a few bad days in court, anyway." Harry Weldon laughed.

Ames became serious. "What worries me a little, though, is that I am sure there are lots of folks in town who aren't convinced deep down in their hearts that I really believe Holcome is innocent."

He looked at Harry, and Harry nodded.

"Convicting a man about whose guilt there is a reasonable doubt," Ames went on, "is injustice. If I can prevent it, I mustn't let it happen, no matter how many people suspect me of ulterior motives."

"Harry," he went on, "I look on you as an honest man. Let me ask you this: Did you feel that there was a reasonable doubt about George Holcome's guilt?"

"Of course I did," Harry said. "I was defending him."

Ames shrugged. "Then I'm sure you understand how I could feel the same way."

He turned and saw that Gay had been sitting at a card table near him. She had heard everything that was said, and when he turned around, their eyes met. He knew, then, that there was at least one person in the room who didn't believe him.

WHEN THE LAST GUEST had gone, Ames and Gay stood a moment in silence in the empty hall. He looked squarely at her without smiling. "You think I was lying, don't you?"

She nodded without hesitation.

Ames shrugged. "I guess there's nothing for me to say, then."

She smiled, and it was a gentle smile. She said, "There's nothing for anybody to say. But maybe there's one point I ought to clear up. My deciding to marry you."

"It wasn't the wrong decision, was it?"

She didn't answer that. She said, "What I meant was that I made the decision quite a while before you thought I did. A couple of weeks after you arrived in Ozarkanna, to be exact. I fell in love with what you were — everything."

"But you might have been wrong on one or two points?" he asked.

"If I was," she answered, "and if they were important points —" She stopped.

He looked at her. "It would be the moment to take her in my arms," he thought. "Only, she isn't a woman you sweep off her feet. I know that now. I thought I married a woman. What I really married was a whole world, and you don't sweep a world off its feet."

THE NEXT DAY a telephone call came to Ames's office. It was the Governor, asking if Ames could come up to the capital the next day for a little talk. Ames said he certainly could.

He hung up and sat at his desk, wondering why he felt no elation. Wondering why something cold and like fear touched him at the pit of the stomach. But he didn't have to wonder long. His subconscious mind knew, even before he did, that tomorrow was the twelfth of the month — the day Rolly Henderson would finish his sentence for the purloining of the bar examination questions and go on trial for perjury, maximum sentence, seven years.

He had an impulse to sit down and talk the whole thing over with Gay. But this wasn't one of those workaday problems that a man discusses with his wife. This was his entire career. This was his marriage and his son and his future as he had planned it so long and so carefully. If Gay had lived through it all with him, she could understand how he felt now; but it was hard to explain.... He told her only that he was going to River City to see the Governor.

"And," he said, "it would be a good chance for you to come along and do some shopping."

"It would, wouldn't it?" she answered. "I don't think I will this time though, thanks. Too much to do here."

He nodded, taking this in silence. Then he said, "I can't help feeling this is something we ought to talk about, Gay. The Governor may have something in mind. Something that might have quite a bearing on our future."

She said, "I go where my husband goes. There's nothing to discuss."

They looked at each other, and he felt, suddenly, a wave of anger at being put in this position.

"If you think I made a grandstand play in the Holcome case," he burst out, "why don't you say so?"

"It isn't necessary for me to keep talking about it. You know."

"Look here!" The words burst from him in exasperation. "Do you mean to say you'd let a thing like my dismissing a case affect anything between us?"

"The only thing that could affect anything between us," she said, "is one of us."

"I'm not different from what I was then."

"If that's true, then I made a mistake."

He looked at her unbelievingly. "This can't be happening," he said finally. "You can't be — kissing me off."

"No." She shook her head slowly. "It's a bit hard to explain how I feel. I just don't see anything to be gained for either of us by me clearing out."

"Clearing out!" he exploded. "Good lord, Gay —!"

"There isn't anybody else I want to marry," she went on. "And it would make Dad unhappy. It wouldn't do your career any good, either — we haven't been married but a little while. We'll let things stay this way; nobody needs to know anything we don't want to tell them.

THERE WAS A LONG SILENCE while Ames tried to take this in.

Gay went on, "You had your life all planned, but there weren't any other people in your plans. Just milestones to be passed. You didn't think that your wife might be just as much a person as you are. Well, I've got my ideas of the man I want for a husband. I've got pretty definite ideas about the man who's going to be the father of any children I have, too." For the first time her chin set, and a light almost of hardness came into her eyes. "No son of mine is going to be just a milestone in anybody's life."

She went out. After that, Ames paced the living-room floor for an hour. He would have said he was thinking, but he wasn't. His mind had stopped before something it couldn't grasp. Gay drove him to the train the next morning.

"It still isn't too late," he said. "You could come along."

"Thanks," she said. "I've got a million things to do here. Honest."

There was a silence, and then he said, "You still feel the way you said you did last night?"

"Yes," she said. "I don't like feeling that way, but that's the way I do. You made a subtle play in the Holcome case. You did the unpolitic things deliberately, to get a reputation for integrity. A false one, of course."

"I suppose I should have tried to send the guy up because he was rich. Even if he couldn't see the sign!"

"Ames," Gay said wearily, "I know you tore down the sign. I went by there fifteen minutes after Holcome. The sign was all right. And I know you went out there and tore it down and then took the picture."

"Why didn't you say so?"

"Remember, Ames: *for better or worse?* I wish you hadn't torn down my heart."

The train came before he could answer.

THE GOVERNOR was most flattering. "This Crime Commission," he said, "is really no more than an idea at this stage, but it's going to be important, and it occurred to me that it would be wise to do the planning from the start with the man who is to be the head of it."

Ames listened with half his mind. He was looking at the calendar on the Governor's desk. The twelfth day of the month. Seven years for perjury. There might be time off for good behavior, and anybody was eligible for parole after a stipulated time. But it would be tougher for a man like Rolly Henderson. The Chairman of the Governor's Crime Commission could see to it that Henderson's case didn't come up too favorably before the Parole Board. Before seven years had passed, Ames might be sitting at the desk in this very room. Governor Conroy. It was a dream; it was right there on the schedule.

It wasn't as if Rolly Henderson were being deprived of anything. If he got out of jail, he'd be in trouble again soon enough. It was the nature of the man.

So when the Governor paused, Ames said, "I don't have to tell you how deeply honored I am, sir. But I'm going to have to ask you to wait."

The Governor was surprised. "Wait?"

"Only for a couple of hours," Ames said. "There are some facts not yet in your possession. They might affect your choice in this appointment. I'd feel better it you knew all there was to know before you decide."

The Governor was puzzled. He said, "Am I to understand that you may refuse the appointment?"

"Never in the world," he said. "I'm merely pleading for a stay. A couple of hours — until you have all the facts."

He went out after that to walk the streets of River City. To walk and walk endlessly until he reached some sort of clarification.

That was the way he pictured it, but that wasn't the way it happened. Actually, he walked only a couple of hundred yards, down the State House corridor to the chambers of the Chief Justice of the State Supreme Court.

His welcome there was as cordial as it had been in the Governor's office. Ames wasn't thinking now about what he was doing; some impulse he could not recognize was making him act.

He said, "You remember my appearance before your court about a year ago?"

The Chief Justice remembered.

"You probably haven't kept track," Ames said, "but I have. The other man in the case, a man named Henderson, begins a term for perjury today. The same day, the Governor invited me here to discuss my heading his proposed Crime Commission. It's a coincidence, but I've got an idea I'd have to come to see you, anyway." He smiled. "I came in to give myself up."

The Chief Justice's eyebrows went up politely. He didn't understand.

"I don't think," Ames went on, "that *I* can be convicted of perjury in the matter. I defended myself, if you recall, and I did it pretty well. I let Henderson convict himself. But I did buy bar examination questions from him. They turned out to be the wrong questions, but that doesn't alter the fact that I bought them."

There was a long silence. The Chief Justice looked at him steadily. At last he said, "Why did you tell me this?"

"I don't know that I could explain it," Ames told him. "It isn't my conscience. I built a house —" He stopped and shrugged. After a moment he went on, as if talking to himself. "I got to know a girl," he said, "and she married me. She married me because she thought I was on the square. She wanted to believe I was on the square, even though the evidence was against believing that sometimes." He paused. "I used a phrase a minute ago, a corny phrase: 'To give myself up.' But it says what I want to say."

The Chief Justice kept looking at him, not smiling. "You know what it means?"

"Sure," Ames said. "Disbarment."

The Chief Justice frowned.

"Well —" Ames got to his feet. "It's happened before in the family." There was a short silence. "If you do me one favor, sir," Ames said.

The Chief Justice said nothing.

"If you'd notify the Governor for me," Ames said.

HE WENT OUT of the office, down the stairs, and out of the State House. He didn't feel any different, and he didn't think. He didn't dare, just yet.

He got a room at the same hotel where he and Gay had stayed on their honeymoon. He didn't let his mind think about that, either; he hadn't meant it that way — it just happened. He got a bottle of whiskey and sat down carefully near the window. He drank slowly and systematically, and after a while any danger of thinking passed. He went to sleep in the chair, and when he roused himself at daylight there was still some whiskey in the bottle. He finished that and went to bed.

It was late afternoon when he woke up the second time. He remembered that he hadn't let Gay know he wasn't coming back to Ozarkanna the night before, but he felt too horrible to let that bother him.

He went into the bathroom and looked at himself. The reflection was about as bad as he felt — haggard eyes, unshaven face. "The perfect picture of the disbarred lawyer," he thought. "This must be the way the old man felt — something I never appreciated until now. I wonder if it would have made any difference to him if I had. Probably not."

He shaved and showered, and went back to lie on the bed until he felt better. It got dark after a while.

The cocktail lounge downstairs was still uncrowded when he went into it. There was a row of booths along the wall, and at the one nearest the door he stopped. Gay was sitting at the table. She said, "Hello, darling. Sit down."

He sat down and automatically ordered a drink. "What are you doing here?" he asked.

Gay said, "I came up to find my guy."

He looked at her, then at the table. "I didn't get the appointment," he said.

"I know," she told him. "The Governor called me. He's an old friend of Dad's."

Ames sighed. "I don't have to tell you the story, then."

"No. I heard it."

"Disbarment," he said.

"I don't know about that," Gay said quickly. "I have a lawyer working on it. It creates an interesting legal point. Can a man be disbarred for something which he did before he became a member of the bar and which actually had nothing to do with his becoming a member of the bar?"

"A lawyer working on it —?"

"You can call Holcome in the morning. You can't reopen that case, but you can see that Holcome takes good care of the boy he ran over."

"Of course," he said dully. "But you said a lawyer —"

"My father." She paused, and her eyes were wet. "Don't you know your family is going to fight for you — now?"

THERE WAS A LONG SILENCE, during which the waiter returned. Ames picked up his drink, looked at it carefully, and put it down again.

Finally Gay said, "Look — suppose you didn't have a son. Suppose it turned out to be a girl."

Ames thought about that. "A girl would be wonderful," he said. "The only thing I'd care about — I wouldn't want her to be ashamed of me."

She wouldn't be," Gay said. "She'd think you were the greatest guy in the world."

They both sipped their drinks, with great deliberation.

"Have you had dinner?" Ames asked.

Gay shook her head. "I drove down," she said. "We could get something to eat on the way." She reached over and touched his hand, "Let's go home," she said.

Ames nodded. He took a five-dollar bill out of his pocket and put it on the table. He hoped, in an obscure way, that the waiter would always remember this occasion.

"All right," he said. "That's the only thing I ever really wanted, I guess, all my life. Just to go home."

Find Volume I of
THE MASTERPIECES OF EUSTACE COCKRELL
in bookstores and at Amazon

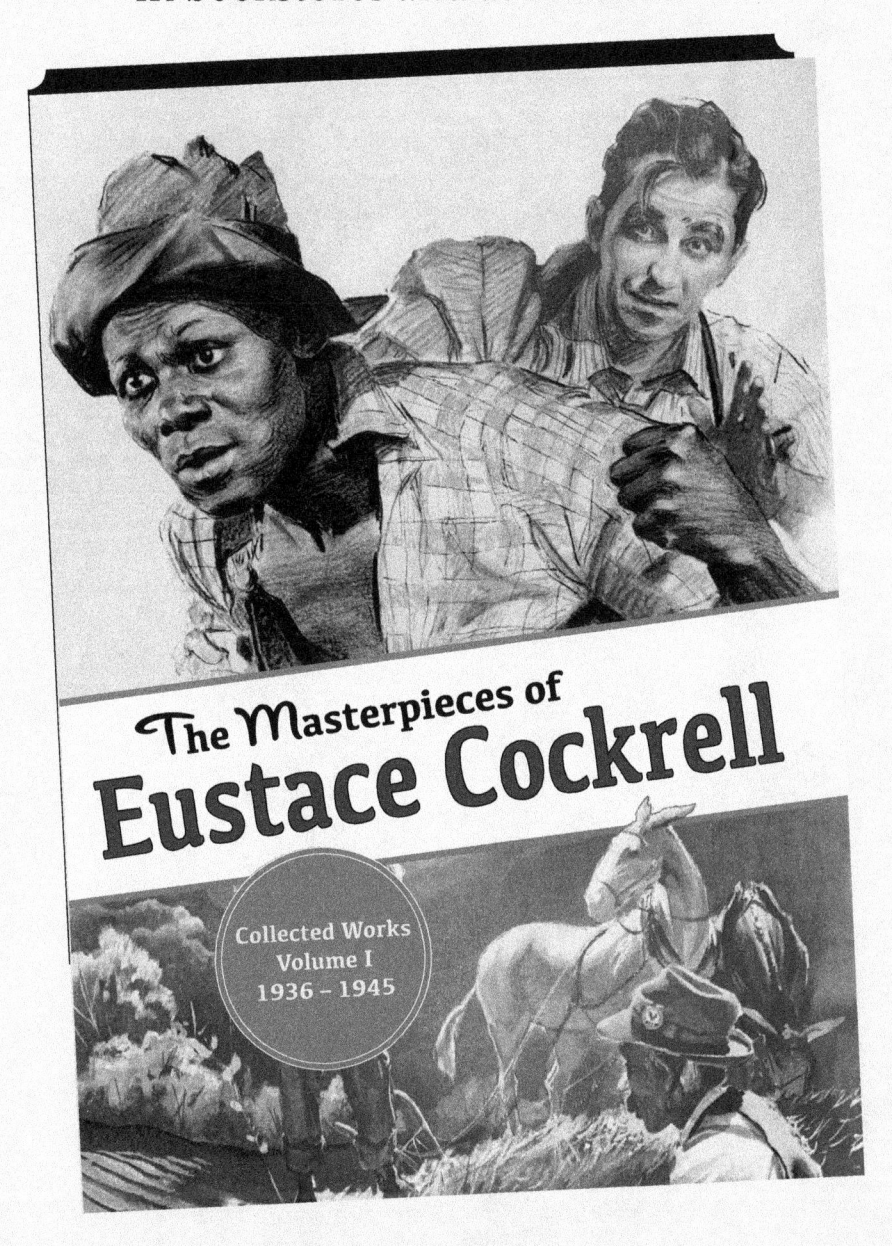

The Masterpieces of Eustace Cockrell

Collected Works
Volume I
1936 – 1945

Eustace Cockrell's stories are filled with memorable characters, the population of a lively era: jockeys, politicians, newspapermen, girls-about-town, medums, and even St. Peter. They struggle against expectations, the worst instincts of their fellows, and often enough of their own inclinations, to arrive, somehow, generally a bit worse for wear, at a life in some way renewed. First published in magazines from Argosy and Bluebook to Cosmopolitan and Collier's, these stories constitute a time portal to the middle years of the twentieth century.

—AMANDA COCKRELL, niece of Eustace Cockrell, and author of *Border Wars*

CPSIA information can be obtained
at www.ICGtesting.com
Printed in the USA
BVHW061731010822
643540BV00006B/494

9 781958 363119